D1444080

American Musicological Society
Music Library Association Reprint Series

Dover Publications, Inc., New York, in cooperation with the American Musicological Society and the Music Library Association, has undertaken to bring back into print a select list of scholarly musical works long unavailable to the researcher, student, and performer. A distinguished Committee representing both these professional organizations has been appointed to plan and supervise the series, which will include facsimile editions of indispensable historical, theoretical and bibliographical studies as well as important collections of music and translations of basic texts. To make the reprints more useful and to bring them up to date, new introductions, supplementary indexes and bibliographies, etc., will be prepared by qualified specialists.

Sir John Hawkins, *A General History of the Science and Practice of Music*
W. H., A. F., and A. E. Hill, *Antonio Stradivari, His Life and Work*
Curt Sachs, *Real-Lexikon der Musikinstrumente,* new revised, enlarged edition
The Complete Works of Franz Schubert (19 volumes), the Breitkopf & Härtel
    Critical Edition of 1884-1897 *(Franz Schubert's Werke. Kritisch*
    durchgesehene Gesammtausgabe.)
Charles Read Baskervill, *The Elizabethan Jig and Related Song Drama*
George Ashdown Audsley, *The Art of Organ-Building,* corrected edition
Emanuel Winternitz, *Musical Autographs from Monteverdi to Hindemith,*
    corrected edition
William Chappell, *Popular Music of the Olden Time,* 1859 edition
F. T. Arnold, *The Art of Accompaniment from a Thorough-Bass as*
    Practised in the 17th and 18th Centuries
The Breitkopf Thematic Catalogue, 1762-1787, with new introduction and
    indexes by B. S. Brook
Otto Kinkeldey, *Orgel und Klavier in der Musik des 16. Jahrhunderts*
Andreas Ornithoparcus, *Musice active micrologus,* together with
    John Dowland's translation, *A. O. his Micrologus, or Introduction,*
    Containing the Art of Singing
O. G. T. Sonneck, *Early Concert-life in America (1731-1800)*
Giambattista Mancini, *Practical Reflections on the Figurative Art of Singing*
    (translated by Pietro Buzzi)
Denis Stevens, *Thomas Tomkins, 1572-1656*
Thoinot Arbeau, *Orchesography* (translated by Mary Stewart Evans)
Edmond vander Straeten, *La Musique aux Pays-Bas avant le XIXᵉ siècle*
Frits Noske, *La Mélodie française de Berlioz à Duparc* (translated
    by Rita Benton)
Board of Music Trade, *Complete Catalogue of Sheet Music and*
    Musical Works (1870)

THOMAS TOMKINS

1572–1656

Internal view of Worcester Cathedral, drawn and engraved
by James Ross of Worcester especially for Valentine Green's
history of the city

THOMAS TOMKINS
1572–1656

BY

DENIS STEVENS

DOVER PUBLICATIONS, INC.
NEW YORK

Published in Canada by General Publishing Com-
pany, Ltd., 30 Lesmill Road, Don Mills, Toronto,
Ontario.
Published in the United Kingdom by Constable
and Company, Ltd., 10 Orange Street, London
W. C. 2.

This Dover edition, first published in 1967, is an
unabridged and corrected republication of the work
first published by Macmillan & Co. Ltd., London, in
1957. It contains a new Preface and Discography by
the author.

Library of Congress Catalog Card Number: 66-25706

Manufactured in the United States of America
Dover Publications, Inc.
180 Varick Street
New York, N.Y. 10014

IN MEMORIAM

STEPHEN DAVIDSON TUTTLE

PREFACE TO THE DOVER EDITION

WHEN, in the summer of 1956, I was engaged in a final revision of this book in preparation for the printer, the thought entered my mind from time to time that such sins of omission and commission for which I might subsequently be found liable could, if I were fortunate, be conveniently hidden away between that tercentenary commemoration of Tomkins's death and the quatercentenary of his birth due to be celebrated in 1972. I little thought that a new edition would be called for at a halfway stage. But, as the composer himself tells us in the first of his three-part *Songs*,

> Hours into days, days into years are gone;

and the passing of time renders obsolete a work of reference or scholarship that is not continually brought up to date, corrected, and amplified. To my own files containing modifications and additions of all types came welcome notes and queries from readers kind enough to respond to the open invitation following upon my original Preface, and in thanking them now for their interest and help I must ask them — as well as new readers — to excuse my inability to correct everything in these pages that needs correction. For the purposes of the present offset republication, it was wisest to avoid complex resetting with its attendant and inevitable changes in pagination and indexing. In particular the tabular matter of lists and editions has been left largely as it stood in the 1957 publication.

I have therefore decided, as an interim measure which I trust may prove acceptable, to mention the most outstanding matters here and now, but before I do so it is my pleasant duty to acknowledge scholarly assistance from Mr. Maurice Bevan, Mr. Douglas Cleverdon, Professor Theodore Finney, Mr. W. K. Ford, Mr. John Harvey, Lady Susi Jeans, Dr. Peter le Huray, Mr. Charles Morgenstern, Mr. Richard Newton, Mr. R. L. Rickard, Dr. Bernard Rose, Mr. Albi Rosenthal, Dr. H. J. Steele, and Mr. E. E. Wright.

Caught up during the course of my research by the numerous and proliferating branches of the Tomkins family tree, I realized at the time how hopeless a task it was to produce a perfect account of the history and genealogy of this widespread clan of musicians. I was particularly glad, for this reason, to hear and read of new information about the destinies of one or the other of the Tomkinses, such as Mr. Rickard's letter telling me the details of the change in surname from Tomkins to Berkeley in the year 1832. These details amplify and improve upon the references to Richard Tomkins on p. 126. Apparently the last of the family to bear the name Tomkins was another Richard, son of the Reverend Richard (1712 –89). This younger Richard, a Fellow of New College, Oxford, from 1787 until 1817, was presented by the College to the living of Great Horwood, Bucks, on June 27, 1816. He assumed the name Berkeley (which was his mother's maiden name) on October 9, 1832, by Royal Licence. The family name was however continued in that branch of the family presided over by Thomas, a brother of the Reverend Richard Tomkins. The portraits of this Thomas, and of his son Packington George Tomkins, are now in the private collection of Mr. John Riley, at the Manoir de la Trinité, Jersey, in the Channel Islands.

For many years an advocate of the fruitful nature of certain inter-relationships between music and musicology, I nevertheless derived an especial pleasure from my correspondence with Mr. Maurice Bevan. In a broadcast performance of some of Tomkins's anthems which I conducted in 1956, the baritone solo part of *Thou art my king, O God*, was sung with consummate artistry by Mr. Bevan, who told me afterwards of his belief that he might be a descendant of the Tomkins family. The particular branch, he thought, was that of John Tomkins, organist of St. Paul's Cathedral from 1619 until his death in 1638; and by a remarkable coincidence Mr. Bevan was a lay vicar of St. Paul's at the time. Indeed, his interest in Tomkins led him to discover in the Cathedral Library a hitherto unrecorded copy of a bassus part-book of *Musica Deo Sacra*.

By 1958 Mr. Bevan was able to assure me that his surmise was unquestionably true, and that research into his own family records and the corroboration of Duncumb's *History of the County of Hereford* revealed certain variants in names and marriages when compared with the sources available to me. Although Mr. Bevan felt that Duncumb's information may not have been completely accurate, it is worthwhile to list the variants in so far as they affect the tables on p. 12 and on p. 204. According to Duncumb, John Tomkins (b. 1631) married Margaret Eyre, and they settled at Buckenhill in the county of Hereford. The full name of their son was Nathaniel Thomas, and it was he who married Elizabeth Baynham. The wife of their son Packington is said to have been Mary Bohun, not Elizabeth Bohun.

Mr. Bevan traced his descent through one of their children, Thomas (1719–88), who married Anne Handley.

They had seven children, one of whom, Packington George Tomkins, D.D. (1761–1825) married a Margaret Green and raised a family of eleven children. Louisa Tomkins, one of five daughters, married Captain John Molesworth, whose son Samuel became eighth Viscount Molesworth. A daughter, Charlotte, married Henry Bevan, Archdeacon of Middlesex, who was a grandfather of Maurice Bevan. The reason for the two portraits finding their way to Jersey was a decision of one of the Molesworths to sell them to a relative whose name is known to users of the *English Hymnal*, Athelstan Riley, one of the founder-members of the Plainsong and Mediaeval Music Society. As I was then Secretary of the Society, I welcomed the opportunity to visit Mr. John Riley, the present Seigneur de la Trinité, who kindly gave me permission to see and photograph the two portraits. Disappointing as it was to find that the portrait of Thomas Tomkins was not that of the great composer, but of a distant descendant, the visit nevertheless helped to clear up minor details in the genealogy.

Among the new documents that have come to light recently are a none too complimentary reference to the composer's father, Thomas Tomkins (*c.* 1545–1627), in the Chapter Acts of St. David's Cathedral; and a letter written by the composer to Dr. Richard Baylie, President of St. John's College, Oxford. The St. David's records, now at the National Library of Wales, Aberystwyth, include several large volumes or registers of which the one marked 'A' (1560–1577) offers the following information on p. 236:

Thomas Tomkins was monished by Mr. Chanter etc. . . . to procure and get home his wedded wife as is supposed betwixt this present day and one fortnight after Lammas Day next: and for his sinful act committed with his maidservant etc., though he seem, from the bottom of his heart, to be sorry for his offence, yet to give to the poor namely to David Glover 3s. 4d. to pray for him upon pain of deprivation of his stall and living thereunto belonging.

This order, dated July 14, 1571, presumably had the required effect on the erring organist, for no further complaints were made, and his house was set in order by the following year, when Thomas the composer was born. The other document, dated March 4, 1638, is an autograph letter to the President of St. John's College, Oxford, concerning the appointment of a young Worcester organist named Richard Brown who, after a few years at Oxford, apparently returned to his home town to assist Tomkins.

Thomas Tomkins to Dr. Richard Baylie:

Worthy Sir:

My humble duty and service I present you with. I understand by my worthy friend Mr. Boughton Subdean of His Majesty's Chapel that it hath pleased my Lord Grace of Canterbury to confer upon one Richard Brown, a youth of mine, the organist's place of your College of St. John's, and to that effect caused Mr. Subdean to write a letter unto me to send him forthwith unto you. The letter came unto my hands but on Friday last: I thought fit as to acquaint you therewith so to desire your favour towards him. I must thank you also for a brother of mine that is under your verger at Salisbury. If you had any occasions into these parts as formerly you have had, my son would be glad to be your host, and you should be truly attended with both our persons and love. If Mr. Dr. Walker come unto you while my letter is in memory and not forgotten, you would be pleased to remember the respects of them that truly love him. About the 12 or 13 of this present, your organist shall attend you, God willing. You will be pleased to pardon my errors, and I shall ever remain

the servant of your command,
Thomas Tomkins, Organist of Worcester.

This letter, in the College Muniments (LX. 35), shows that a good pupil of a well-known cathedral organist could occasionally count on opportunities for employment in collegiate chapels as a method of gaining professional experience and biding time until a more important appointment might become available. The benevolent influence in this case was undoubtedly Tomkins himself, for he was a senior and respected member of the Chapel Royal, and had only to mention youthful talent to his "worthy friend" the Subdean for it to be passed on to higher authority, whence came appointments such as that of the organist of St. John's. The letter is also of interest because of the composer's references to his half-brother Giles Tomkins at Salisbury, his son Nathaniel at Worcester, and Dr. Walker, who (in view of the request for conveying respects and affection) may possibly be the William Walker to whom the madrigal *No more will I thy love importune* was dedicated in 1622.

* * * * *

Any scholar who tries to establish a complete catalogue of the works of a composer, of whatever epoch or nationality, knows how impossible it is to offer a definitive work in printed form. No sooner has the catalogue appeared than a number of compositions turn up from unexpected sources, including private owners who cannot be blamed for failing to divulge their treasures, and the entire business of cataloguing and collating must begin again. I have already stated that technical considerations were a factor in my decision not to bring the List of Works and their Sources completely up to date. But mention should be made of some of the most useful and important among the new discoveries.

Dr. Peter le Huray, whose unrivalled knowledge of anthems in the seventeenth century may soon be available in book form, was generous enough to send me a brief account of sources which do not appear in my List. These sources, all of which are manuscripts, comprise a set of part-books (medius and contratenor cantoris missing) at Pembroke College, Cambridge; a bassus book (written *c.* 1630) in Lambeth Palace Library, MS 764; a complete set of part-books (which Professor Finney links with the missing Rimbault set, formerly in the library of John Evelyn) now in the New York Public Library, Drexel MSS 4180–5; and various single books at Windsor, Gloucester Cathedral, and York Minster. All of these add materially to the concordances of verse and full anthems, but the only new title I could add was that of a verse anthem for St. Thomas, beginning *Almighty and everlasting God*, in the so-called *Batten Organ Book*, which Dr. le Huray thinks may really have been written by Giles Tomkins. Evidence of the often convenient invisibility of the dividing line between sacred and secular music may be found in a different kind of discovery, that the full anthem *Who shall ascend the hill of God* is musically identical with the madrigal *When I observe those beauty's wonderments*. Those scholars and musicians wishing to consult original copies of *Musica Deo Sacra* may care to know that in addition to the sets listed on p. 176, there are also copies (not always complete, unfortunately) in the University Library, Cambridge; the Bodleian Library, Oxford; Gloucester Cathedral Library; St. Paul's Cathedral Library; the Library of St. John's College, Oxford; and the Public Library of Manchester.

One of the most complex bibliographical aspects of Tomkins's music is surely that which deals with the concordances of his works for consort of viols. A complete picture will emerge only when every single part-book is

transcribed and collated, for works which share a common
title and a common treble part may be found to differ very
considerably in their inner or bass parts. For help in this
matter I am greatly indebted to Mr. Richard Newton, who
sent me much information from his own extensive files, as
well as a gentle warning that the task was still not complete.

To give an example of the kind of problem encountered, and the relatively ineffective nature of the usual brief
thematic incipit such as one uses for catalogue purposes,
the first of the five-part *Pavans* in my list is also known in a
four-part version (Marsh's Library, Dublin, MS Z.3.4;
Bodleian Library, Oxford, MS C 64–9). This is not
simply a reduction of the five-part *Pavan*, however, but a
completely new version as far as the inner parts are concerned. In both sources the *Pavan* is followed directly by
an *Alman* in the same key (F), and Mr. Newton suggests
(very plausibly, I think) that Tomkins may have intended
them as paired dances, after the fashion of the pavan and
galliard.

My listing of *Pavan No. 8* should be amplified to include a concordance in the Bodleian MS E 415, which I
missed since it is there transposed down a minor third and
referred to as No. 2. The difference in pitch may have to
do with the growing habit of accompanying a consort of
viols with a small chamber organ. The *Ut re mi*, according to Mr. Newton, is also to be found in a set of part-
books containing only this work in the Library of York
Minster, and there is a strong possibility that this may be a
Tomkins autograph. Mention should be made here of a
set of part-books described in Rosenthal's Catalogue
No. 10 (*Rare Music*), which was issued in 1948. Item 75
is a set of fantasias by Gibbons, Facio, Jenkins, and Withy,

with one by Tomkins, corresponding to that on p. 167 of
the Bodleian MS D 246.

*   *   *   *   *

Understandably, the past few years have brought forth
a spate of new practical editions of music by Tomkins, but
these cannot here be discussed or evaluated individually.
One worthy project deserves to be brought to the attention
of all readers, nevertheless; it is the complete publication
of *Musica Deo Sacra*, edited by Dr. Bernard Rose, in the
series *Early English Church Music*. Apart from its interest
as a summing-up of Tomkins's achievements in the field of
church music, this set of volumes will also stand as one of
the greatest single monuments of Anglican music in the
Stuart era. With *Musica Deo Sacra*, the *Songs*, and the
keyboard music available, we need only a complete edition
of the consort music to round out the picture of Tomkins's
artistic endeavours. What we see and hear is already
enough to demonstrate that he was a composer of no little
importance in the history of English music, but there will
always be room for minor adjustments in the hierarchy as
long as there is music untranscribed and unheard.

DENIS STEVENS

COLUMBIA UNIVERSITY
IN THE CITY OF NEW YORK,
DECEMBER 1965

PREFACE TO THE FIRST EDITION

IN spite of the generally acknowledged excellence of Elizabethan, Jacobean, and Caroline music, the number of monographs on composers responsible for this music is piteously small. Tomkins, through his association with all three of these great epochs, has always seemed to me especially deserving in this respect, and I hope that this short account of his life, his family, and his work will encourage other scholars to deal with the more eminent of his contemporaries.

Since this book was written many thousands of miles from musical and biographical source materials, difficulties arose at many stages. For help in surmounting these difficulties, I wish to thank many kind friends whose prompt and courteous replies to my queries were a source of pleasure as well as of information: Mr. Robert Donington, Mr. Vincent Duckles, Monsieur Jean Jacquot, Mr. A. Hyatt King, Mr. Jeremy Noble, Dr. Bertram Schofield, Mr. David Willcocks, and Mr. Franklin Zimmerman.

I am grateful also to various libraries and institutions for sending me photographic copies of music and documents, and for permission to reproduce certain pages: the Public Record Office, the Principal Probate Registry at Somerset House, the Music Library of London University, Magdalen College Library and the Bodleian Library, Oxford; and in America, the University and departmental libraries of Columbia, Cornell, and Harvard. Lastly, I should like to express my sincere appreciation of the enthusiastic way in which many of my graduate students at Cornell and Columbia sang and played Tomkins's music, and of the devoted way in which my wife assisted me in the preparation of both bibliography and list of works.

DENIS STEVENS

NEW YORK, 1956

Since the above was written, a visit to England has enabled me to add a few details to the List of Works and their Sources. Such lists are, in the nature of things, rarely faultless on their first appearance, and for this reason I shall welcome any additions or corrections that may be offered.

During the past year, many performances of works by Thomas Tomkins have confirmed his high reputation and enhanced his fame. Especially memorable in this respect was the Tomkins Festival at St. David's in the summer of 1956, when Mr. Peter Boorman (the cathedral organist) and the Venerable Carl Witton-Davies (then Dean of St. David's) provided many opportunities to hear the composer's music against a background of his birthplace. Thanks are also due to the BBC's Transcription Service, General Overseas Service, and Third Programme, and to all those artists who took part, for helping to make the tercentenary year a success.

D. S.

CONTENTS

ILLUSTRATIONS

Internal view of Worcester Cathedral, drawn and engraved by James Ross of Worcester especially for Valentine Green's history of the city. *Frontispiece*

Additions, mostly in the hand of Thomas Tomkins, to his own copy of Morley's *Plain and Easy Introduction to Practical Music*. The names added by Tomkins are those of Bevin, Mudd, Blitheman, Mundy, Bull, Hooper, Morley, Carleton, Gibbons, Warwick, and John Tomkins. (The Library of Magdalen College, Oxford) *facing page* 29

Warrant of Charles I for the appointment of Thomas Tomkins as Composer-in-Ordinary. (London, Public Record Office, S.P. 39–23–53) *between pages* 52 *and* 53

Certificate of the Mayor and Aldermen of Worcester, dated June 17, 1650, showing that Thomas Tomkins was 78 years of age in that year. (London, Public Record Office, S.P. 23–124–273) *facing page* 61

The ending of the *Offertory*, signed 'Mr Thomas Tomkins:— organist of His Majesty's Chapel, 1637'. Two short pieces 'for Edward'— Edward Thornbrough, Archdeacon of Worcester. (Oxford, Bodleian Library, MS [Mus. Sch.] C 93, f. 80) *facing page* 141

A Sad Pavan: for these distracted times, dated February 14, 1649. Charles I was executed on January 30, 1649. (Paris, Bibliothèque du Conservatoire, Rés. 1122, pp. 136, 137) *between pages* 148 *and* 149

THE TOMKINS FAMILY

The Tomkins family produced more able musicians during the sixteenth and seventeenth centuries than any other which England can boast.

CHARLES BURNEY, *General History of Music* (1776).

NO account of Thomas Tomkins and his music would be complete without reference to his family. It was a musical family, to be sure, in the same sense as the families of Ferrabosco, Couperin, and Bach were musical, but it differed from these in one important way. Whereas the Ferraboscos, Couperins, and Bachs have left us music written by different generations of the same family, the influence (or lack of it) of father upon son being thereby the more clearly perceptible, the Tomkins family has not preserved any music from the pen of Thomas senior, Precentor of Gloucester Cathedral, or of Nathaniel, Canon of Worcester Cathedral. There is, moreover, no extant music by the three sons of John Tomkins, organist of St. Paul's, the three sons of Giles Tomkins, organist of Salisbury Cathedral, or the three sons of Peregrine Tomkins.[1] It seems that creative effort of lasting value was confined to one generation, that of Thomas, organist of Worcester Cathedral, and of his half-brothers John, Robert, and Giles, or else that

---

[1] With the possible exception of *Fine young folly*, a song for three voices in *Select Musical Ayres & Dialogues* (1653) and in Lawes' *Treasury of Music* (1669) i, 103, ascribed to William Tomkins. Perhaps this was William, son of Peregrine Tomkins, but there is no direct evidence.

fate has been unkind to manuscripts containing music by
their forebears or descendants.

Documentary evidence in the form of two pedigrees
confirms the Cornish origin of the Tomkins family, first
pointed out by Anthony à Wood.[1] Further confirmation
may be found in the frequent appearance in old Cornish
wills and records of various forms of the family name —
Thomkins, Tompkins, Tonkins, are the principal variants
of the more usual spelling which Thomas himself used
consistently throughout his life. A further link with
Cornwall may be seen in one of Thomas's keyboard
pieces, the *Toy: made at Poole Court*, which he may have
composed at the country house of the Trelawny family,
not far from Lostwithiel, where his father was born.

Both the father and the grandfather of Thomas senior
bore the name Ralph, but the pedigrees give no details
of this early Tudor root of the family tree. Thomas
senior was born during the last years of Henry VIII's
reign, grew up in Cornwall and married there, probably
in the year 1566. His wife, Margaret Pore or Poher,
bore him three children, two of them being named
Thomas. The pedigree of 1683 tells us that Thomas
senior

sold his Estate in Cornwall and came into Gloucestershire, being
a Divine

but it gives us no idea when the northward move took
place. The first mention of Thomas senior in the Chapter
Act Book of St. David's Cathedral, Pembrokeshire, is
dated July 12, 1571, and it shows that he was then a
Vicar Choral.[2] Six years later he is referred to in the
same source as Master of the Choristers and Organist,

---

[1] *Fasti Oxonienses*, i, 320.   [2] Atkins, p. 39.

but this promotion appears to have given him little financial satisfaction:

Whereas Thomas Tomkins, Master of the Choristers and Organ Player in this Church, as well by his own report as by the testimony of others, declareth that he hath not so great wages as others have had who occupied his place and office heretofore; and also credibly affirmeth that he is not able to live and continue a member of this Church upon such wages and commodity as he now enjoyeth, but must of necessity be obliged to leave this Church, and to accept such place, as with greater commodity, wages and living, is elsewhere offered unto him. It is therefore ordered, constituted and appointed by the Reverend Father in God Richard, Bishop of St. Davids and Mr. Lewis Gwyn, deputies unto the Most Reverend Father in God Edmund [Grindale], by God's Providence Archbishop of Canterbury and Metropolitan of England, in His Grace's Visitation within the Diocese of St. Davids, executed by the foresaid Deputies or Delegates, that Thomas Tomkins the younger, Son unto the foresaid Thomas Tomkins the elder, now being one of the Choristers of this Church, shall from henceforth, to the end that his poor Father, at whose finding he is, may thereby the rather be relieved, have a Vicar's Stall in the said Cathedral Church of St. Davids which one Richard Johnson lately held, and is now void, and from the Feast of the Nativity of St. John the Baptist next coming, shall and may enjoy all profits and commodities belonging to the same stall and place of Vicar Choral, without defalcation, according to the custom of the Church. And it is further appointed, constituted and decreed by the foresaid Delegates or Deputies that there is now but one chorister in this Church, besides the said Tomkins the younger (the Statute requiring six in all) two other children of years, voice and aptitudes, likely to do God's service, as appertaineth to a Chorister of the foresaid Church, shall be appointed by the Chanter and Chapter, so that at least there may be three of them continually kept and maintained.[1]

The 'Thomas Tomkins the younger' was the son born about the year 1567, before the move to St. David's

---

[1] Atkins, pp. 39-40. Spelling and punctuation have been modernized in this as in all subsequent citations from early documents.

took place. At the time when the document was written (April 29, 1577) the other son named Thomas — destined to become organist of Worcester Cathedral — was only 5 years old. Between the two Thomases was another child, whose identity is by no means clear. The pedigree of 1634 makes no mention of this child, while that of 1683 simply says 'Thomas and another son died unmarried'. It is highly probable that those responsible for drawing up the pedigree of 1683 had either lost sight of or misunderstood these early ramifications of the family tree, for the will of Anne Tomkins, second wife of Thomas senior, makes it clear that the child was a girl and not 'another son'. This will [1] enumerates certain bequests to seven children: five sons and two daughters. They are referred to by Anne as her 'own natural children', as opposed, of course, to the children born of the first marriage.

The latter part of the will deals with bequests to these other children, first of all to her 'late husband's son Thomas Tomkins and . . . his daughter Ursula' and then to her daughter Bridget Tomkins, who is named as sole executrix. Two facts emerge from this will, and point towards Bridget as the third of the three children born of the marriage of Thomas senior and Margaret Pore. First, Bridget's name is not included among those who are specifically called the natural children of Anne; it is, however, coupled with the name of the only other surviving child of the first marriage. Secondly, Bridget is made sole executrix of Anne's will, and this indicates some measure of seniority, agreeing with the proposed date of birth, *c.* 1570. Thus Bridget would have been twenty-five to thirty years older than the other

[1] See p. 8.

daughters, Margaret and Elizabeth, who were born of the second marriage, and about whom very little is known.

The children of the first marriage may tentatively be assigned to the following years:

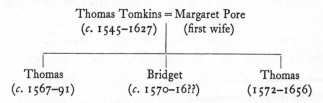

Thomas Tomkins = Margaret Pore
(*c.* 1545–1627) | (first wife)

| Thomas | Bridget | Thomas |
| (*c.* 1567–91) | (*c.* 1570–16??) | (1572–1656) |

As shown by the Acts of Chapter, the elder son was granted a vicar's stall at St. David's in order to augment the family income, which in 1577 had to support three children. The boy does not appear to have taken his duties very seriously, for even before this grant, a complaint about his absence from a special meeting of the Commissioners was noted in the Acts of Chapter for April 23, 1577.[1] What went on between this date and the date of the final document concerning the boy is largely a matter for conjecture, but it seems that his conduct grew steadily worse, for the entry under January 22, 1586, tersely states:

> Thomas Tomkins, junior, a Vicar Choral, having grossly misbehaved, is expelled, and his stall, having been declared vacant, is given to David Thomas.[2]

Atkins cites an opinion that this expulsion (which took place in the same year as the birth of John, first son of Thomas senior's second marriage) was probably for insubordination, and did not reflect on the boy's moral character.[3] His high spirits and longing for a life

---

[1] Atkins, p. 39.   [2] Atkins, p. 40.   [3] Atkins, p. 40 (note).

of adventure led him to go to sea, but the pedigree of 1634 communicates the sad news that he died in the *Revenge*, when this ship was involved in a hopeless action with fifty-three Spanish ships in 1591. Sir Richard Grenville, who was described on one occasion as a man of intolerable pride and insatiable ambition, brought his 150 men into the midst of 5000 Spaniards, a foolhardy deed which on land would have resulted in lightning massacre. At sea, the fighting continued for fifteen hours, and few of the British lived to tell the tale of desperate hand-to-hand encounter, with the odds overwhelmingly against them. Grenville was wounded and moved from the ill-fated *Revenge* to another ship, where he died the following day.

Perhaps the death of Thomas, both in its tragic and heroic aspects, helped cleanse the blot of summary dismissal from the family escutcheon; but his dismissal meant more than shame for his father and mother. It caused the family income to shrivel once more to its former size, whilst the family itself increased, first with John, then with Robert, Giles, Nicholas, Peregrine, Margaret, and Elizabeth. The move to Gloucester, which seems to have taken place prior to 1594, was undertaken for reasons of economy and living-space as well as a desire to start life afresh. A contributing factor to this attitude on the part of Thomas senior was the death of his first wife, and his eventual re-marriage with Anne, probably daughter or sister of Richard Hargest, who lived at Penarthur farm, near St. David's.

It is not known when Thomas senior took Holy Orders, but he is listed as a Minor Canon in the Chapter Accounts of Gloucester Cathedral for the year 1594.[1]

---

[1] Atkins, *Addenda et Corrigenda*, facing p. 1.

Two years later he is described as Vicar of St. Mary de Lode, an old church quite near the cathedral,[1] to whose Dean and Chapter he owed the appointment. In 1610 the records show that he was Precentor, an office which he held continuously until 1625. Thus economic pressure compelled him to give up a musical career in favour of ecclesiastical preferment, and ironically enough his music has suffered the same fate as his work on church history — total loss. In the musical library of his son Thomas, there was a book listed A in a set running from A to H, dated 1600,[2] but no trace of this has been found. It is listed as the property of Thomas Farington Tomkins, obviously referring to Thomas senior, although there is no other extant mention of this middle name Farington. Similarly, the account which he wrote of the Bishops of Gloucester, used by Browne Willis,[3] has been lost or destroyed. He died in March or April, 1627, and his will (preserved among the Consistory Court Records of the Diocese of Gloucester) was proved on April 19:

Memorandum that in the month of March 1626 according to the computation of the Church of England Thomas Tomkins one of the petty canons of the cathedral church of Gloucester and chanter of the same being sick and weak in body but of perfect memory being asked how he would dispose of his estate and goods said divers and sundry times all that I have I give unto Anne Tomkins my wife to dispose thereof as she sees good and her I make my executrix. Witnesses present: Richard Broadgate, one petty canon of the cathedral church of Gloucester, Elizabeth Chap[man].

His wife survived him by only six months, and her will is to be found among the same diocesan records.

[1] Fosbroke, *History of Gloucester*, p. 173.   [2] See p. 129.
[3] *A Survey of the Cathedrals*, ii, 723.

It is dated November 29, 1627, and was proved on December 14 of that year:

> I, Anne Tomkins of the city of Gloucester Widow [bequeath] to my son John Tomkins, unto my son Robert, to my son Nicholas, to my son Giles, to my son Peregrine, unto my daughter Margaret, and unto my daughter Elizabeth Smith mine own natural children a piece of gold of 11s. a piece to make each of them a ring for a motherly remembrance. Also I give unto my late husband's son Thomas Tomkins and unto his daughter Ursula 10s. each. The residue of my goods I give unto my daughter Bridget Tomkins whom I make my sole executrix.[1]

It is very probable that Anne Tomkins named her children in order of seniority, but if this is accepted as true, the order given in the pedigrees of 1634 and 1683 must be abandoned, and the children of the second marriage ranged thus:

Thomas Tomkins = Anne Hargest
(*c.* 1545–1627) | (second wife)

| John | Robert | Nicholas | Giles | Peregrine | Margaret | Elizabeth |
| (1586–1638) | | | (d. 1668) | (d. 1659) | | |

The daughters were placed after the sons for legal reasons, and were not necessarily born after the five sons. In all, then, nine children born of two marriages were alive when Anne made her will. It was a solid beginning to a vast family, whose descendants have been traced as far as the early part of the nineteenth century.

* * * * *

John Tomkins, besides being the eldest of the five brothers, is by far the most outstanding musically, and deserves to be mentioned in the same breath or (as Charles Butler did) in the same sentence as Thomas. He was 8 years old when the family moved to Gloucester,

[1] This will, and the previous one, from Atkins, p. 44.

and probably sang in the choir there, later proceeding
to Cambridge where he became a scholar of King's
College and, in 1606, organist of the chapel. Two years
later, he received the degree of B.Mus., and remained
in Cambridge until 1619. He was a great friend of
Phineas Fletcher, then a Fellow of King's, and many of
Fletcher's poems refer to John by the thinly disguised
name of Thomalin. The voices of nature are invoked by
Fletcher in an elaborate eulogy of his friend's organ-
playing:

> Thomalin my lief, thy music strains to hear,
> More wraps my soul, than when the swelling winds
> On craggy rocks their whistling voices tear;
> Or when the sea, if stopped his course he finds,
> With broken murmurs thinks weak shores to fear,
> Scorning such sandy cords his proud head binds:
> More than where rivers in the summer's ray
> (Through covert glades cutting their shady way)
> Run tumbling down the lawns, and with the pebbles play.

The bucolic charms of Jacobean Cambridge were
not, however, strong enough to restrain the youthful and
pleasure-loving John from frequent visits to London
during vacations. Besides meeting his brother Thomas
there, he was able to see something of the musical
activity of city and court, and although he had to wait
several years for his London appointments, his time was
obviously not wasted. Fletcher's commentary on these
gay but necessary escapes from the sleepiness of academic life is at the same time gentle yet pointed:

> To thee I here bequeath the courtly joys,
> Seeing to court my Thomalin is bent:
> Take from thy Thirsil these his idle toys;
> Here I will end my looser merriment:
> And when thou singst them to the wanton boys,
> Among the courtly lasses' blandishment,

Think of thy Thirsil's love that never spends;
And softly say, his love still better mends:
Ah too unlike the love of court, or courtly friends![1]

In 1616, intrigue of one kind or another succeeded in depriving Fletcher of his fellowship, and thereafter he served as private chaplain to Sir Henry Willoughby at Risley, Derbyshire, then as rector of Hilgay in Norfolk. John Tomkins remained in Cambridge for three more years, but continued to keep closely in touch with London musical life, gaining steady renown as a composer and keyboard player. It was thought at one time that he also wrote music for masques and plays, a production of *Albumazar* at Cambridge being frequently cited as his work; the advocates of this theory were not, however, unduly perturbed by the fact that it was the text, rather than the music, whose authorship was being ascribed to John. Eventually it came out that another Tomkins, not related to the musical family, was the true author of the play.[2] John is sometimes wrongly credited with the authorship of certain prefatory verses to Edmund Elys's *Dia Poemata*, published in 1665, but this task was actually performed by his sons John (b. 1631) and Thomas (b. 1638). His ability to write commendatory verse of fair quality is nevertheless confirmed by the short poem to his brother Thomas, printed in the *Songs* of 1622.

In 1619 he settled in London as organist of St. Paul's, and it was not long before his services came to be sought after for the Chapel Royal. He was sworn in as gentleman extraordinary in 1625, with the promise of a place as organist, but he is not mentioned in connec-

[1] Fletcher, *Poems*, ed. Grosart, iii, 219-23.
[2] *Notes and Queries*, 3rd series, ix, 259-60; xii, 155.

tion with this office until several years later. His rapid promotion from pisteler and gospeller to gentleman, in the space of less than a year, is shown by the records in the Cheque Book:

1626. Francis Wiborowe died at Ely the 28th of October, and John Tomkins, organist of St. Paul's, was sworn in his place the third of November following, pisteler, and Richard Boughton gospeller, and Henry Lawes gentleman.

1626. Memorandum, that Crue Sharpe died the 21st of December, and Thomas Rayment, a bass from Salisbury, was sworn pisteler in his place the 30th day of January following, and John Tomkins gospeller, and Richard Boughton gentleman.

1627. Mr. Luke Jones, Clerk, gentleman of His Majesty's Chapel and Sub-Dean of St. Paul's London, died the 18th day of July, and Richard Sandy, a contra tenor of St. Paul's, was sworne pisteler in his place the 19th day following, and Thomas Rayment gospeller, and John Tomkins gentleman.[1]

Soon after this appointment John married Margaret Griffiths, daughter of Dr. Sylvanus Griffiths, Dean of Hereford Cathedral. Three sons were born to them during the succeeding ten years: John, named after his father; Sylvanus, named after his grandfather in Hereford; and Thomas, whose name was by then a highly-respected feature of the Tomkins family. Both John and Sylvanus were sent to Worcester for their education and musical training, and although they both married in their early thirties, the male line of descendants issued from the union of John Tomkins and Elizabeth Baynham, daughter of a Hereford squire. Son, like father, chose a Hereford lady for his bride, and the family continued to flourish in the counties of Hereford and Worcester for several generations. The third son, Thomas, was born in 1638 (the year in which his father died) and he

[1] *Cheque Book*, pp. 11-12.

was brought up and educated at Worcester by Nathaniel Tomkins, only son of Thomas who was then organist of the cathedral there.[1] The younger Thomas, who never married, had a brilliant academic career after studying at Balliol College, Oxford. He was elected a Fellow of All Souls, gained the degree of D.D., and subsequently became Chancellor of Exeter Cathedral and chaplain to the Archbishop of Canterbury. It seems that he was not endowed with any special musical gifts, and it is unlikely that he had anything to do with the publication of *Musica Deo Sacra*.[2] From 1586 to 1840, this branch of the Tomkins family can be traced without interruption:[3]

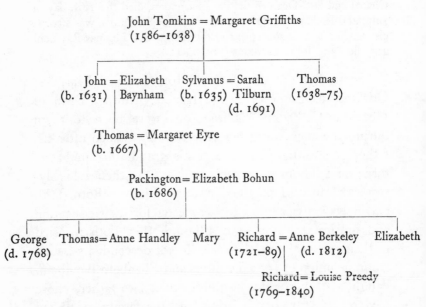

[1] Prattinton MS, Society of Antiquaries.

[2] A contrary opinion is expressed in the *Dictionary of National Biography* (Thomas Tomkins); but see Atkins, p. 58, and Wood, *Athenae Oxonienses*, iv, col. 1046.

[3] The Rev. Richard Tomkins assumed the name of Berkeley, and succeeded at Cotheridge on the death of his uncle, Henry Berkeley.

John Tomkins senior is listed together with his brother Giles as joint organist of the Chapel in 1633, when they accompanied King Charles on his visit to Scotland.[1] As senior organist of the chapel, it was Thomas rather than John who should have undertaken this journey; but he was at that time over 60 years of age, and probably asked that his younger brother might be allowed to serve in his place. In the same year Ravenscroft included one of John's psalm tunes — *Gloucester* — in his increasingly popular collection of hymns and chants. Few of his compositions have been preserved, although there are words of six anthems in a Chapel Royal anthem book,[2] a single part of *Have mercy upon me* in a part-book at Tenbury dated 1617,[3] a madrigal *O thrice blessed* in Myriell's anthology,[4] a setting of *Cantate Domino*,[5] and a single keyboard piece, probably a solo for the virginals, entitled *John come kiss me now*.[6] When he died in 1638, he was buried in the north aisle of St. Paul's Cathedral, his grave being surmounted by a tablet bearing the following lines:

Johannes Tomkins, Musicae Baccalaureus, Organista sui temporis celeberrimus, postquam Capellae regali, per annos duodecem, huic autem Ecclesiae per novemdecem sedulo inservisset, ad coelestem chorum migravit Septembris 27, Anno Domini 1638. Aetatis suae 52. Cujus desiderium moerens uxor hoc testatur Marmore.[7]

His praises were sung by his friend and colleague William Lawes, whose brother Henry published this and

[1] *King's Musick*, p. 85.
[2] British Museum, Harley MS 6346.
[3] Tenbury, St. Michael's College, MS 1382.
[4] British Museum, Add. MSS 29372-7, also in 29427.
[5] *Ibid*. Add. MSS 29366-8, 18936-9.
[6] *Ibid*. Add. MS 29996.   [7] Dugdale, *Old St. Paul's*, p. 101.

other compositions in the *Choice Psalms put into Musick for Three Voices* of 1648:

ELEGY ON THE DEATH OF JOHN TOMKINS

Musick, the master of thy art is dead,
And with him all thy ravished sweets are fled:
Then bear a part in thine own tragedy,
Let's celebrate strange grief with harmony;
Instead of tears shed on his mournful hearse,
Let's howl sad notes stol'n from his own pure verse.

*   *   *   *   *

Occasionally a fourth son, named Robert, is postulated, although neither of the pedigrees mentions more than John junior, Sylvanus, and Thomas.[1] The only Robert in the family was the one mentioned second in the will of Anne Tomkins, but his date of birth remains unknown, as does the year of his death. He was a viol player, and may have inspired much of the consort music written by his half-brother Thomas. On March 28, 1633, he was appointed musician for the consort in place of Robert Kyndersley,[2] and two years later was receiving a salary of £46 per annum as viol player in the service of King Charles,[3] a position which is still confirmed in 1640.[4] In a list of 1641, he is named along with his

---

[1] Rimbault (*Cheque Book*, p. 209) talks of 'another son, Robert, who was one of the Royal Musicians in 1641', and this (in spite of Eitner's guarded statement — 'Seine Verwandtschaft ist unsicher' — in *Quellen-Lexicon*, ix, 425) misled Fellowes so far as to list this mysterious son as Robert (6) in Grove's *Dictionary*, 5th edition, viii, 497. Robert (6) and Robert (9) should combine to form one person. There is also a John Tomkins whose career is briefly described by Atkins (p. 30) and whose son, also named John, sang in the choir at Worcester in 1611 (p. 45, note). No definite connection between this family and the main Tomkins family can be established.

[2] *King's Musick*, pp. 83, 89.

[3] Nagel, *Annalen der englischen Hofmusik*, pp. 43, 45.

[4] Public Record Office, S.P. 16/474 (2), ff. 6-7.

brother Giles as one of the musicians for the lutes, viols, and voices,[1] but he must have died before the Restoration because the earliest available list of the new musical establishment at court, dated 1660, states that his place in the broken consort has been taken by Henry Hawes.[2] He seems to have composed no consort music, though the organ parts of three anthems are to be found in Batten's manuscript,[3] these titles (*Thou art fairer*; *Hear me, O God*; *Like as the hart*) occurring also in the Chapel Royal anthem book. Six further anthems are attributed to Robert Tomkins in the latter source, and in many ways it is a pity that the words only are preserved. Batten's organ parts, interesting as they may be to the historian, give us no idea of the quality of Robert's music.

* * * * *

Nicholas, the third son, died a bachelor as his brother Robert did, if we are to accept the evidence of the 1683 pedigree. According to Anthony à Wood,[4] he was musical, though by no means a professional; like his brothers, he contrived to find a place at court, and is described in the 1634 pedigree as 'one of the Gentlemen of the Privy Chamber to his Majesty'.

* * * * *

Giles Tomkins appears to have been a particular favourite of King Charles, and an adept at serving both court and cathedral, even though these were as far distant as London and Salisbury. No music by Giles has come down to us, but there are words for two of his anthems in the same Chapel Royal anthem book that provides us

---

[1] *King's Musick*, p. 111.   [2] *Ibid.* pp. 117, 125.
[3] Tenbury, St. Michael's College, MS 791.   [4] *Fasti Oxonienses*, i, 320.

with the titles of works by Robert, John, and Thomas. It is very probable that he found the performance of music more agreeable than composition, even though his half-brother Thomas had set him such a shining example by being skilled in both. After his early musical training at Gloucester, Giles was sent to Cambridge, where he succeeded in 1624 to the post of organist at King's College, which his brother John had relinquished some five years earlier. There is no doubt that he made excellent use, as John did, of the time during which his actual presence in Cambridge was not subject to statutory demands. Although there is no direct evidence of his having spent a considerable amount of time in London, it is very significant that his court appointment came about at exactly the same time as the settlement of the dispute in Salisbury.

The subject of the dispute was Thomas Holmes, whose father had been Master of the Choristers of Salisbury Cathedral until his death in January, 1629.[1] Certain members of the Chapter were in favour of appointing Holmes in place of his father, but the Dean proposed Giles Tomkins, and was supported by one of the canons, Giles Thornborough, whose brother Edward was archdeacon of Worcester and a great friend of the Tomkins family. The Bishop of Salisbury, however, was determined to have Holmes appointed, and he so far intervened as to claim a vote in the meetings of the Dean and Chapter, which resulted in a clash between Dean and Bishop over questions of ecclesiastical procedure. The Dean attempted to avoid the deadlock by

---

[1] John Holmes is said to have been organist from 1602 to 1610, and although this is denied in some reference books it is perfectly possible that he acted as assistant when needed.

proposing Tomkins as a lay vicar, but the Bishop replied by claiming that the proposal was null and void because Tomkins had never appeared for a voice trial. The Custos of the Choristers, Dr. Barnston, supported the Bishop by emphasizing Tomkins's unsuitability for singing the psalms or for 'the artifice of singing called pricksong'. Whether Dr. Barnston based his evidence on hearsay, or upon personal knowledge of Giles Tomkins's vocal abilities, does not appear. Not only he, but the Bishop also, was over-ruled when the Dean calmly went ahead and appointed Giles as a lay vicar, referring the question of who was to instruct the choristers to the Archbishop of Canterbury.

The Archbishop, aided by a committee of four bishops and a dean, found that a firm decision was by no means easy to arrive at, and accordingly wrote to the King on June 22, 1629:

May it please your most excellent Majesty according to your gracious reference we whose names are underwritten have several times met and endeavoured to accommodate the differences between the Bishop on the one side, and the Dean and Chapter of Salisbury on the other side but not being able to prevail with both parties as we desired we have held it our duty to certify your Majesty that upon the whole hearing of both sides we find not reason to think otherwise than that Giles Tomkins was lawfully elected unto the places now in question and that he ought to be admitted into the possession of the same yet notwithstanding we submit all unto your princely pleasure.[1]

The reply which arrived a week later, signed by the King's secretary, Viscount Dorchester, betrayed something of Charles's innate unwillingness to give a clear answer to a straightforward question. He supported the attitude of the Archbishop and his committee, but gave

[1] Robertson, *Sarum Close*, p. 180, from Salisbury Chapter documents.

the impression that the appointment was to be provisional:

His Majesty having seen the report whereof this is a true copy doth require that the within-named Giles Tomkins be admitted by way of provision into the place now in question. But for the validity of the election and right of voice in the Chapter with their dependencies his Majesty leaveth the same unto a trial at law in such course as is accustomed in cases of like nature. . . .[1]

On October 8, the Dean gained final control over his adversaries by claiming the office of Custos of the Choristers, and although a lawsuit was instituted the outcome of it is not known.[2] It is quite possible that the whole affair died a natural death, for Giles was formally installed in the chorister's house in 1630, and thereupon began to restore the shattered morale of the choir.

His court appointment was dated April 2, 1630, and he was designated 'Musician for the Virginals, vice R. Dering, deceased'. On April 20 his wages were fixed at £40 per annum, and two months later he received the usual warrant for livery.[3] His companions among the court musicians at this time were the Ferraboscos, the Laniers, Daniel Farrant, Thomas Day, and Robert Johnson, besides many others of less renown. Livery payments continue until 1642,[4] and there are two references to additional appointments in 1633 (the Scottish journey, already mentioned in connection with brother John) and in 1641, when his name appears among those

---

[1] Robertson, *Sarum Close*, p. 181 (Shuter's Memorials, p. 102, in Salisbury Chapter documents). Atkins (p. 64, note) reads 'honest' for 'accustomed'.

[2] *Ibid.* p. 184, quotes a document (C.2. Ch.I S 9.9.22) which unfortunately tells only half the story. Atkins (p. 65, note) points out that the Court of Arches decided, on the point of law, in favour of Holmes.

[3] *King's Musick*, pp. 71, 73.

[4] *Ibid.* pp. 75, 78, 81, 89, 101, 106, 107.

musicians who played the lutes and viols, or sang.[1] In 1660 his appointment was renewed, the other virginal player at the time being Christopher Gibbons,[2] but three years later he again appears among the musicians for the lutes and voices, so perhaps he was not such a poor singer as Dr. Barnston of Salisbury had made out.[3]

The travelling to and from London must have been something of a trial as time went on, for complaints begin to appear in 1634, when Laud's Visitation Articles for Salisbury were drawn up and approved. Regarding the choristers, the following paragraph tells its own tale:

One Giles Tomkins hath the charge of instructing them in the art of singing, which he protesteth he doth carefully, and I believe he doth. He hath been blamed lately for leaving them without a guide and teacher once or twice when he went to wait at court, but he promiseth he will do no more so, yet protesteth that they all save two sing their parts perfectly, and need no teacher in his absence.[4]

When the warrant for livery was issued on the Feast of St. Andrew, 1668, Giles Tomkins was noted as *mortuus ante diem*, and his place was taken by John Blow.[5] He left a wife and three children, two of which had been born of an earlier marriage:

```
(first wife)   =  Giles Tomkins  =  (second wife)
     ┌──────────────┤                 │
Thomas          Giles  = Margaret  John
(b. 1631)      (1633–1725)  Winns  (b. 1637)
```

The second son, Giles, was given the very difficult task of following in his uncle's footsteps as organist of Worcester Cathedral, the document of appointment

[1] *Ibid.* pp. 85, 111.   [2] *Ibid.* pp. 113, 121.   [3] *Ibid.* p. 164.
[4] *Wiltshire Notes and Queries*, March, 1893.
[5] *King's Musick*, pp. 205, 210.

(August 28, 1661) describing him cautiously as a student in music.[1] He was not a success, in spite of the fact that he had many friends who encouraged and helped him. Nathaniel Tomkins was then a canon, and Giles Thornborough, who had been at Salisbury with Giles Tomkins senior, had come to Worcester as sub-dean. Giles junior was apparently much given to absence when presence would have been more in keeping with his office, and eventually the Dean had to declare the appointment terminated, naming Richard Brown (a minor canon) as his successor.[2] His musical career at an end, Giles followed the example of his grandfather: he entered the Church, was presented to the living of Martin Hussingtree, married, and had six children.[3] His span of life even exceeded that of his uncle, for he was 93 at the time of his death in 1725. His death and burial are recorded in the parish registers of Martin Hussingtree, whose church he had served as rector for more than half a century.

* * * * *

Peregrine, fifth son of Thomas senior and his second wife, does not appear from the available records to have been particularly musical. He was, however, known in musical circles, as his witnessing of the will of John Patten (father-in-law to Orlando Gibbons) indicates. This took place in 1623, shortly before his marriage to Jane, daughter of Sir Henry Hastings, whose four farms at Humberston in Leicestershire yielded a considerable sum of money by way of a dowry. This money was heavily taxed in 1646, when the Committee for Compounding of Delinquents, intent on raising money for

[1] Atkins, p. 65.   [2] Atkins, p. 68.
[3] Richard, organist of St. David's in 1719, may have been one of these.

the army, heard of Peregrine's journey to Oxford, when he was said to be 'in arms against the Parliament' and 'a servant in attendance on the King'.[1] He was then described as being 'of London, and Dronfield, co. Derby', and the fine was £90. Three years later Peregrine begged that his delinquency might be taken off, or his fine reduced so that he might be able to pay it without ruin. The remark about his having been in arms against the Parliament, interlined in the former certificate, was objected to as contrary to his consent. There is a further plea stating that the £600 secured from the farms at Humberston was his wife's dowry and that he was under oath not to touch the money.[2] On January 8, 1649, the fine was reduced to £10.[3]

Later that year he issued a further plea concerning goods in the possession of John Markett of St. Martin-in-the-Fields, also accused of delinquency; but the outcome of this suit is not known.[4] He had three sons, William, John, and Charles, and it is possible that the first of these is to be identified as the composer of a short item in *The Treasury of Musick*, published in 1669. Peregrine died shortly before the Restoration, his will being proved in 1659.[5]

*   *   *   *   *

One other branch of the family remains to be considered, and one member of that branch is especially important in the affairs of the Tomkinses: Nathaniel, son of Thomas Tomkins and Alice Hassard. There was also

---

[1] State Papers, Committee for Compounding, ii, 1378 (G 184, p. 172).
[2] *Ibid.* (G 184, p. 175).   [3] *Ibid.* (G 5, p. 43).
[4] *Ibid.* (G 124, p. 270; G 11, p. 75).
[5] P. C. C. Pell, f. 437.

a daughter, Ursula, who was alive in 1627,[1] but nothing further is known of her. Nathaniel, however, was prominent in Worcestershire history from the time when he became a canon of the cathedral in 1629, having then graduated from Balliol College, Oxford, with the degree of B.D. From the very first he was a popular figure, active both in the affairs of the cathedral and in the near-by school, where he encouraged the choirboy plays that had been a legacy from Tudor times.[2] But his strong Royalist and high-church sympathies, which were shared by the Dean and many of his colleagues, gradually changed his reputation in the eyes of the townsfolk, as the following letter shows:

To the Most Reverend and Right Honourable the Lord
    Archbishop of Canterbury.

My Most Honoured Lord,

    . . . I most humbly beseech your Grace to hear our grievances . . . [The Bishop] hates and speaks most unworthily of Mr. Tomkins our Prebend, who is as worthy, honest and true-hearted a churchman as any is of his quality in England. And the Bishop's hatred hath so inflamed the citizens, that this good and worthy man is made amongst them their matter of sport and contempt, all the injuries and affronts possible put upon him by their very boys, nay by our own School boys, to whom we give exhibition. Very lately, coming out from choir service as he was doing his adoration to God, purposely to hinder him in that action, the boys came thrusting and thronging upon him (who was then senior at home and had my authority) in such an insolent fashion that he was forced to hit one a box on the ear. The town triumphs at this, and the boy's father means to sue him for striking in the church. If our Bishop have the hearing of the business it will be

---

[1] Cf. the will of Anne Tomkins, p. 8.

[2] Ede, *The Cathedral Church of Worcester*, p. 136. Fellowes suggests in the preface to his edition of Ferrabosco's *Ayres* (1609) that the N. Tomkins who wrote some Latin alcaics in praise of Ferrabosco was the son of Thomas Tomkins. But Nathaniel Tomkins of Worcester was only 10 years old in 1609. A more likely candidate would be one of the Northamptonshire Tomkinses.

a heinous matter. But I know your Grace will relieve him, if there be need. In the meanwhile, I will do justice upon that saucy lad, and turn him out of his exhibition.

CHRISTOPHER POTTER

January 25, 1636.[1]

There was a further dispute over the seats in the cathedral, for they were used by certain citizens as a rallying point for those who objected to choral services, and the Dean was in favour of having at least the temporary seats removed. Once more came the danger of opposition from the Bishop, so Dr. Potter wrote to the Archbishop again, mentioning the three members of the Chapter who were desperately trying to maintain dignity and order:

> The complying of our weak silly bishop and these silly weak ones of my company . . . has put [the townspeople] into such a fury and malice against me, Mr. Boughton and Mr. Tomkins, as is hardly to be imagined.[2]

Nathaniel's loyalty remained unshaken, and from 1642 he was made responsible for raising sums of money for the Royalist army, on one occasion even receiving a request from the King himself, who ordered payment of £200 'for church rent' to Captain Francis Blunt.[3] As a relief from the trials of administration Nathaniel must often have turned to music, for he had been trained as a chorister at the cathedral and as an organist at the hands of his father. A letter from Bishop Skinner to Sheldon, Archbishop of Canterbury, mentions Nathaniel's skill as an organist and the fact that he had a chamber organ in

---

[1] State Papers (Domestic) Charles I [1636], vol. 344, no. 107.

[2] State Papers (Domestic) Charles I [1639], vol. 432, no. 80.

[3] Townshend, *Diary*, ii, 57, 99, 159, 163, 217. Historical Manuscripts Commission, XIVth Report, Appendix, Part VIII [1895], p. 200.

his house.[1]   The truth of this may be seen in a playful
exaggeration which was current during Nathaniel's lifetime — that he could play better on the organ than on
a text.[2]

He left no music of his own, preferring the rôle of
performer or editor to that of composer.   Had it not been
for Nathaniel's zeal for his father's work, *Musica Deo
Sacra* might never have appeared in print, and the history
of English church music would be that much the poorer.
Had it not been for Nathaniel's care, his father might
have suffered far more than he did during the troubled
times of the siege of Worcester and the years of the
Commonwealth.   With the cathedral silent, their lands
sequestered, and their positions abolished, father and son
must sometimes have been near to despair.   When his
first wife Theodosia died, despair was tempered with
grief;   but a second marriage restored Nathaniel's spirit
as well as his fortune, for Isabella Folliot brought as her
marriage portion the manor of Martin Hussingtree and
the patronage of its church.   The marriage, which was
Isabella's third and Nathaniel's second, took place in
January, 1654.   When Isabella died eight years later,
the property passed into the Tomkins family, where it
remained for many generations.   Nathaniel died on
October 20, 1681, aged 82 years, according to a memorial
tablet formerly in Martin Hussingtree church.

[1] Bodleian Library, MS Tanner 45, f. 19.
[2] Smith and Onslow, *Diocesan History of Worcester*, p. 262, note.

THE LIFE OF THOMAS TOMKINS

Let him heedfully examine, observe, and imitate the Artificial
works of the best Authors, such as Clemens non Papa, Horatio
Vecchi, Orlando di Lasso, Alfonso Ferrabosco, Luca Marenzio,
G. Croce, Doctor Fayrfax, Doctor Tye, Mr. BYRD, Mr. White,
Mr. Morley, and now excelling Mr. Thomas and John Tomkins
(that Aureum par Musicorum).

CHARLES BUTLER, *The Principles of Music* (1636).

ALMOST until his coming of age, Thomas Tomkins
must have lived in the shadow of his elder brother,
whose fiery and impulsive temperament had caused
trouble at St. David's and afterwards precipitated a
brief but glorious career at sea. The young Thomas, of
completely different character, retained the virtues of
gentleness, devotion, and industry to the very end of his
distinguished musical career; and although he progressed
slowly, he did so surely. That he was born in Pembrokeshire we know from his preface to the *Songs* of 1622.[1]
He was the third of three children by his father's first
wife, Margaret, and was born within a year of the
family's arrival in St. David's, whither they had removed
from Cornwall. Although officially designated as Organ
Player, Tomkins senior did not necessarily enjoy an additional salary or stipend beyond that given to him as Master
of the Choristers, and this may have been one of the
reasons why his somewhat unruly elder son was granted
a vicar's stall by understandably unwilling authorities.

[1] Quoted in full on pp. 39-40.

The statutory six choirboys had dwindled to two, and although there was an attempt to raise the number to three the general musical atmosphere of the cathedral could not have been particularly stimulating. The younger Thomas probably joined the choir in 1578 or the following year, for this would be the obvious way in which his father could implement the decision of the authorities and at the same time start his son on a musical career. After the death of Margaret, the father married again, and Anne (*née* Hargest) proved to be a reliable and not unsympathetic stepmother. Her first child, John, later to become organist of King's College, Cambridge, and St. Paul's Cathedral, was born in the same year that the elder Thomas was expelled from St. David's. Thomas the younger was then 14 years old, and had reached the end of his days as a boy treble.

In the course of the next few years four brothers and two sisters augmented the family circle. Its only diminution was due to the death of the bold and unruly Thomas on board the *Revenge*, which fought a hopeless action against the Spaniards in 1591. The time had almost come for removal to more spacious quarters, and for seeking a more ample source of income. By 1594 the family had installed itself in Gloucester, where Tomkins senior was a minor canon of the cathedral and later vicar of the near-by church of St. Mary de Lode. Having been compelled by economic circumstances to sacrifice a musical career himself, the father saw to it that his sons were well trained. There was now only one son by the name of Thomas, and since he was the eldest boy it was only natural that he should be the first to go to London for further training.

That he must have gone to London is shown by his

own admission, in the *Songs*, of his indebtedness to Byrd. Nearly all of the individual dedications of these songs are simple and straightforward: 'To Master Thomas Day', 'To my brother Mr. Nicholas Tomkins'; the one exception is no. 14 (*Too much I once lamented*) where the inscription is unusually full and fulsome: 'To my ancient, and much reverenced master, William Byrd'. In order to study with Byrd, he would have had to go to London, and this short period from 1594 to 1596 is the only time he could have done so, unless we assume (as Atkins does) that Thomas went to the Chapel Royal as a chorister, for which there is no evidence. Cheque Book listings of appointments usually mention the fact when the person appointed had his boyhood training in the Chapel Royal:

1585. Tho. Tallis died the 23rd of November, and Henry Eveseed sworn in his place the last of the same. Child there.

1585. Jo. Bull sworn the . . . of January in Mr. Boding-hurst['s] place. Child there.[1]

When Tomkins's appointment is listed in 1621, there is no mention of his having been a child of the Chapel Royal, and it may therefore be more likely that he came to London only when he was 21 or 22 years old. This agrees very closely with the record of his Oxford degree of B.Mus., taken when he was 35 and 'fourteen years student in music'.

The accounts of the treasurer of Worcester Cathedral give us our first glimpse of Tomkins after his period of training in London:

1596–97. Et in stipend —— Tomkins instructoris Choristarum cantand. infra eccl^{iam} cath^{em} predict. ad xj^{li} vj^s viij^d per ann.   xj^{li} vj^s viij^d

[1] Rimbault, *Cheque Book*, p. 4.

He succeeded John Fido, a temporary replacement for Nathaniel Patrick, who died in March, 1595, after a comparatively short term of office. Patrick's widow, who within two years of married life had lost first her infant son Francis and then, a few months later, her husband, found consolation for her grief in the friendship of Thomas Tomkins. She was some eight or nine years his senior, if we are to believe John Toy's sermon which states that she was 'near fourscore' at the time of her death in 1642, but the two were married in 1597. They had two children, Nathaniel and Ursula. Nathaniel, named after his mother's first husband and his father's predecessor at the cathedral, was born in 1599. The date of Ursula's birth is not known, but she is mentioned in the will of Anne Tomkins, the second wife of Thomas's father.

In spite of his duties at Worcester, Thomas kept in touch with musical affairs in London, and may occasionally have visited the city as a gentleman extraordinary of the Chapel Royal. There was a renowned gentleman extraordinary not far away at Tewkesbury in Gloucestershire, and the pages of the Cheque Book tell us of the circumstances of his appointment:

Mr. William Phelps of the Town of Tewkesbury in the county of Gloucester, being trained up in the noble science of Music, and also for that he did show a most rare kindness to Mr. Doctor Bull in his great distress, being robbed in those parts, is at his humble suit admitted by me . . . an extraordinary gentleman of her Majesty's most honourable Chapel, and sworn thereto accordingly the 29 day of May 1592. . . .[1]

Gentlemen admitted in this way usually had to promise not to try to secure for themselves a regular,

[1] Rimbault, *Cheque Book*, p. 32.

Authors whose authorities be either cited or vsed in this booke.

Such as haue written of the Art of Musicke.

Late Writers.

Iacobus faber stapulensis.
Franchinus Gaufurius
John Spataro.
Peter Aron.
Author quatuor principal.
Francho.
Robertus de Haulo.
Andreas Ornitoparchus.
Incertus impressus Basileæ
Ludouicus Zaccone.
Iosepho Zarlino.
Henric. loritus Glareanus
Lucas Lossius.
Ioannes Listenius.
Ioannes Thomas freigius.
Fredericus Beurhusius.
Sethus Caluisius.
Andreas Rasselius.
Nicolaus Faber.
Ioannes Magirus.
Mansredus Barbarinus Coregiensis.

Ancient Writers.

Psellus.
Boëthius.

Cited by Franchinus.
{ *Ptolomæus.*
{ *Aristoxenus.*
{ *Guido Aretinus.*

Practicioners, the moste parte of whose works we haue diligently perused, for finding the true vse of the Moods.

Iusquin.
Io. Okenheim
Iacobus Obrecht
Clement Ianequin
Petrus Platensis
Nicolas Craen
Iohannes Ghiselin

Antonius Brumel
Iohannes Mouton
Adamus a Fulda
Lutauich sensti
Iohannes Richaforte
Feuin
Sixtus dietrich
De orto
Gerardus de salice
Vaquieras
Nicolas Payen
Passereau
Francoys lagendre
Andræas syluanus
Antonius a vinea
Grogorius Meyer
Thomas Tzamen
Iacques de vert
Iacques du pont
Nicholas Gomberte
Clemens non papa
Certon
Damianus a goes
Adam Luyre
Iohannes vannius
Hurteur
Rinaldo del mel
Alexander Vtendal
Horatio ingelini
Lælio Bertani
Horatio vecchi
Orlando de Lassus
Alfonso Ferrabosco
Cyprian de rore
Alessandro striggio
Philippo de monte
Hieronimo Conuersi.
Io. Battista Lucatello
Io. pierluigi palestina
Stephano venturi
Ioan. de macque
Hippolito Baccuse

Paulo quagliati
Luca Marenzo

Englishmen.

M. Pashe.
Robert Iones.
Io. Dunstable
Leonel Power
Robert Orwel
M. Wilkinson.
Io. Guinneth.
Robert Dauis.
M. Risby.
D. Farfax.
D. Kirby.
Morgan Grig
Tho. Ashwell.
M. Sturton.
Iacket.
Corbrand.
Testwood.
Vngle.
Beech.
Bramston.
S. Io. Mason.
Ludford.
Farding.
Cornish.
Pyggot.
Tauerner.
Redford.
Hodges.
Selby.
Thorne.
Oclande.
Auerie.
D. Tie.
D. Cooper
D. Newton
M. Tallis.
M. White.
M. Persons
M. Byrde.

Additions, mostly in the hand of Thomas Tomkins, to his own copy of Morley's *Plain and Easy Introduction to Practical Music.* The names added by Tomkins are those of Bevin, Mudd, Blitheman, Mundy, Bull, Hooper, Morley, Carleton, Gibbons, Warwick, and John Tomkins

The Library of Magdalen College, Oxford. By permission of the President and Fellows

paid position in the chapel, but many of them were later appointed, after having served on special occasions when an unusually large number of singers was required. Whether or not Mr. Phelps of Tewkesbury suggested the name of his not-so-distant neighbour is of no great importance, though we may be sure that Tomkins's growing reputation was brought to the notice of the Sub-Dean by an influential friend in London musical circles. Tomkins's circle of friends was a wide and resplendent one, although its importance has hitherto received less emphasis than it deserves. It began to influence his career at the close of the sixteenth century, and secured for him a place in the illustrious group of composers who contributed madrigals to *The Triumphs of Oriana*, published in 1601 under the editorship of Thomas Morley.

Tomkins's madrigal *The fauns and satyrs tripping* was at one time attributed to the composer's father, probably because its technical excellence appeared to be far in advance of the capabilities of a youth of 25 or 26. Now that the year of birth is known to be 1572,[1] and the composer's age 29 when the madrigal was published, there seems nothing unusual about this early essay in a style that he was later to work at even more assiduously. As a gesture of thanks for Morley's invitation, and because of an undoubtedly genuine desire to improve his knowledge of theory, Tomkins invested in a copy of the *Plain and Easy Introduction to Practical Music*, first printed in 1597. This copy, complete with annotations by Tomkins, has fortunately survived to the present day thanks to the care with which it was looked after by successive owners, of whom the most recent were W. H. Monk, A. H. Mann, and E. H. W. Meyerstein. Dr.

[1] Document cited on p. 63.

Mann, in a note affixed to the fly-leaf of the volume, justly extolled its virtues and importance:

I regard this example of a famous book as one of the most valuable copies in existence. Certainly up to the present moment I have not seen one anywhere, to compare with it in any way whatsoever.[1]

The interest of the book lies not so much in its comments on the text (for not all of these are in Tomkins's hand) as in the four canons which he has written in the margins of pages 100 and 101, and the additions he has made to the last page of the book. This page contains a list of theorists and composers upon whom Morley drew, or pretended to draw, for his information. To the Englishmen, Tomkins adds the following names: Bevin, Mudd, Blitheman, Munday, Bull, Hooper, Morley, Carlton, Gibbons, Warwick, and John Tomkins. The last four were also dedicatees of songs in the composer's publication of 1622. After the name of John Tomkins, a later hand, perhaps that of the antiquary John Stafford Smith, has added the name of Thomas Tomkins.

In *Musica Deo Sacra*, there is a coronation anthem entitled *O Lord grant the King a long life*, and since this does not appear among the anthems sung at the coronations of Charles I and James I [2] there is every probability that it was specially written for local use at Worcester. Also in *Musica Deo Sacra* is a splendid full anthem for 7-part choir, *Be strong and of good courage* (the *Confortare*). An anthem beginning with these words is cited in the Lambeth MS, edited by Wickham Legg, of the Order of James I's Coronation in 1603. It may well be identical

---

[1] Meyerstein left this book to his Alma Mater, Magdalen College, Oxford, to which Thomas Tomkins was affiliated when he took his degree in 1607.

[2] *Cheque Book*, p. 157; Wickham Legg, *The Coronation Order of King James I*, p. 10 ff.

with the one composed by Tomkins, who was then 31 years old. The music for this coronation was in the very capable hands of Nathaniel Giles, a former organist of Worcester, and John Bull, whose name Tomkins had added to the list in his copy of *A Plain and Easy Introduction*. Two of the gentlemen of the chapel were William Byrd and John Stevens: the former had taught Tomkins, and the latter had befriended him during his early years in London. Both appear as dedicatees in the *Songs* of 1622, and it is therefore not impossible that these four men, Giles, Bull, Byrd, and Stevens, who either knew Tomkins personally or were conscious of his growing reputation as a composer, may have been influential in having him invited to compose one of the coronation anthems. Certainly the music is worthy of a great occasion and a fine performance.

Thomas has sometimes been confused with a student and usher of Magdalen College who was in residence from 1604 until 1610. This gentleman was a Northamptonshire Tomkins, and so far as is known, was not related to the Tomkins family of Cornwall.[1] The reason for this confusion is the affiliation of Thomas to Magdalen College, Oxford, for the purpose of taking his B.Mus. degree. Residence was not required at that time for a degree of this nature, although membership in a college was necessary in order to supplicate for the degree. The main part of Anthony à Wood's account appears under the year 1606, which is probably a mistake for 1607, as the University Registers show:

THOMAS TOMKINS OF MAGDALEN COLLEGE

This eminent and learned musician was son of *Thomas Tomkins* Chauntor of the Choir at *Gloucester*, descended from those of

[1] See the corrections in the notes to Bloxam's *Registers*, viii, 139.

his name at *Lostwithiel* in *Cornwall*, educated under the famous musician *William Byrd* and afterwards for his merits was made Gentleman of His Majesty's Chapel Royal, and at length Organist of the Cathedral Church at *Worcester*. . . .[1]

The account in the Registers, although more brief, gives the actual date of the degree:

Thomas Tomkins, Magdalen College.   14 years student in Music; supplicated B.Mus. 6 June, admitted 11 July 1607.[2]

There is no indication that this degree helped to advance the composer's fortunes and reputation in any way.   He had already held the post at Worcester for ten years, and his renown among the musical circles of London was due largely to his compositions and his brilliant prowess at the keyboard.   The appointment of his father to the rank and dignity of Precentor at Gloucester in 1609 must have been a source of pleasure to him, as was the progress of his son Nathaniel, who served as Bible clerk in Worcester Cathedral during the year 1610, and chorister in 1611.

Tomkins, together with Coperario, Ward, and other prominent musicians of the time was called upon to write an anthem for the funeral of Prince Henry, whose death in 1612 had saddened the whole of England.   When the body of the Prince was brought to the Chapel Royal, the choir sang 'several anthems to the organs and other wind instruments'.[3]   One of these anthems was undoubtedly the highly chromatic and expressive *Know you not* which Tomkins had hurriedly but devotedly composed for the occasion:

[1] Wood, *Athenae Oxonienses*, i, 321.
[2] *Registers of the University of Oxford*, vol. ii, part I, p. 147.   Atkins (p. 47) suggests that *When David heard* was written for this degree, but there is no evidence for this.
[3] Birch, *The Life of Prince Henry*, p. 362.

Great Britain mourn, let every family mourn; O family of David, O family of Levi, sorrowing for him as for thy first-born, sob and sing, sigh and cry.

The fact that this was a verse anthem, or 'anthem to the organs' as the description has it, demonstrates the rapidity with which English composers followed the lead set by Byrd in his *Psalms, songs, and sonnets* of 1611. Tomkins not only followed his master's example but also gathered supporters in Worcestershire for the renewal of the organ in the cathedral, since it was obvious that the new style of anthem would call for an elaborate and important organ part.

In all, there were 112 individuals and corporate bodies who contributed towards the cost of the organ, which was built by Thomas Dallam in 1613–14. Sums of money ranging from £20 to 2s. 6d. enabled Tomkins to draw up specifications for a two-manual instrument with thirteen stops, the organ itself costing £211 and the gallery, case, and painting of escutcheons £170.[1] In the same document that provides these details, there is an inventory of the thirteen stops:

The Particulars of the Great Organ

2 open diapasons of metal	[8]
CC fa ut — a pipe of 10 feet long [2]	
2 principals of metal	[4]
2 small principals, or fifteenths, of metal	[2]
1 twelfth, of metal	[$2\frac{2}{3}$]
1 recorder, of metal — a stopt pipe	[8]

---

[1] Treasurer's Accounts, D. 248 ('Organs, 1614'). There is a more detailed account of the instrument in a letter written by Nathaniel Tomkins to John Sayer in May, 1665. (Bodleian Library, Add. C 304a, f. 141.)

[2] A brief note on p. xvi of *Musica Britannica*, v, suggests that the organ was tuned 'about a major third below the international pitch of the present time'. A supplement to *Musica Deo Sacra* shows that the pitch of an organ was a minor third *higher* than nowadays. This is borne out by the letter from

In the Choir Organ

1 principal, of metal	[4]
1 diapason, of wood	[4]
1 flute, of wood	[4]
1 small principal, or fifteenth, of metal	[2]
1 two-and-twentieth, of metal	[1]

One of the earliest descriptions of this noble instrument is to be found in Habington's *Survey of Worcestershire*, compiled between 1606 and 1647. This account dates from 1639:

At the west end and highest ascent into the Choir is mounted aloft a most fair and excellent organ, adorned with imperial crowns, red roses, including the white fleur-de-lys, pomegranates, being all royal badges. Towards the top are two stars, with the one, W. Parry, Episcopus; with the other A. Lake, Decanus; and written about the organ, By the meditation and mediation of Thomas Tomkins, organist here unto the Right Reverend Bishop and Venerable Dean, who gave these munificent gifts and invited their friends by the industry of the said Thomas Tomkins.[1]

Habington follows this with details of some of the more important among the coats-of-arms. He then quotes an inscription which once appeared above the fifty-seven coats of arms on the organ case:

These honourable and worshipful gentlemen whose arms are here placed, were contributors towards these organs. Anno Domini 1614.[2]

It is interesting to compare this early description with a later one by Green, who still refers to the nine (really eight) stops on the great organ, and five on the

Nathaniel Tomkins to Sayer, where the lowest note of the Worcester organ is said to sound a 10-ft. pipe (FFF). CC (an 8-ft. pipe nowadays) would then have been 6⅔ ft., thus the organ was a high-pitched instrument in spite of the extra keys and pipes below CC.

[1] Habington, *Survey*, ii, 462.   [2] *Ibid*. 463.

choir, but differs from Habington in his reading of the inscription, which was on the west front of the gallery, on the cornice. Instead of 'contributors towards these organs' Green has 'contributors towards this gallery', and this may have been due to an alteration in the wording of the inscription between 1661, when the instrument was rebuilt, and 1796, when Green's book was published. This alteration would have been called for by the destruction of the organ at the time of the second siege of Worcester, and the subsequent building of a new instrument by George Dallam in 1661, with enlargements by Thomas Harrison in 1666.

Tomkins may well have been proud of the organ, for it served the cathedral well for thirty-two years in its original state, and did further duty after the Restoration, when a few surviving ranks of pipes were pressed into service by Dallam and Harrison. These ranks may still have been in use when Green heard the organ in the late eighteenth century:

> The great characteristic of this noble instrument is its sweetness and fullness of tone, to which this part of the cathedral, well adapted for sound, does the amplest justice. . . .[1]

Two of the compositions by Tomkins included in *Tristitiae Remedium*, a musical anthology compiled in 1616 by his friend Thomas Myriell, were later printed in *Musica Deo Sacra* as verse anthems; and though Myriell's part-books [2] contain no organ score, it is perfectly clear that strings or wind instruments, or a mixed consort of both, were expected to play along with

---

[1] Green, *A History of Worcester*, i, 114.

[2] British Museum, Add. MSS 29372-7, *Tristitiae Remedium. Cantiones selectissimae diversorum tum authorum tum argumentorum labore et manu exaratae.* Thomas Myriell. A.D. 1616.

the voice-parts. Thus, in spite of the composer's enthusiasm for the new organ at the cathedral, he found it desirable to encourage the performance of verse anthems, and even full anthems, with instrumental accompaniment. One of the full anthems in this anthology is the justly famous *When David heard*, which appeared in the *Songs* of 1622 with a dedication to Myriell, and again in *Musica Deo Sacra*. Although neither the manuscript copy nor the two printed versions contain any hint of instrumental participation, a comment by Charles Butler [1] proves that mixed consorts were very much the order of the day:

> Of this mode [the Lydian] is that passionate lamentation of the musical king for the death of his son *Absalom*, composed in five parts by Mr. Thomas Tomkins, now organist of His Majesty's chapel. The melodious harmony of which, when I heard it in the Music-School (Oxon), whether I should more admire the sweet well-governed voices, with consonant instruments, of the singers, or the exquisite invention, wit, and art of the composer, it was hard to determine.

There is little doubt that the best of Tomkins's anthems were written during the first two or three decades of the seventeenth century. Both Worcester and the Chapel Royal needed music in the polyphonic, conservative idiom that lent dignity to the services and honour to a great tradition. At the Restoration, that tradition had given way to the pressing claims of new foreign styles, and when at last Tomkins's anthems were collected together and published as *Musica Deo Sacra* (1668) they were looked upon, just as the liturgical polyphony printed by Byrd and Tallis in the previous century had been, as a monument to the glories of a past tradition rather than

[1] *The Principles of Music*, p. 5.

an offering to the gods of present usefulness. But during the reign of James I, and for a few years beyond, these anthems were a vital part of Tomkins's creative activity. No fewer than eleven of the anthems in *Musica Deo Sacra* appear in a manuscript written before 1617,[1] and these together with the ones in Myriell's collection show how mature the composer's technique then was.

In 1617 Tomkins was prosperous enough to take on a lease, conjointly with a city bailiff named Foulke Broughton, of a house not far from the cathedral. This lease, dated November 26, 1617, was drawn up between the new Dean, Dr. Joseph Hall

of the one part and Foulke Broughton of the city of Worcester gent. and Thomas Tomkins dwelling within the precincts of the said church, gent. of the other, of a tenement and garden situate, lying and being within the parish of St. Michael Bedwardine for 40 years at 10s. a year.

Interest in local affairs and property did not, however, distract Tomkins from the very substantial attractions of the metropolis, and he probably became a gentleman of the Chapel Royal at some time between 1617 and 1620. The actual date of appointment is not recorded in the Cheque Book, although his name appears among the gentlemen present on June 29, 1620, when Thomas Peirs was sworn gentleman in place of James Davies.[2] In the following year Tomkins was appointed as one of the organists, his immediate senior being Orlando Gibbons:

1621. Edmund Hooper, Organist, died the 14th day of July, and Thomas Tomkins, Organist of Worcester, was sworn in his place the second day of August following.[3]

[1] Tenbury MS 1382.   [2] *Cheque Book*, p. 47.   [3] *Ibid.* p. 10.

The duties of Chapel Royal organists were arranged in rotation, and in theory the Sub-Dean and Clerk of the Cheque were supposed to be informed of the comings and goings of the gentlemen concerned. A document drawn up by the Bishop of Bath and Wells [1] devotes an entire paragraph to the organists, but gently hints that they are free to make their own arrangements:

> If there be above two organists at once, two shall always attend; if there be but two in all, then they shall wait by course, one after another, weekly or monthly, as they shall agree betwixt themselves, giving notice to the Sub-Dean and the Clerk of the Check how they do dispose of their waiting, that thereby it may be known who is at all times to be expected for the service, and they shall be subject to such orders, and to such checks, in the same manner as the other gentlemen are.

The very vagueness of this injunction led to trouble, for we find evidence of disagreement among the organists in 1615, and this gave rise to a new order by the Bishop, which was presumably still in force when Tomkins was appointed:

> . . . the most ancient organist shall serve the eve and day of every principal feast, as namely the eves and days of the feasts of Christmas, Easter, St. George, and Whitsuntide, the next organist in place to serve the second day, and so likewise the third for the third day, if there be so many organists, and for all other festival days in the year, those to be performed by the organists as they shall fall out in their several weeks of waiting; the feasts being ended, he that did or should begin the Saturday before shall finish up the same week, according to former custom, and the other to follow, except the feast of Christmas, for then they change every day, as the choir doth during the whole twelve days. [2]

Leave to take up these temporary duties was freely granted by cathedral authorities, who doubtless felt some

---

[1] Orders for the Attendance of the Gentlemen of His Majesty's Chapel, *Cheque Book*, p. 71.   [2] *Ibid.* p. 73.

pride at being musically represented in the Chapel Royal. During Tomkins's periods of duty in London, or where-ever the Chapel Royal might be, his place at Worcester was taken by John Fido, a somewhat difficult individual who had been organist from 1595 to 1596. Fido, whose alternate attachments to Hereford and Worcester appear to have been regulated by his being *persona non grata* at each of these cathedrals in turn, eventually became a minor canon of Worcester, where he remained until his death in 1640.[1]

The years 1621 and 1622 were marked by publica-tions: first the psalm tunes *Dunfermline* and *Worcester* printed in Ravenscroft's *The Whole Book of Psalms*, and then the *Songs of 3. 4. 5. and 6 .parts*. The name of Thomas Tomkins was beginning to resound in the man-sion as well as the manse, and his *Songs* show how careful he was to avoid being put either in the one category or the other; like the anthologies of his teacher, William Byrd, the *Songs* included both sacred and secular compositions, and their quality made an immediate appeal to musicians of varied station and taste. The recent appointment of Tomkins as organist of the Chapel Royal may well have helped to publicize the book, which was dedicated to the Earl of Pembroke:

My very good Lord

Though it may seem a presumptuous and improper thing for me to present your Honour with a Song, who are daily busied in the great and weighty Counsels and affairs of the King and King-dom: yet have not my thoughts been wound up to this height, without an appearing reason to myself, of excuse, and pardon at the least, if not of fittingness, and hope of acceptation.

For though your Lordship's employments be daily, yet hath the Day many hours, and if you should bestow all of them on sad

---

[1] For a full account of Fido, see Atkins, pp. 35-7.

and serious matters, you might shorten them, and deprive us too soon of the benefit both of your Counsels and Actions. Besides (if I may presume to give your Lordship any account of my poor self) I first breathed, and beheld the sun, in that Country, to which your Lordship'gives the greatest lustre, taking the Title of your Earldom from it, and even therefore have always (I know not by what secret power of natural affection) ever honoured and wished your Lordship's prosperity. To which considerations may be added that goodness of nature, eminent in your Lordship, which was ever a friend to Music, and the known virtues of your mind, which seems to be best in tune, in those who love Music best, as being least distracted by low cogitations, and your often frequenting and favourable attention to the Music in the Chapel, which useth sometimes to raise the soul above her Companions, Flesh, and Blood; as also the place which you hold under His Majesty, which consequently renders you, a Patron and Protector of Music.

Concerning the Songs, if they shall be found answerable to the desire and affection of their indulgent parent: I beseech your Honour to consider, that as there are few men absolutely perfect, save only in contemplation; so neither is more clearness to be expected in the rivers, than in the spring, not more perfection, in imperfect men's contemplations, or works of this kind.

For the lightness of some of the words I can only plead an old (but ill) custom, which I wish were abrogated: although the Songs of these books will be even in that point, suitable to the people of the world, wherein the rich and poor, sound and lame, sad and fantastical, dwell together.

Lastly, I do again most humbly beseech your Lordship to pardon my presumption, and to accept of these my imperfect offers, who will offer my prayers to God for your Lordship, that you may enjoy a happy and blessed Harmony in the whole course of your life, (between yourself and your friends, your body and mind) to the end that you may have content (which is the best kind of Music) here, and the Music of the Angels hereafter. This is, and shall be, the prayer of

Your Honour's most humbly devoted
in all observance and duty,

THOMAS TOMKINS.

William Herbert, third Earl of Pembroke, was referred to by Aubrey as 'the greatest Maecenas to learned men of any peer of his time or since'.[1] The nephew of Sir Philip Sidney, he was an intimate friend of Donne, Massinger, and Inigo Jones. He was the dedicatee of Davison's *Poetical Rhapsody* and (with his brother Philip) of the First Folio edition of Shakespeare. Tomkins's preface gives us knowledge of the Earl's musical interests, which are not widely appreciated even though he is said to have taken part in the Court Masque on St. John's Day, 1604. Henry Lawes and Nicholas Lanier set his poems to music, and it is probable that he encouraged musicians as much as poets and dramatists.

The *Songs* are unique among the publications of the English madrigalists in that they are dedicated individually to the composer's family and to his friends, as well as collectively to the Earl of Pembroke. In this Tomkins was following the practice of many of his contemporaries in Italy, who inscribed their songs and instrumental pieces to friends and colleagues.[2] He begins the collection with a song dedicated 'To my dear Father Mr. Thomas Tomkins' and ends it with an anthem 'To my son Nathaniel Tomkins': interspersed among the twenty-eight items the names of his five brothers — Giles, John, Nicholas, Peregrine, and Robert — are to be found.

The names of some of the greatest composers of the time also appear: the paired lyrics which serve the first two of the four-part songs are dedicated to two great lutenists, Dowland and Danyel, while the next is 'To Master John Coperario'. William Byrd and Orlando

---

[1] Aubrey, *Brief Lives*, p. 145.
[2] See Sartori, *Une Pratique des musiciens lombards* (1582–1639).

Gibbons are there, so too are John Ward and Nicholas Carlton, who (in his will dated 1630) named Thomas as his 'singular and esteemed good friend' and made him co-executor of his estate in Beoley, Worcestershire.[1] Other Worcestershire friends include Humphrey Withy, who was a chorister at the cathedral in 1611, subsequently becoming lay clerk, Sub-Deacon and Librarian, Deacon and Sub-Treasurer, and finally Clerk of the Works and Verger; Henry Molle, Headmaster of the King's School at Worcester; and Nathaniel Giles, who was a native of the city and one of Thomas's predecessors as organist of the cathedral.[2]

Thomas would have known Nathaniel Giles at the Chapel Royal, and was later to become acquainted with his son, also called Nathaniel, who came to Worcester as a canon in 1626. It is significant that many members of the Chapel Royal appear as dedicatees of these songs, for besides Byrd and Gibbons, who have already been mentioned, we find the names of William Cross, Thomas Day, John Stevens, and Thomas Warwick. Cross was associated with the gentlemen of the Chapel Royal as early as 1603, when he signed an admonition prepared by the Sub-Dean; his name is found again, along with that of Thomas Tomkins, in the document dated June 29, 1620, to which reference has already been made. Day's name is appended to the same document: he seems to have joined the choir in 1615, after having been in the establishment of Prince Henry. He served as organist of Westminster Abbey from 1625 until 1632, becoming Master of the Children of the Chapel Royal in 1636. John Stevens was one of the senior members of the choir. He was sworn in place of Thomas Wiles, in

---

[1] Dawes, *Nicholas Carlton*.　　　　[2] Atkins, pp. 26-9.

1590, and is often named 'Recorder of Songs', which means that he copied much of the music used in the Chapel. It was he who copied Tomkins's coronation anthems written in 1625, receiving 30s. for his pains. Tomkins, the composer of the music, received only 40s. Thomas Warwick, one of whose Pavans is included in the *Fitzwilliam Virginal Book*, was chosen for the difficult task of succeeding Orlando Gibbons, and subsequently lost a month's pay for presuming

to play verses on the organ at service time, being formerly inhibited by the Dean from doing the same, by reason of his insufficiency for that solemn service.[1]

Five other dedicatees remain to be mentioned,[2] and all were important men in musical, literary, academic, or ecclesiastical circles. Thomas Myriell, the compiler of *Tristitiae Remedium*, studied at Pembroke Hall, Cambridge, and subsequently became archdeacon of Norfolk. He was a very discerning music-lover, and included some of the finest compositions, both sacred and secular, in his anthology. Besides the anthems of Tomkins, there are two by William White of Durham, another member of this far-flung circle of friends. White was in the choir of Westminster Abbey at the time of Queen Elizabeth's funeral,[3] and it is fairly certain that he got to know Tomkins when the two were together in London on some occasion of state. One of his Fancies for strings is dated 1641, and he is mentioned by both Simpson and Mace.[4]

The poet and divine, Phineas Fletcher, was probably

[1] *Cheque Book*, p. 78.

[2] William Walker and Robert Chetwode have not yet been conclusively identified.

[3] La Fontaine, *The King's Musick*, p. 44.

[4] Simpson, *Compendium*; Mace, *Music's Monument*.

a closer friend of John than of Thomas Tomkins; educated at Eton and King's, Fletcher became a Fellow of his college in 1611, but intrigues against him brought about his retirement five years later. John Tomkins was organist of King's College at this time, and his name appears as 'Thomalin' in some of Fletcher's poems. Although there is no direct evidence that Thomas Tomkins ever met Fletcher, he must have held him in high esteem since he appears as the dedicatee of *Fusca, in thy starry eyes*, a particularly fine five-part madrigal. In later life Fletcher served as chaplain to Sir Henry Willoughby at Risley in Derbyshire, and rector of Hilgay, Norfolk.

'Mr. Doctor Heather', as Tomkins calls him, was a native of Harmondsworth, Middlesex, and he perpetuated his name in the professorship of music at Oxford, which he founded in 1626, the year before his death. Although Heather was not formally admitted to the Chapel Royal until 1614, his connection with it must date from the early part of the century since he signed a document prepared by the Sub-Dean in 1603.[1] Aylmer, like Heather, enjoys the prefix 'Mr. Doctor', but his doctorate was in divinity, not music. Theophilus Aylmer was a son of John Aylmer, Bishop of London (the family name is variously spelt Ailmer or Aelmer). A prebendary of St. Paul's in 1583, he served for a short time as rector of Much Hadham in Hertfordshire before coming to London as archdeacon. He was a prominent figure in the city for nearly thirty-five years, and although his connection with Thomas Tomkins is not a particularly direct or musical one, it is clear that the two were well acquainted.

[1] *Cheque Book*, p. 70.

The importance of this discussion of the twenty-eight separate dedicatees in the *Songs* lies in the picture it gives of the composer's friends and acquaintances both within and outside the family circle. These people, unlike the Earl of Pembroke, were on roughly the same social level as Tomkins; they were men with whom he may have spent many a pleasant hour in music-making and conversation. In a sense, they reflect the breadth of his interests and the excellence of the company he kept, besides showing something of the esteem in which an organist of his eminence was then held. There is a charming sequel to all this in the prefatory poem, written by John Tomkins 'To my Brother the Author':

> *Yet* thou wert mortal: now begin to *live*,
>   And end with only *Time*. Thy Muses give
>   What Nature hath denied, *Eternity*:
> Gladly my younger Muse doth honour thee,
> But mine's no praise. A large increase *it* has
> That's multiplied through strong affection's glass.
> Yet is thy worth the same, and were no other
> Though as a *Judge* I spake, not as a *Brother*.
> This comfort have, this *Art's* so *great*, so *free*,
>   None but the *good* can reach to *censure* thee.

Thomas Tomkins was in his early fifties when King James died in 1625, and the double duty of attending to the music for the funeral in May of that year, and for the coronation of Charles I during the following February, taxed his energies very severely. The death of Gibbons in June, 1625, dealt the Chapel a serious blow, and undoubtedly led the authorities to look to Tomkins for musical guidance and inspiration. That the duties of the gentlemen of the Chapel Royal were exceptionally heavy

at times like these is borne out by the Sub-Dean's account
of the order of the royal funeral:

> Two days before the day of the funerals the corpse was brought
> into the said Chapel in great solemnity with an anthem, and set
> under a hearse of velvet, and the gentlemen of the Chapel from
> that time waited there, and performed solemn service with the
> organs brought thither for that purpose; they also waited with the
> corpse by course night and day: by night first decani side, and
> next cantoris side, and twice in the night, viz. at nine of the clock
> and at midnight, they had prayers with a first and second chapters,
> and ended with an anthem.[1]

Tomkins, as organist, was assisted by three senior
members of the Chapel: William Heather, Nathaniel
Giles, who was then Master of the Children, and John
Stevens, recorder of songs.[2] This same group of tried
and experienced musicians attended to the details of the
coronation music, a good deal of which was composed
by Tomkins although nothing has survived apart from
the text of *Sadock the Priest*, preserved in a manuscript
collection of words of anthems used in the Chapel
Royal.[3] This text is to be found among the eight anthems
listed in the Cheque Book:

> To Mr. Tomkins xl[s.] for composing of many songs against
> the coronation of King Charles. To Mr. Stevens for pricking
> those songs xxx[s.].[4]

John Tomkins joined the Chapel as organist in 1626,
and it is more than possible that his elder brother envied
him the short distance between St. Paul's and Whitehall.
In those days, the journey from Worcester to London used
to take the best part of a week. Thomas found much to

---

[1] *Cheque Boook,* p. 154.   [2] *King's Musick,* p. 57.
[3] British Museum, Harleian MS 6346.
[4] *Cheque Book,* p. 58. The anthems are mentioned on pp. 157 f.

occupy his mind at Worcester, however, for the Dean and Chapter granted him two leases, both dated November 25, 1627. The first lease, extending over a period of twenty-one years, was for eleven acres of pasture land in St. Clement's parish.[1] The second was a lease for forty years of four bays and a half of buildings within the precincts of the cathedral, and as these buildings were old and decayed Tomkins had every intention of renovating or replacing them. A clause in the lease tells us that if he were to be dispossessed through no fault of his own, the Dean and Chapter would repay him

the value of all timber, boards, bricks, tiles, iron, lead, tin, sand, clay, and other building stuff whatsoever, bestowed or to be bestowed in reparation or new building of the said houses or buildings, also all charges of workmanship.[2]

Besides attending to these leases Tomkins had to visit Gloucester frequently, for his father had died earlier in the year, and his stepmother did not long survive her husband. Perhaps, on those journeys between the two cathedral cities, Thomas would call to mind the text of the madrigal which he had dedicated, five years previously, to his dear father:

> Our hasty life away doth post,
> Before we know what we have lost;
> Hours into days, days into years are gone,
> Years make a life, which straight is none.
> Thus soon is man's short story told:
> We scarce are young when we are waxed old.

In March, 1628, Tomkins was the unfortunate victim of a typical administrative error of the court of Charles I, whereby one and the same post had been promised to two different people. The following

[1] Cathedral Records, A vii 10, f. 123.   [2] *Ibid.* f. 133.

document was drawn up in the first place, by order
of the Bishop of Bath and Wells:

Charles by the grace of God &c. To all men to whom &c
Greeting. Know ye that we for certain good causes and considerations us hereunto especially moving of our especial grace certain
knowledge and mere motion have given and granted and by these
presents for us our heirs and successors do give and grant unto our
wellbeloved Thomas Tomkins the room and place of composer
of our music in ordinary. And him the said Thomas Tomkins
composer of our music in ordinary we do make nominate and
appoint by these presents, Which said room and place Alfonso
Ferrabosco deceased late had and enjoyed, To have hold and enjoy
the said room and place of composer of our music in ordinary to
the said Thomas Tomkins during his natural life. And further
of our more ample grace we have given and granted and by these
presents for us our heirs and successors we do give and grant unto
the said Thomas Tomkins for his attendance in the exercise of
the said room and place the wages and fee of forty pounds by the
year, To have receive and take the said wages and fee of forty
pounds by the year to the said Thomas Tomkins and his assigns
from the time of the death of the said Alfonso Ferrabosco during
the natural life of him the said Thomas Tomkins out of the treasure
of us our heirs and successors at the receipt of the exchequer of
us our heirs and successors by the hands of the Treasurer and
Under-treasurer of us our heirs and successors there for the time
being, At the four usual feasts or terms of the year, that is to say at
the feasts of the Annunciation of our Blessed Virgin Mary, the
Nativity of St. John Baptist, St. Michael the Archangel and the
Birth of our Lord God by even and equal portions quarterly to be
paid together with all such other entertainments as the said Alfonso
Ferrabosco late had and enjoyed or ought to have had and enjoyed
for the same. Although express mention &c. In witness &c.
witness &c.

Immediately beneath these legal *longueurs* there
appears a brief summary of the matter:

This containeth Your Majesty's grant to Thomas Tomkins
during his life of the room and place of composer of music in
ordinary with the fee of forty pounds by the year from the death

of Alfonso Ferrabosco. And is done by the order of the Lord
Bishop of Bath and Wells.[1]

WINDEBANK

Whether this appointment was a belated expression
of thanks to Tomkins for the important part he played
in the coronation music is not absolutely clear. As far
as is known, no other attempt at a royal reward was ever
made, perhaps for the very good reason that the composer was approaching 60 years of age, and could hardly
be expected to make frequent journeys between Worcester
and London. Nevertheless, the situation carried with it
a certain aura of importance and responsibility, so that
when the revocation of the grant became known, Tomkins
must have felt some disappointment. The letter of
revocation was sent from the Lord Chamberlain, then
Philip Herbert, Earl of Montgomery, to Sir John Coke,
and pointed out that that place had already been promised
to Ferrabosco's son.[2]

Later during the same year Thomas's name appears
with that of his brother John among the gentlemen of
the Chapel,[3] and the presence of two brothers with talents
such as theirs must have ensured a high standard of
music-making. Somehow the Tomkins family always
managed to keep together in groups of two or three, no
matter what the sphere of their activities. In 1629,
Thomas's son Nathaniel became a canon of the cathedral,
adding to the small but enthusiastic circle of musicians
which included Humphrey Withy and Edward Thornborough. The latter was collated archdeacon of Worcester on August 3, 1629, and appears to have been a

[1] Public Record Office, S.P. 39/23/53.
[2] Historical Manuscripts Commission, 12th Report, i, 341 (Coke MSS,
property of the Earl Cowper, K.G., Melbourne Hall, Derbyshire).
[3] *King's Musick*, p. 65.

special friend of the organist, who inscribed a small group
of keyboard pieces to him.[1]

The next few years passed quietly enough, although
Thomas lost a good friend when Nicholas Carlton died
in 1630, at Beoley in Worcestershire. Four years later,
the Visitation of the County of Worcester was responsible
for the first of two pedigrees of the Tomkins family,[2]
besides having certain repercussions which reflect upon
the state of the choir. The Dean and Chapter were
warned

that none be admitted to any place of your choir before he be first
approved of for his voice and skill in singing, by such of your
church as are able to judge thereof, and that the places there, as
they fall void, be supplied with men of such voices as your statutes
require.[3]

The pecuniary difficulties of keeping together an
efficient choir loomed as large in the early seventeenth
century as they do to-day. Yet there is no reason to
believe that Tomkins was satisfied with anything less
than the best in singing and musicianship, for his close
contact with the Chapel Royal and its high standards
would serve to keep his critical ear well attuned. The
injunction conformed to a general pattern, and did not
reflect directly on the state of affairs at Worcester, where
these things were better ordered than in many another
provincial cathedral. At least the supply of choirboys
was in some measure guaranteed by the near proximity
of the school, whose teaching staff was largely composed
of clergy from the cathedral. One schoolmaster and
minor canon, John Toy, seems to have been a close

---

[1] See p. 153 for a description of these pieces.
[2] London, College of Heralds, MS C.30, f. 74 (Atkins, p. 41).
[3] Historical Manuscripts Commission 3, House of Lords MSS, p. 158.

friend and admirer of Thomas, for he published in his *Worcester Elegy and Eulogy* (1638) the following tribute to the sixty-six year old organist:

> And thou, great Master of melodious skill,
> This holy harmony didst help to fill;
> When in this dismal Cadence, no sound else
> Was heard but Mournful groans, and mortal bells.
> Thy hand an Organ was of ample good
> To set in tune, and cheer the mourning mood.
> According to thy Tenor, thou didst lend
> Us Meanes, our low, and base state to mend.
> T'accomplish now this song of courtesy,
> In triple time our thanks shall trebles be.
> These lines are Brief, but know, thy Restless song
> Of fame, shall stand in notes both large and long.

The punning use of musical terms shows that Toy was well acquainted with the technical vocabulary of music, if not with the art itself. He may well have been a performer on the viol, for there is musical evidence for consort-playing in Worcester at about this time,[1] and a pursuit such as this would have surely appealed to Toy's artistic and intellectual outlook on life. Apart from the musical references, there is one phrase — 'mournful groans and mortal bells' — that refers to the plague in the city of Worcester, and it may be more than mere coincidence that the worst year of the plague, 1637, coincides with the date of the vast and propitiatory keyboard *Offertory*.[2]

By 1639 a recovery had been made, and the time was ripe for the first of brother John's children to come up to Worcester as a chorister. Sylvanus, named after his

[1] In an incomplete set of part-books at Oxford (Bodleian Library, [MS] Mus. Sch. E 415-18) the names of Thomas Tomkins, Humphrey Withy, and John Withy (son of Humphrey ?) are to be found along with the dates 1641 and 1642.   [2] Printed in *Musica Britannica*, v, no. 21.

grandfather, Dr. Sylvanus Griffiths, Dean of Hereford probably made the journey in the company of Thomas, returning from a spell of duty at the Chapel Royal. The latter, besides bringing back his nephew, also brought some plate at the request of the cathedral authorities:

Paid for carriage of the old plate to London and bringing down the new, according to Mr. Thomas Tomkins' bill, 19s. 7d.[1]

Sylvanus, like a dutiful nephew, tried out his signature in at least one of Thomas's books, and had no difficulty in persuading his brother John (who arrived a few years later as chorister and King's Scholar) to do the same.[2] The two boys were sent to Worcester for more than purely musical reasons, however, for their father had died in 1638, and there were two younger children to be looked after at home in London.

Thomas continued to be occupied by musical affairs both within the cathedral and outside it. In addition to his normal duties, he played daily for morning prayers held at 6 A.M. in the Lady Chapel, receiving each quarter a small additional fee.[3] His advice was sought by the Dean and Chapter of Gloucester with regard to a new organ in the cathedral, and he journeyed there to inspect the instrument and give further advice in 1640. But the tension between the Laudian or high-church party, to which he and his son belonged, and the citizens of Worcester (who found a powerful ally in the Bishop) began to complicate and upset the normally peaceful life of the cathedral close. Minor outbreaks of violence, in which Nathaniel was involved, ended in a petition sent to Parliament by the citizens, complaining about

---

[1] Treasurer's Accounts (1639) A, xxvi, 66.
[2] Paris, Bibliothèque du Conservatoire, Rés. 1122, p. i.
[3] Treasurer's Accounts (1639) A, xxvi, 66.

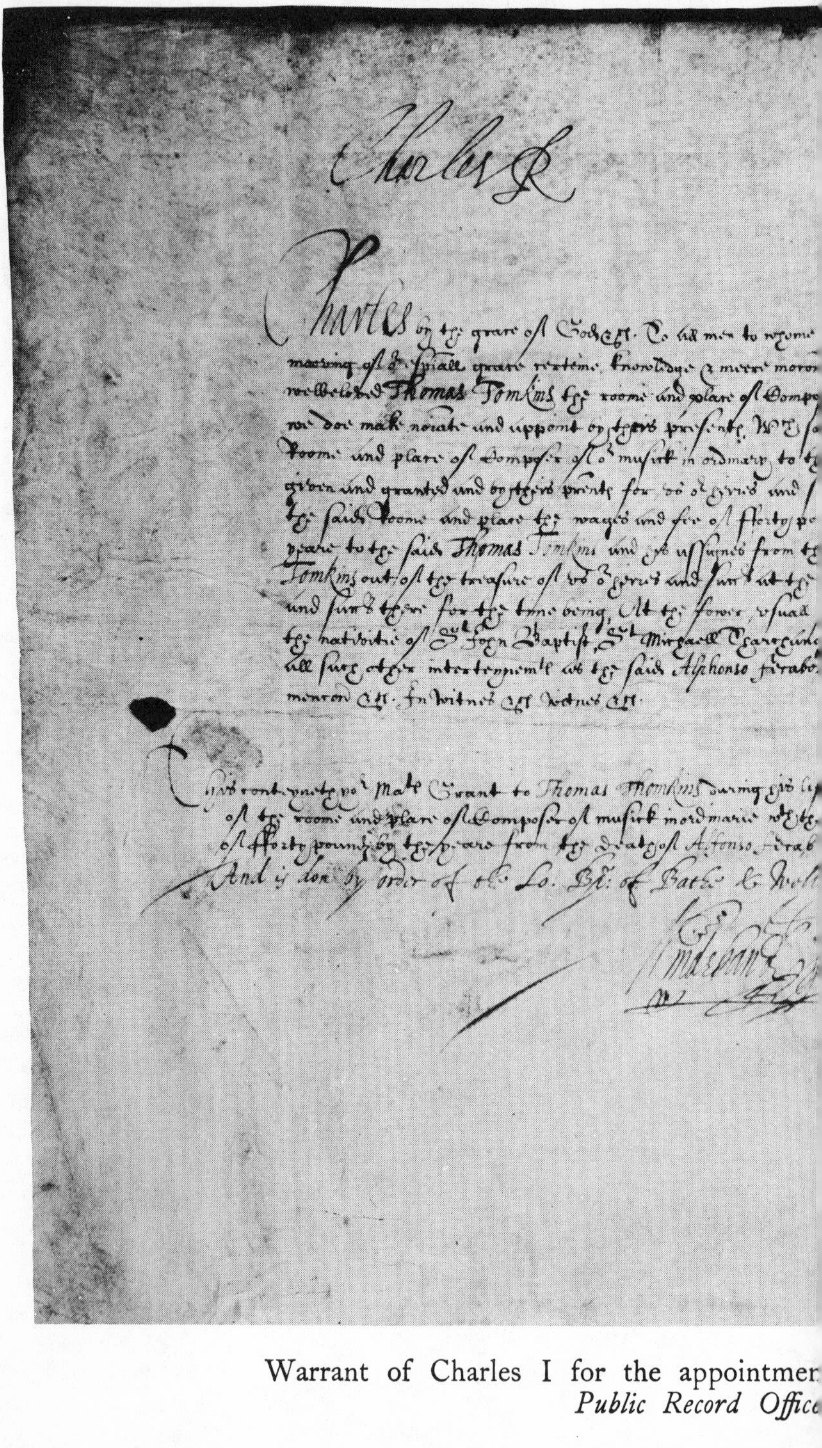

Warrant of Charles I for the appointmen
Public Record Offic

...tinā Knowe yee that w... for certaine good causes... consideratio... vs g... vnto... e... speria... ...
...en and granted and by the... p...nts for vs... o... and su... do... giue and grant vnto o...
...r Musick in ordinarie. And g... the said Thomas Tomkins composer of o... musick in ordinary...
...and plac... Alfonso ferabosco decease... late said... enioye... To haue hold... enioy the said...
...homas Tomkins during his naturall life. And further of our more ample grant w... haue...
...or giue and grant vnto the said Thomas Tomkins for his attendance in the exercise of...
...yeare, To haue receiue and take the said wages and fee of fortie pound... of...
...the death of the said Alfonso ferabosco during the naturall life of g... the said Thomas...
...the fortie of vs o... heires and su... by the hands of the Cost... and treasurer of vs o... heires...
...termes of the yeare, that is to say at the feaste of the annunc... of o... blessed virgin Mary...
...the birth of o... lord God by even and equall portions quarterly to be paid, together with...
...ad and enioyed or ought to haue had and enioyed for the same. Although expresse...

β

Thomas Tomkins as Composer-in-Ordinary
...don, S.P. 39—23—53

the behaviour of the Dean and Chapter. The official reply to this petition gives us slight but precious evidence of one aspect of Thomas's character — his generosity to the poor:

Mr. [Nathaniel] Tomkins knows not wherein he hath offended any of the city in word or deed. His father hath been very charitable to the poor, and so has he.[1]

Nathaniel's statement is borne out by a rough set of accounts in one of his father's music-books — the same book, in fact, that bears the scribbled signatures of the choristers Sylvanus and John. Along with various amounts of money paid to friends and dealers, there is a small but eloquent entry: 'To the poor, 10s.'. There is further evidence of the generosity of both Thomas and his wife in the sermon which John Toy preached on February 2, 1642, at the funeral of Alice Tomkins.

By the death of his wife, Thomas lost a faithful companionship that had been his for forty-five years; he lost a tolerant and devoted helpmate whose virtues were justly extolled by all who had met and spoken with her. Her gravestone, fragments of which are even now to be seen in the crypt of the cathedral, was originally in the Lady Chapel:

Alicia, or
Ales, the wife of Thomas Tomkins,
One of the Gentlemen of His Majesty's
Chapel Royal, a woman full
of faith and good works. She
died the 29 January, 1641 [2]

Toy's sermon has often been mentioned, but never quoted; and since it offers some of the few available

---

[1] Noake, *Monastery and Cathedral of Worcester*, p. 559.

[2] Abingdon, *Antiquities of Worcester Cathedral*, p. 7. The date, 1641, is in accordance with the old style of reckoning. Cf. the burial entry in the Registers of St. Michael's.

testimonies of a personal nature, its importance cannot be over-estimated. It is, of course, only in the peroration that Toy refers to Alicia and her sorrowing husband:

We are met here to do the last honour to our departed Sister, and in her name I thank this worthy Assembly that come to wait on her deserved Obsequies; would she had a better Orator, this presence, especially this subject deserved it; my happiness is the goodness of the subject will help out my imperfect Oratory. I know by her no infirmities that I should need to hide or colour; I need not rack, or torture my invention to force her a praise; I need not strain or dissemble a syllable; she hath filled my mouth with true and real honour.

This text is true in her, we have our time, and she had hers, God be thanked a time of peace and plenty; our time is short, 'tis true, hers was near fourscore, almost two lustres beyond the age of man, if we reckon the number of days, and innumerable grievances of life; she lived long I must confess, but if we measure her life by the affection of her friends, and neighbours, they will I know confess with me, that hers was too too short, she died much too soon. Our time is appointed, so was hers; she was not cut off by untimely chance, she shortened not her days by intemperate diet, she long enjoyed a quiet and entire old age, and like an undisturbed taper burnt out to the last week, yea a good while since with prophetic prediction she points out the time of her departure. We shall have our change, she hath waned some few weeks and now hath hers, from corruptible to incorruption, from mortal life to life immortal, from the light of this world, by which we see a world of misery, to the light of heaven, and Righteousness, which shall never be changed, obscured, nor eclipsed.

This for her we may well presume, for my own part I desire from my soul my last end may be like unto hers, with firm faith, cheerful hope, settled patience, and perpetual preparation, she waited, expected, called, and invited Christ. So far with my Text, but I should wrong her much to say no more, she was an excellent neighbour, I speak it before them that know it, and have most ingeniously confessed it, she was grateful to the best, gracious to the poor, peaceable, officious, and affable to all.

She was an excellent wife, witness the many tears her husband shed, truer tears I dare say never fell at funeral; witness his charge, and charity to bring her home with honour. She like that Emblem of a good Housewife was seldom far from home, at home most neatly industrious, but especially so loving to her husband, that where to pattern such sweet conjugal Society I profess I know not; Let us learn it, (beloved,) believe it, it is a great advantage for heaven to be well skilled in the duty of marriage; this marriage is but for a time, death will divorce it, the second time we should be married to Christ, and will he wed them to himself whom he knew froward and unchaste to a former Spouse? This true good tree hath borne good fruit to the honour and good of this Church, they that have tasted it truly, have praised it for a fragrant and gracious savour, not many Orchards afford the like; she was happy in it to the last.

But which is above all, she was a very good Christian, witness her meekness, one of the truest marks of a Christian, meek she was as appeared by her Matron-like plainness; so meek, that she scorned not to hold discourse with a Child that could scarce speak again to her, an argument of that childish innocency by which we attain heaven.

A good Christian she was, witness that great Example of her devotion, she lived like *Anna* as it were continually in the Temple, twice a day for many decades of years, she attended the worship of God Almighty in this Church, nor would she leave that holy use, for age and weakness, but spite of sickness, as if she meant to sacrifice her life to God, she came still, till the heavy weight of death detained her in her bed.

For her Charity, a main part of the essence of a *Christian*; I must say for that part of Charity that pertains to the tongue, in judging and censuring, she did excel, she loved not to hear, she abhorred to speak evil, of any, she would give fair and candid constructions to all actions, loving and reverent counsel to all that came near her. As for the Charity of her purse, I know not what it was, nor indeed was it her desire that any should know; but this know, she bred up Orphans, sent often meat, and money to her sick neighbours, her servant hath been seen to distribute good pieces of money to many poor families from year to year, from house to house, I am sure if it were known who sent it, it was the servant's fault, for she charged her the contrary; she loved (happy

woman) to hide her treasure, and keep the left hand ignorant of
what the right had done. I am fain to glean and guess at her
Charity, surely if all were known, it would amount to a great
sum, and her great glory, she rather desired that God might have
the glory, to whom of due it belongs. Go to the Earth blessed
Earth, and sleep there sweetly, till the Resurrection, thy other
part is ere this safe arrived to the bosom of *Abraham*: Blessed
Lord, give us grace so to follow her holy example, that we may at
last come to those unspeakable joys, which thou hast prepared for
all them that unfeignedly love thee, and expect thy coming. *Even
so come Lord Jesus.* AMEN.

The value of Toy's tribute lies in its considered, even
though slightly exaggerated reflection of the peace and
goodwill that reigned in the Tomkins household. There
is no reason to doubt the sincerity of his remarks, for he
had long known the family and was thus able to speak
as an active witness and observer as well as out of duty
and friendship. It is through his description of the
character and virtues of Alicia Tomkins that we gain some
insight into the life of her husband, and ultimately of his
thoughts and ideals.

Many of those ideals were entirely at one with the
policies of the high-church party and the supporters of
King Charles, but unfortunately for Worcester the
Parliamentarians were gradually gaining the upper hand.
They had succeeded in forcing Charles's hand in the
matter of the execution in May, 1641, of Earl Strafford,
whose political power had until then been far-reaching
and highly efficacious. But when he was led out to the
scaffold, his most loyal supporters knew that the Royalist
cause was irremediably endangered. Archbishop Laud,
from his prison window, moved as if to bless the doomed
Earl as he passed by, but fell back from faintness and
over-wrought emotions. Laud met his end four years

after Strafford, and Charles himself four years after Laud. The final price was paid for a policy of weakness and variability.

The effect of these happenings on the loyal citizens of Worcester was, in the early stages, to increase their hatred of the Parliamentarians and to bolster up their courage. The cathedral, however, suffered considerable damage when Essex and his ill-controlled troops arrived:

the first thing that they there did was the profanation of the Cathedral; destroying the organ, breaking into pieces divers beautiful windows. . . .[1]

A later report tells of how one soldier, intent on dismantling the Dallam organ, fell and broke his neck. Yet Green did not apparently realize that the instrument had been in any way damaged:

The organ appears to have survived the outrages committed upon the others found in the cathedral at the time of the great rebellion, without much damage: no account of its being removed or repaired occurring till the early part of Dean Waugh's time . . . [*c.* 1752][2]

In 1642 there was an attempt to repair the old organ, 9s. 5d. being spent on candles, glue, leather, and whipcord for the 'great organ bellows'[3] but eventually it was realized that the only solution to the problem was the removal of the old organ from the west end of the nave into the Lady Chapel, and this was done in due course for the sum of 15s. 9d.[4] A slightly larger sum was spent at the same time on repairs to Tomkins's house, but in

[1] Dugdale, *Short View of the Late Troubles in England*, p. 557.

[2] Green, i, 114.

[3] Treasurer's Accounts (1642) A, xxvi, 23. Music was also bought at the same time.

[4] *Ibid.* (1642) A, xxvi, 22.

spite of these precautions further damage was done in the following year:

> To the Mason for tiles, lime and work done in reparation of Mr. Organist's house, ruined by a cannon shot when Waller attempted the taking of the city, May 29, 1643.   4s. 4d.[1]

The same set of accounts gives the name of Mr. Brown — perhaps John Brown, a lay clerk, or Richard Brown, a minor canon who later became organist — as instructor of the choristers, an indication that the aged and bereaved organist had at last delegated some part of his authority to a younger helper. Thomas found much solace in the composition of keyboard music, most of which dates from the time of the siege until two years before his death. Somehow he managed to find enough peace to write in the midst of turmoil and danger.

During the siege of 1646, the removal of all organs in the cathedral followed very soon after the signing of the articles of surrender. Townshend's Diary gives a pertinent anecdote:

> July 20. The organs were this day taken down out of the cathedral church. Some parliamenters hearing the music of the church at service, walking in the aisle, fell a-skipping about and dancing as it were in derision. Others, seeing the workmen taking them down said: 'You might have spared that labour; we would have done it for you.' 'No,' said a merry lad (about ten years old) 'for when the Earl of Essex was here the first man of yours that plucked down and spoiled the organs broke his neck here, and they will not prevent the like misfortune.' [2]

Three days later the services were suspended; fourteen years were to elapse before they were resumed at the time of the Restoration:

> July 23. This day at 6 of the clock prayers, many Gentlemen went to take their last farewell and meeting at the College at the

---

[1] Treasurer's Accounts (1643) A, xxviii, 66.   [2] Townshend, *Diary*, i, 191.

Common prayers of the Church, and to receive the Bishop's blessing, saying 'The Grace of our Lord' &c.[1]

With the cathedral dark and silent, and the city delivered over to Colonel Raynsborough and the Parliamentarian army, there was little that Thomas could do to bring cheer to this sad phase of the city's history. He still had to keep an avuncular eye on Sylvanus and John, and concerned himself from time to time with mundane but necessary tasks, such as laying up stores. In his autograph book of keyboard music, one of the flyleaves is thus marked:

October 1647. Received of Mr. Wood three bushels of wheat xxv[s.] vi[d.]. Then paid John Bullock for all reckonings and for two bushels of mooncorn xv[s.].

To that same month of October belongs the extended version of *Earl Strafford's Pavan*, a musical memorial to a man who had perished six years previously. The *Pavan: Lord Canterbury* dates from the same year, 1647, and these two touching *tombeaux* seem to have started the 75-year-old composer on a new and yet reminiscent phase of musical activity. Works couched in forms and styles that were current in the early part of Elizabeth's reign began to fill the pages of his music-book: the youthful emotions recollected there in the tranquillity of old age lent a feeling of controlled brilliance at once sober and lively. The third memorial came in 1649, when Thomas penned his *Sad Pavan: for these distracted times*, out of respect for Charles I, whose execution had saddened every loyalist in the realm. Much of this music was probably written in the 'high turret or study' in his

[1] *Ibid.* 192.

house on College Green, which is described in the Parliamentary Survey of 1649:

Thomas Tomkins by Indenture of Lease bearing date the 17th day of November in the 16th year of the late King Charles from Christopher Potter late dean of the Cathedral Church of Christ and Mary the Virgin of Worcester and the Chapter of the same church Holdeth to him and his assignees All those 2 messuages and tenements newly built lying and being within the precincts of the said Cathedral Church consisting of about 4 bays and half of building together with the soil and ground thereunto adjoining and a little stable situate between the Songschool and the late stable of Doctor Thornton and Doctor Wight containing in length north and south 9 foot and 6 inches and in breadth east and west 8 foot and 7 inches. All which said 2 houses newly built and all the ground and soil whereupon the old houses and buildings did stand containing in length westward from the wall of the old brewhouse in the occupation of Thomas Giles 27 yards or thereabouts from the east end thereof unto a room or bay parcel of the same building now in the tenure of Richard Hall gentleman situate and being eastward and westward between the said brew-house and the house of the said Richard Hall and having on the south part thereof the Castle of Worcester and on the north the common ground of the said church To have and to hold all the said premises from the ensealing of the Lease for and during the term of 40 years next ensuing at the yearly rent of 5s. payable the 24th July only. One of which messuages aforesaid being now in the tenure and possession of the said Thomas Tomkins containing in breadth 18 foot and in length 34 foot.

And the same consisteth of a hall, a kitchen, a buttery five chambers above stairs and a garret over them the staircase leading to a high turret or study. Also a garden in breadth 34 foot and in length 42 foot with a pump of water therein likewise a wood-house or coalhouse.

All which said messuage in possession of him the said Thomas Tomkins before rented is worth per annum above the said rent of 5s., £5 00s. 00d. The other messuage or tenement is now in the tenure of Thomas Giles and was built by him the said Thomas Giles upon the soil and ground before mentioned and we are credibly informed that the said Thomas Tomkins was trusted by

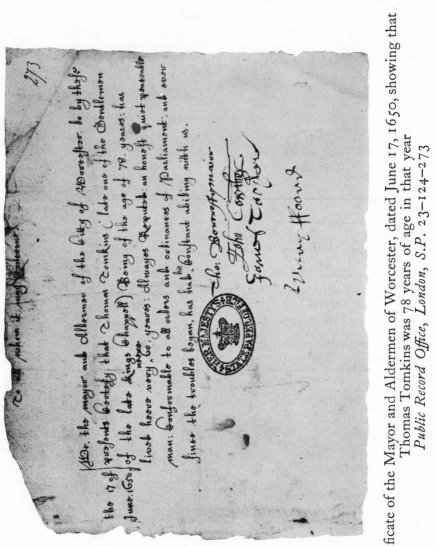

Certificate of the Mayor and Aldermen of Worcester, dated June 17, 1650, showing that Thomas Tomkins was 78 years of age in that year

Public Record Office, London, S.P. 23–124–273

the said Thomas Giles to purchase the same for him, the said Thomas Giles, but contrary to that trust the said Mr. Tomkins did take it in his own name after such time as the said Thomas Giles had built thereon, to his great cost and charges; and therefore humbly craves he may be admitted to purchase the inheritance thereof.

The site of which last recite messuage or tenement containing in breadth 18 foot and in length 33 foot having the castle on the south a gatehouse there on the north Mr. Tomkins on the west and the brewhouse of the said Thomas Giles on the east. And the same house of Thomas Giles aforesaid consisteth of a kitchen a parlour and 3 chambers with a garret over them which said tenement is worth by the year to be let £3 00s. 00d.[1]

Although the name of the person with whom this misunderstanding arose is spelt 'Chiles' in the survey, the Thomas Giles mentioned on page 185 of the autograph keyboard manuscript is undoubtedly the same man. He may have been a son of the Nathaniel Giles who had died in 1633, but if this was so, Tomkins evidently held the son in less esteem than the father. Whether Giles was successful in his appeal is not known; but in view of the terms of the lease dated 1627, it is possible that Tomkins remained master of the situation. His house, later known as the 'High House' because of the turret or study, was leased in 1666 to his nephew John, who had by then married and settled down in Buckenhill, Herefordshire.

The same survey also mentions a former residence of the organist:

An old house called the Singing School late Thomas Tomkins organist in the possession of Widow Hill situate and being within the precincts of the college adjoining to the garden late Nathaniel Tomkins and now Daniel Dobbyns on the east and the College Green on the west consisting of a hall, a parlour, a cellar, a chamber

---

[1] Atkins, pp. 54, 55. Noake (*Monastery*, p. 370) takes a serious view of all this, and states that Tomkins was 'exposed for alleged dishonesty'.

below and 2 chambers over with a little buttery worth per annum to be let £1 10s. 0d.[1]

This building, although rebuilt and enlarged in the eighteenth century, is still to be seen on the south-west side of the Edgar Tower. Thus there is some part extant of both houses occupied by Tomkins, three centuries after his death.

The last few years of his life were relatively un-troubled, except for an attempt to sequestrate certain property and interests at Dodderhill, which he shared with his son Nathaniel. Since Nathaniel was a minor canon, and therefore liable to be dispossessed of his property, Thomas was understandably anxious that his own part of the estate should remain in the possession of the family. Even the Bishop of Worcester, John Prideaux, had suffered hardship and deprivation as a result of the new Parliamentary laws, and he died in 1650 almost penniless. Nathaniel Tomkins tried to appeal against the sequestration, but did not succeed, as the following summary of the case shows:

30 October 1649. Nathaniel Tomkins being unable to prosecute his appeal against sequestration, now before the Barons of the Exchequer, begs to compound for his estate. Is sequestered on pretence of delinquency. 20 March 1650. Fine at $\frac{1}{6}$, £208 16s. 8d.

9 April 1650. The Committee for Compounding being informed of an undervalue, require a certificate thereof.

9 July 1650. Thomas Tomkins complaining that demesne lands and tithes in Dodderhill are sequestered as the estate of his son Nathaniel, who has no interest therein, the County Committee are to certify.

23 July 1650. Begs that the profits of his sequestered lands may be secured in the tenant's hands undisposed of, till the hearing of his case.

[1] Atkins, p. 56.

30 July 1650. County Committee to show proofs why they consider the estate in question to belong to Nathaniel Tomkins.

26 September 1650. The County Committee to discharge the sequestration, with arrears from 24 December last, if they do not forthwith show cause to the contrary.[1]

Perhaps there was some support for Thomas's case in a certificate signed on June 17, 1650, by the Mayor and Aldermen of the city; he was undoubtedly thought well of, and respected as much for his age as for his gentle character:

To all whom it may concern: We, the Mayor and Aldermen of the city of Worcester do by these presents certify that Thomas Tomkins (late one of the Gentlemen of the late King's chapel) being of the age of 78 years, has lived here very near 60 years. Always reputed an honest quiet peaceable man, conformable to all orders and ordinances of Parliament, and ever since the troubles began has had his constant abiding with us.[2]

> THOMAS BERCROFT, Mayor.
> JOHN COWTHER
> JAMES TAYLOR
> HENRY FOORD

It is this document that enables us to place Tomkins's date of birth in the year 1572; and it is also noteworthy that the figure given for his period of residence in Worcester, although not precisely coincidental with the date of his appointment as organist, does give the impression that he was considered an old and venerable inhabitant.

Pavans, verses, and settings of *In nomine* continued to be added to the music-book, whose later leaves show a fast deteriorating hand and a strong desire to make use

[1] Calendar of State Papers (Committee for Compounding), 1643–60, iii, p. 2132: 'Thomas Tomkins, late King's Chaplain and Nathaniel Tomkins, Elmridge, Co. Worcs., his Son'.

[2] London, Public Record Office, SP 23/124/273. Quoted by Emden, *Lives of Elizabethan Song Composers.*

of every inch of paper, even if staves have to be drawn at right angles to one another. The same book contains a list of debts dated May 24, 1651. The tailor, smith, carpenter, mason, shoemaker, and mercer are all included, together with certain private persons who were then his neighbours. Edward Pennell is named, so too is Thomas Giles. Pennell was one of the few commissioners who performed his duties in a satisfactory way, if we are to believe Henry Townshend,[1] and it may have been for this reason that he still held office in 1660, at the first quarter-sessions of Charles II. Perhaps the Marjorie Taylor and Mrs. Boughton named in the same list were related to Canon Taylor and Canon Boughton. Whether the debts were ever discharged is not clear, though it is certain that both he and Nathaniel were in some financial difficulty.

It was Nathaniel who found a solution to the problem, in January of 1654. Himself a widower, he decided to re-marry, for he was only 55 and was tired of his lonely existence out at Elmridge. His new wife, Isabella, was a daughter of Guthlake Folliot, who had been chapter clerk of the cathedral. She had been twice married before meeting Nathaniel, and had inherited the manor of Merton or Martin and the patronage of Martin Hussingtree Church from her first husband, John Haselock. It was this wealthy and amiable widow who provided shelter for Nathaniel and his father, and though Habington calls it a 'meane Manor' he may have been referring to its size rather than its character or aspect.[2] The village was only a few miles from Worcester, and the three elderly people found it isolated but ideal for their enforced retirement.

---

[1] *Diary*, i, 138.   [2] *Survey*, i, 349.

Thomas had wound up his affairs in Worcester, though not without the expected worries in disposing of personal property and furniture. A recent bequest had provided him with rather more than he needed in the way of household articles, but he had not wished to refuse.[1] The kind of life he was to lead at Martin Hussingtree was in some ways more simple, but that much less sheltered from the elements. He survived until 1656, a bad year according to the reports of Townshend:

Since the middle of March to the . . . of April never remembered such strong cold winds, storm, snow, sleet and slobbery weather — to so great hindrance of the countryman's sowing.

From middle of May until . . . except one whole day in middle of June, so great a drought that hay is £40 the load. Grass mostly burnt up.

July. This hot, dry year has caused great sickness, especially the small pox and measles, whereof many have died in all places.[2]

Thomas was laid to rest in the churchyard at Martin Hussingtree, where several of his relatives were later buried. Under the date of June 9, 1656, the registers of the church have the following entry:

Mr. Thomas Tomkins organist of the King's Chapel and of the Cathedral Church of Worcester was buried the 9th day of June 1656.

[1] See list in *Musica Britannica*, v, 159. [2] *Diary*, i, 32.

MUSICA DEO SACRA

And I think he hath not a mind well tempered, whose zeal is not inflamed by a heavenly anthem.

OWEN FELTHAM, *Resolves* (1628).

IT is highly probable that Tomkins regarded his church music as the most important single branch of his widely varied musical activities. Unlike his secular music, which may be assigned to definite phases in his career, or else affords its own evidence of sporadic, even occasional interest, the church music appears as an almost lifelong task, pervading all times and all places, and still remaining in the foreground of his thoughts even when circumstances brought about by political and military manœuvres denied him the *raison d'être* for its continued composition. The lines engraved beneath the frontispiece of Lawes' *Treasury of Musick*, published in 1669, aptly sum up a situation which Tomkins had known and suffered from 1642 until the end of his days:

> Although the cannon, and the churlish drum
> Have struck the choir mute, and the organs dumb,
> Yet music's art, with air and string and voice,
> Makes glad the sad, and sorrow to rejoice.

He began writing music for the Anglican church in his early twenties, when he was first appointed organist at Worcester, and for the next forty-five years the stream of anthems and services flowed on steadily, increasing in quality though not necessarily in complexity, with the

66

result that his son Nathaniel was able to assemble sufficient material for the posthumous publication known to us as *Musica Deo Sacra*.

The idea of such a publication must long have haunted the composer's mind. In 1622 he had so far modified the conventional contents of a madrigal book as to include four anthems, one of which was later reprinted in *Musica Deo Sacra*, but after that date he saw nothing of his own through the press. The times were unpropitious for the publication of church music, and in spite of Barnard's excellent anthology of services and anthems published in 1641, public interest was at a low ebb. Barnard had transcribed enough material to enable him to plan a further publication, which would have included works by composers then living, among them Thomas Tomkins, but this ambitious project never matured. Meticulously copied volumes, still in existence,[1] testify the industry of Barnard and the apathy of his clientèle, besides indirectly confirming the all-powerful influence of the manual copyist, whose work was undoubtedly cheaper and occasionally even more accurate than that of the printer.

The appearance of Barnard's collection, which was apparently not acquired by Worcester Cathedral until twenty years after the date of publication,[2] may, however, have raised Tomkins's hopes to a certain extent, while at the same time acting as a deterrent. It must have been obvious that a large-scale collection of music by one composer could not follow too closely upon an anthology of the magnitude of John Barnard's *Selected Church Music*. As his keyboard music shows, Tomkins was a

[1] R.C.M. MSS 1045-51, now in the British Museum.
[2] Atkins, p. 63.

conscientious compiler of his own music, and there is no reason to believe that he was less conscientious when it came to the preservation and classification of anthems and services. Like many of his fellow-organists, he compiled an organ book containing accompaniments for use both in choir practice and at service time, the folio volume marked 'E' in his private collection of manuscript books [1] being a very likely candidate. Nathaniel Tomkins would naturally have used this book as the basic text for the Pars Organica of *Musica Deo Sacra*, unique in being the only printed organ book in seventeenth-century England, although manuscript organ books are quite common.[2]

There can be no doubt that the hope of publication receded from Thomas's mind as the long and empty years of the Commonwealth wore on. From the time of the second siege of Worcester, last of the royalist cities to hold out against the Parliamentarian troops, he had turned more and more towards the composition of keyboard music, almost to the extent of turning a deaf ear to the entreaties and encouragements of his son. The desire to publish, once strong in the father, passed naturally to the son; and as the father became more absorbed in his clavichord and his chamber organ, so the son lost his youthful enthusiasm for keyboard instruments and directed his thoughts to the collection and collation of that vastly impressive corpus of church music

---

[1] See p. 129.
[2] Durham Cathedral MS A 1-5; St. Michael's College, Tenbury, MS 791 (Adrian Batten); Christ Church Library, Oxford, MS 1001; Ely Cathedral, MS 1 (John Ferrabosco and James Hawkins); General Library of the University of California at Berkeley, M2 C645 Case B (? Thomas Cappell of Chichester). I have to thank Professor Anthony Lewis for drawing my attention to the last-mentioned manuscript.

which was practically a family heirloom. The death of Thomas in 1656 brought matters to a climax: from then onwards Nathaniel knew that his bounden duty was to create an imperishable musical memorial to his father's skill and piety. At that time Nathaniel was the only person who could adequately perform such a task, for he had inherited most, if not all, of his father's manuscripts, and had lived with him long enough to understand and carry out his wishes. It has sometimes been suggested that Thomas Tomkins (1638–75), Chancellor of Exeter Cathedral, was responsible for editing *Musica Deo Sacra* and seeing it through the press,[1] but there is no proof that this eminent and learned divine had any great knowledge of music or deep interest in it.

Documentary evidence also favours Nathaniel's claim as editor, for he wrote on the verso of a long letter to John Sayer of the Chapel Royal, in May, 1665, a message for William Godbid, the music printer of Aldersgate Street:

Sir I pray you speak to Mr. Godbid to send me one sheet of the bass of I.i. or fol.121.122.123.124 of the mean of Q.q. or fol.147.148.149.150.[2]

It was William Godbid who printed *Musica Deo Sacra* in 1668, and the bass and mean mentioned by Nathaniel refer to the bassus and medius parts, which he presumably was reading in proof three years before the date of publication. That he performed this difficult and tiring task extremely well, if a little mechanically, is proved by the relatively small number of corrections ('Notes which may be added by the pen') which appear at the end of each part-book, as well as by the consolidated

---

[1] *Dictionary of National Biography*, article on Thomas Tomkins.

[2] Bodleian Library, MS Add. C 304ᵃ f. 141v. I am indebted to Mr. Jeremy Noble for the loan of his transcript of this series of letters.

judgement of the editors of *Tudor Church Music*, who found the printing of the notes singularly accurate in all four vocal part-books.[1]

The same editors are, with some justification, less pleased with Nathaniel's care in seeing to the correct underlay of text to music. It is highly unlikely that he had a score of the anthems and services before him, although he did have an organ score, and so was able to check vocal and organ parts which (apart from very few exceptions) correspond satisfactorily. In order to secure a really musical and singable underlay, Nathaniel would have had to sing through, not once but several times, every voice-part of every work in *Musica Deo Sacra*, and amend the printer's copy accordingly. Nathaniel, in spite of his genuine devotion to his task, might understandably have baulked at such a proposition, for he was a fine organist but not an especially good singer. He was, according to Bishop Skinner,

bred in his cradle, and all his life among organs; . . . an excellent organist, and hath ever maintained an organ in his house.[2]

He evidently placed his trust, not unwisely, in the ability of singers to adapt the text in a convincing and artistic manner to the varying lengths of the musical phrases. They were not all like the common singing men of whom John Earle, in the genial vituperation of his *Microcosmographie*, said:

they are so religiously addicted that they serve God oftest when they are drunk . . . the old Hebrew names are little beholding to them, for they miscall them worse than one another. Though they never expound the scripture, they handle it much and pollute the gospel with two things, their conversation and their thumbs.

---

[1] *Tudor Church Music*, VIII, xiv.
[2] Bodleian Library, MS Tanner 45, f. 19.

This from a Bishop of Worcester and Salisbury might well be accounted the unprejudiced evidence of an eye- and ear-witness, if it were not for the fact that the *Microcosmographie* of 1629 contains other and equally amusing exaggerations of the same kind.

Musica Deo Sacra has, in its way, been just as much maligned and misunderstood as the singing men who first made its symbols live in sound. Fétis, misled by the reference to Charles I on the title-page, stated that the work appeared in 1623, which was probably a typographical error for the year of Charles's accession. Burney, a little nearer the mark, dated one of the Christ Church copies 1664 [1] and threw much subsequent scholarship into a state of confusion. The greatest confusion of all, however, is brought about by the correct date (1668) and a short title reference; for without the knowledge that Charles I is mentioned on the title-page, the music is apt to be judged by post-Restoration standards, and accounted well-nigh anachronistic. Nathaniel Tomkins probably realized that rapidly changing musical fashions would limit the potential audience for his father's music, and he lost no time in placing an advertisement in the London *Gazette*, the original draft of which reads:

Lately printed, Musica Deo Sacra et ecclesiae Anglicanae; or music dedicated to the honour and service of God and to the use of cathedral and other churches of England, by Thomas Tomkins sometime Gentleman of His Majesty's Chapel Royal and Organist of Worcester: in ten books whereof one is the organ part. They are to be had at the Chanter's House of Westminster. [2]

Why this set of four voice-parts and one organ book should be sold as a set of ten is somewhat mysterious,

---

[1] Burney, ii, 291.   [2] Public Record Office, S.P. 29–187–209.

even when due allowance has been made for the typically generous exaggerations of advertising terminology. A working minimum would be nine, to include two copies each of medius, contratenor, tenor, and bassus, and one copy of Pars Organica. Since the decani and cantoris parts are printed opposite one another in each book, at least two copies of each would be needed by the lay clerks for anthems of normal dimensions, and more if they were to sing the eight-, ten-, and twelve-part anthems in reasonable comfort. Extra copies of the medius part, for the boys, would naturally be copied by hand, since no establishment would want to include the entire contents of *Musica Deo Sacra* in its repertory, and it was therefore easier to duplicate medius parts of whatever works were chosen. Occasionally the printed text was used as the basis of complete sets of parts, again perhaps for reasons of economy, and this explains why certain of the later seventeenth-century manuscript sources (especially the Durham ones mentioned by the editors of *Tudor Church Music*, VIII) contain the same errors as the original publication.

The account books of Worcester Cathedral indicate that the usual method was to acquire a set of printed books, decide upon which anthems and services to use, and then arrange for one of the lay clerks to copy out extra medius parts for the boys. In 1661 the following entry may be seen:

Books bought to furnish the Church.
For a set of printed song-books for the choir,
box and carriage   £12 15   6.[1]

John Brown, one of the four lay clerks who returned

---

[1] Treasurer's Accounts (1661) A, lxxiii, 53.

to the choir at the Restoration, was soon set busily copying:

Joanni Brown laico p[ro] canticis variis depingendis £2   0   0.[1]

Twenty-two years later, the books were still in use, though an inventory of 'plate and other utensils' submitted to the Treasurer makes it quite clear that they were showing signs of age:

Eight new service books, twelve old ones, besides those the singing men have in their boxes.[2]

The 1661 inventory could only refer, of course, to Barnard's *Selected Church Music*, and similarly the 'eight new books' mentioned in the later document must have been *Musica Deo Sacra*. The number eight rather than nine is given because the Pars Organica was undoubtedly up in the organ loft when the list was in process of compilation. Seven part-books are still to be seen in the cathedral library, as well as four of the Barnard set.

One particular set of the *Musica Deo Sacra* part-books is of more than usual interest: it is the copy at St. Michael's College, Tenbury. The Pars Organica, besides possessing the usual three pages of corrections (bound in this instance between the Index and page 1) has yet another page bound into the volume immediately following the last page. The lower third of this leaf presents two items of information concerning the speed and pitch of music. A solitary semibreve, printed on a clefless stave, is thus described:

Sit mensura duorum humani corporis pulsuum, vel globuli penduli, longitudine duorum pedum a centro motus.

---

[1] *Ibid.* (1662) A, xxix, 18.
[2] Noake, *Monastery and Cathedral of Worcester*, p. 547.

The semibreve then appears once more, on the F line of a bass stave, with the following remark:

Sit tonus fistulae apertae longitudine duorum pedum et semissis: sive 30 digitorum Geomet.

Nathaniel clearly added these instructions as an afterthought: he wished to make it understood that absolute values for tempo and pitch could be given; and that his father's music, if it were to be correctly performed, should proceed at thirty-six semibreves to the minute (one semibreve equalling two heartbeats) and at a pitch whose tenor F should correspond to the sound produced by an organ pipe two and a half feet long.

The loss of traditional tempi due to the silencing of choirs, and the undoubtedly vague attitude towards pitch resulting from sub-standard workmanship (in many cases all that was available) in the impoverished organ-building profession, may well have moved Nathaniel to add these instructions as a kind of postscript. Strangely enough, Nathaniel did not dedicate the publication to a private patron, nor did he state explicitly that it was a memorial to his father. There is no preface, and no indication of the editor's identity. Thus the unique instructions in the Tenbury copy are all that remain of Nathaniel's quiet and self-effacing personality.

Musica Deo Sacra contains five services, five psalm tunes, the Preces and two proper psalms, and ninety-four anthems.[1] Among the items not included in this

---

[1] *Tudor Church Music*, VIII, xvii, gives the number as ninety-three, since the Burial Service is counted separately. As many anthems proper to other special services are contained in *Musica Deo Sacra*, it has been thought best to include the music for the Burial Service among the main body of texts, as the original index does. Cavanaugh mentions ninety-five anthems: he counts *Behold I bring you glad tidings* and its chorus 'Glory be to God' as two separate works.

publication are two Evening Services, two psalm tunes, two settings of the Litany and one of the Responses, and eighteen anthems. Of the five services, the first three have become fairly well-established in the cathedral repertory through the publications of Warren, Ouseley, Cook, Atkins, and Ramsbotham. The First and Second are usually classed as 'short services' or relatively simple and straightforward compositions, but in fact the Second Service looks forward to the more complex type ('great service') in its *Te Deum*, where there are verses for *ssatb*.

The First Service is notable for its bold use of a head-motive; a full bar which appears at the beginning of *Te Deum*, *Benedictus*, and *Nunc Dimittis*. Tomkins uses thematic links in all of his services, and may have been consciously following in the footsteps of Tallis and Farrant, both of whom used this technique during the reign of Elizabeth I. Little use, however, is made of contrasts in colour between groups of upper and lower voices. It is not until the *Creed* that the three lower voices have a phrase to themselves ('who for us men') and a little later there is a brief expansion to five-part harmony at 'I acknowledge one Baptism'. The main contrast comes from the alternation of the two sides of the choir, and is thus spatial rather than dynamic or tonal.[1] Usually Tomkins begins and ends the canticles with full choir, using alternation for the body of the texts with the exception of certain phrases which demand more dignified and sonorous treatment. 'Thou art the King of Glory' (*Te Deum*), 'To perform the oath' (*Benedictus*), 'Very God of Very God' (*Creed*), and 'He hath filled the hungry' (*Magnificat*) are a few of the phrases singled out

---

[1] Recordings and broadcasts give no idea of the simple beauty of this effect. Eventually, perhaps, the use of stereophonic tapes will remedy matters.

for performance by both sides of the choir. Similarly those phrases which imply alternation are generally set in that manner: 'To Thee all angels' and 'To Thee Cherubim', as well as 'The glorious company' and 'The goodly fellowship' (*Te Deum*). In neither instance is there any attempt to relate the phrases musically, though at certain points in the *Venite* there are matching, though not mechanically exact, musical phrases. Occasionally madrigalian methods creep in at such obvious places in the *Benedictus* as 'and hath raised up', 'the prophet of the highest', 'the day-spring from on high', all of which are set to ascending scale-passages. Conversely, 'came down from heaven' (*Creed*) bears a descending phrase. There is a particularly graphic illustration of 'he hath put down' in the *Magnificat*, employing subdivision of voices and contrast of timbre as well as spatial contrast:

(Note values are unreduced, as in all subsequent musical examples, except where the contrary is expressly stated.)

Although similar to the First Service in matters of general style, the Second Service has particular differences which set it apart. There is no organ in *Venite* and *Kyrie*, and the intonation of *Te Deum* is set. This time there is a double example of the use of head-motives:

the opening of *Te Deum* occurs again at *Magnificat*, and
that of *Jubilate* at *Nunc Dimittis*. *Jubilate* is set in place
of *Benedictus*, but otherwise the number of separate
canticles or texts is the same for both services. A comparison of the two settings of *Te Deum* is instructive in
that it shows Tomkins to be quite free in his choice of a
scheme of alternation and use of full choir. In the
Second Service, there is a wider range of contrasting
textures, especially noticeable at the two sections which
obtain an effect of gymel by subdividing the trebles at
'When Thou tookest upon Thee to deliver man' and the
counter-tenors at 'Thou sittest at the right hand of God'.
These are in effect verse sections,[1] though it is not until
the *Jubilate* that the use of this technique becomes
decisive ('O go your way'). At many places in the *Creed*
all-pervading homophony is relieved by an active and
interesting tenor part, and there is an effective instance
of cumulative fervency in the use of a rhythmic half-drop
(to borrow a term from the visual arts) at 'and He shall
come again':

The customary ascent is heard at the word 'ascended'
and there is a novel touch at the word 'together [is
worshipped and glorified]' where the two sides of the
choir start singing together in the middle of a phrase.
A similar example of illustration verging on misplaced

---

[1] The second is not so designated in *Tudor Church Music*, VIII, 59.

ingenuity may be seen at 'throughout all generations' in the tenor part of the *Magnificat*. Most successful of all perhaps is the *Nunc Dimittis*, with its beautifully balanced sequence at 'For mine eyes have seen'; and its impressive use of full choir, yet suggestive of antiphony (even of canon), from 'To be a light' to the end.

The Third Service, although one of Tomkins's more complex works, is not quite as overpowering as it appears from the twelve-stave pages in *Tudor Church Music*, VIII. His organ part, present throughout, is not indispensable, but it should be used in any performance which lays claim to historical accuracy. The ten voice-parts often combine to form five, and in fact extended passages of even six-part writing are relatively uncommon. There is, however, a noticeable increase in the overlapping of antiphonal phrases, which creates a tightly woven musical texture and a smoother transmission between decani and cantoris. Doubtless more antiphony was used than is actually marked in *Musica Deo Sacra* and its published transcription, and consequently more verse sections. It is too frequently forgotten that the restoration of such features to church music of this period is as essential aesthetically as the restoration of lacunae caused by missing part-books is essential musically. *Jubilate*, with its joyful waves of sound at the opening, and *Magnificat* and *Nunc Dimittis* (with hinted head-motive) are among Tomkins's loftiest achievements. The quietly reverent way in which each of the latter two canticles begins is an illustration of the fine use to which verse technique can be put; and the skilful deploying of melodic sequences and passages of close imitation comes as yet further proof of Tomkins's unerring instinct for choral sonority. Not

least remarkable is the frequent use of false relations as a
harmonic ingredient rather than a means of expression:

Ex. 3

The organ part in the Fourth and Fifth Services is
an integral part of the texture, and even though Tomkins
gave no more than a sketch of what he would have played,
it is clear that he favoured a greater degree of elaboration
than was common among his contemporaries, chief of
whom in the realm of the verse service were Gibbons
and Byrd. The head-motive which is common to both
the *Magnificat* and *Nunc Dimittis* of the Fourth Service
is indeed taken over from a similar point in Byrd's Second
Service, by way of a tribute from pupil to teacher. It is
no more a 'curious example of plagiarism'[1] than the
parallel quotation of Dowland's *Lachrymae* in *O let me
live for true love* in the *Songs* of 1622. The very beginning
of *Te Deum* is of special significance owing to the para-
phrase of the well-known intonation which was taken
over by the Anglicans from the Sarum liturgy. A link
with the First and Third Services may be seen in the
octave skip at 'heaven and earth', where the organ part
assumes considerable importance.

Madrigalian quirks are present at 'the sharpness of
death', where (in common with the *Te Deum* settings of
all the other four services) chords containing one or more
sharps appear. To the same category belongs the verse

---

[1] Fellowes, *English Cathedral Music*, p. 90.

for two basses in the *Magnificat*: 'He hath put down the mighty'.

Bass verses are a remarkable feature of the Fifth Service, which may well have been composed with some particular singer in mind. Even in the chorus parts there is far more declamation than in the other services, postulating a more intimate *milieu* of performance such as a private chapel. The *Jubilate*, with its short but florid 'Amen', affords one more instance of the composer's

fondness for reminiscence: the phrase at '[O] be joyful in the Lord' echoes that of the *Jubilate* in the Third Service. But the really unique thematic link occurs between the 'Glory be to the Father' of *Magnificat* and *Nunc Dimittis*. The music is almost note for note the same, but the key in the latter canticle is B flat as against G minor of the former. Thus the emotional differences inherent in the two canticles are brought out in a subtle but telling manner.

The five-part Preces and Psalmi Festivales compare

favourably with the best of Jacobean settings, and even though the Preces cannot be used in their entirety owing to slight changes in the liturgy since Tomkins's day, they are a valuable adornment to any service. Psalm xlvii (Whitsun) and Psalm xv (Ascension) are dignified, largely homophonic settings which have so far met with little but deliberate misuse. Fragments from them have been transposed, altered, and underlaid with verses from *Magnificat* and *Nunc Dimittis*; these verses, termed 'fauxbourdon' for no apparent reason, have then been made to alternate with plain-chant verses, a procedure with which Tomkins certainly never became acquainted.[1] In their pristine form, they are splendid examples of artistically contrived psalm-settings, *O clap your hands* being especially noteworthy for its paired verses and alternating use of similar and dissimilar musical material.

The logical division of Tomkins's anthems is into two main categories, full and verse, and the latter of these he chose to call 'songs to the organ'. He learned from his master Byrd the basic technique of verse anthem composition, which (contrary to general supposition) was not something new and revolutionary. Byrd, who was a Catholic, and therefore not unfamiliar with the great achievements of the pre-Reformation masters, knew well that the contrasting of large and small groups of singers was a commonplace occurrence even though it was rarely marked in any special way. In the Eton Choirbook verbal texts are written in red and black in order to differentiate between the two kinds of sonority, the solo group and the ensemble. A generation later, two-, three-, and four-part sections call for soloists through the very

[1] Editions by Burgess and Shore (Novello's Parish Choir Book, nos. 889 and 1037).

difficulty of their execution: witness the second *Agnus Dei*, with its complex proportional notation, in Taverner's *Missa O Michael*. Henrician composers could not, of course, reduce their texture to anything smaller than a duo, but the 'verse anthem' principle was there, and it only needed the organ (which in pre-Reformation times alternated with, rather than accompanied the choir) to usher in the last refinement of all, the verse for solo voice.

There are other divisions, separate from stylistic ones yet not uninfluenced by them, which deserve consideration. Just as the word 'motet' can be made to hide a wide variety of highly individual liturgical forms, so the word 'anthem' covers many different forms and styles. There are, in *Musica Deo Sacra*, at least twenty-one works written for special occasions, including eleven settings of Collects,[1] music for the Burial Service, music for the Communion Service (*Gloria*, *Sanctus*, and Offertory *He that hath pity*), a Coronation anthem for Charles I (*O Lord grant the King a long life*), another — possibly for James I — *Be strong and of good courage*,[2] and four special anthems for St. George, St. Stephen, Christmas, and Easter.

About two-thirds of the total number of anthems in *Musica Deo Sacra* make use of texts from the Psalms. Usually the selection of verses is regular and consecutive, but once in a while Tomkins makes up his own sequence of verses (*Arise O Lord God lift up thine hand*) or draws upon one of the favourites in Sternhold and Hopkins (*My shepherd is the living Lord*). Besides this latter, there are three other poetical texts of unknown authorship: *Above the stars my saviour dwells*,[3] described as 'An

---

[1] *Turn thou us* (for the Commination) is set twice.
[2] Wickham Legg, *The Coronation Order of King James I*.
[3] Also set by Robert Parsons.

Hymn'; *Not in the merits of what I have done*; and *Leave, O my soul, this baser world below.*[1]

One prose text appears to be freely composed: *O Lord do away as the night even so my sins.* It is found among the three-part anthems for men's voices, as are two further texts of more than usual interest. One is a setting of the Preces, employing the same text as the five-part version, but including also the intonations. The responsorial character of the Preces is thus obliterated, yet the music would serve quite satisfactorily as an anthem with text from various Psalms, like *Arise O Lord God.* In *Glory be to the Father*, there is a coda of unusual interest built upon a florid *Alleluia*, suggesting that the composer had an Easter performance in mind. *Alleluia* is also interpolated into the *Sanctus* previously mentioned, but it is unlikely that the two works are closely connected since the setting of *Holy holy holy* is for five voices.[2] Three anthems have double texts, and were probably underlaid in this way when Nathaniel came upon them. He did not apparently stop to unravel the peculiarities of *Blessed is he that considereth the poor*, for these words appear in two of the voice-parts, while *O Lord graciously accept* appears in three others. The bassus has both texts, but it is clear that the second fits badly, and is unlikely ever to have been sanctioned by Thomas Tomkins. Two five-part anthems have Latin texts as well as English,[3] the former being possibly intended for use in the Chapel Royal or in a collegiate chapel where Latin was permitted.

The texture of the full anthems varies from the richly scored *O praise the Lord all ye heathen* (a 12) to

---

[1] Sometimes listed as *Stripped of my merits* and *Hear O my soul*, respectively.

[2] It is freely based on *See, see the shepherd's queen*, in the *Songs* of 1622.

[3] *Why art thou so full of heaviness/Domine tu eruisti animam*; *Lord enter not into judgment/Non nobis Domine.*

the three-part anthems for men's voices, all of these latter being without an organ part. *O praise the Lord*, besides being a *tour de force*, offers lively proof of the Englishman's immunity from the dispersed choirs of the Italian manner. No regrouping is needed in order to perform the work in its most striking and effective manner: Tomkins has divided into three each section of a four-part choir, and the resulting cohesion is as strongly felt in the smooth and dignified counterpoint of the opening bars as it is in the quasi-echo effects of 'for His merciful kindness'. This work may well have been written for some great occasion of state, or possibly for Tomkins's degree exercise in 1607. There is some indication that the anthems for more than six voices were all early works. Certainly *O God the proud are risen* (*a* 8) and *O sing unto the Lord* (*a* 7) may be dated before 1617, for they are both found in the tenor part-book copied by Jarvis Jones of Oxford in that year.[1] The one other full anthem *a* 7 is *Be strong and of good courage*, already mentioned as appearing in the list of anthems used at the coronation of James I in 1603.

Typical of the six-part anthems is *Who shall ascend the hill of God*, with its varied interplay of three, four, and five voices before the full choir is heard at 'from the God of his salvation'. The inevitable ascent of the first phrase contrasts admirably with the almost static homophony supporting 'and stand before His holy seat', whilst later the solidity of salvation is brought home by a long dominant pedal. The coda is repeated, with slight changes in verbal text, after the fashion of the English anthems published by John Day early in the reign of Elizabeth.

The fifteen anthems *a* 5 are among the finest in

[1] Tenbury, MS 1382.

Musica Deo Sacra. Tomkins displays his reverence for
the mood of the text and his delight in the opportunities
offered by salient words and phrases: both the breadth
of design and the finesse of detail are dear to him.
Besides the well-known *When David heard* [1] there is
another, even more expressively dramatic setting of a
verse from the Second Book of Samuel — *Then David
mourned.* Seldom in English church music has there
been so successful a working of the pathetic vein as this:

Ex.5

Both moving and pathetic in a different way are the
ululatory motives at the beginning of *Why art thou so
full of heaviness,* an anthem that is almost entirely lacking
in homophony, perhaps to illustrate the word 'heaviness'
with its relentlessly unfolding counterpoint. Usually
Tomkins introduces passages of homophony at just the
right point, so relieving the ear and throwing the text

[1] Discussed on pp. 111-13.

into relief. The impression is one of solemnity at 'Thou
and the ark of Thy strength' in *Arise O Lord into Thy
resting-place*; of prayerful humility at the opening of
Have mercy upon me O God; of supplication at a similar
point in *O Lord I have loved the habitation of Thine house*.

Occasionally these chordal sections are prefigured by
the uppermost voice; a venerable device to be sure, but
also a remarkably effective one, especially at 'for in Thy
sight' (*Lord enter not into judgment*) and at 'O Lord, let
it be Thy pleasure to deliver me' (*Withdraw not Thou
Thy mercy*):

Ex. 6

This latter anthem assigns a double rôle to the middle
of five voices — as bass of one trio and treble of another —
at the phrase 'for innumerable troubles', and a similar
example may be found in *Great and marvellous*, where
'Who shall not fear Thee O Lord' is passed from a trio
of high voices to one of low voices. *Almighty God the*

fountain of all wisdom is a beautiful setting of the Fifth Collect at the end of the Communion, and is noteworthy for its particularly fine and extended 'Amen'. Both *Arise O Lord God* and *He that hath pity* (an Offertory Sentence from the Communion Service) are prayers for the poor and needy, whose plight was keenly felt and often remedied by Tomkins and his wife Alice.

Among the four-part anthems are several examples of Tomkins's finest workmanship. *Turn thou us* (the Last Collect of the Commination) is an ingenious canon four in one, yet its musical worth far surpasses the brilliance of its construction, and as Burney said it is 'well worthy the disciple of the admirable Byrd'.[1] The music for the Burial Service includes moving and dignified settings of the three texts at the beginning of the ceremony, and of the text to be said or sung after the interment.[2] Liturgically linked with *Turn thou us* is the Collect for Ash Wednesday, which offers two or three instances of Tomkins's fondness for repeating a phrase one note higher for emphasis. *The heavens declare the glory* brings in a touch of madrigalian technique when contrary motion is used to illustrate 'the ends of the world', but it is skilfully written and deserves to be better known. The same might well be said for *O how amiable*, which compares favourably with the excellent setting by Weelkes.

Most of the three-part anthems are based on Psalm texts, and their especial use is confined to smaller, but not necessarily men's choirs. The combinations of voices for these nineteen works without organ vary considerably.

[1] Burney, ii, 114.
[2] This latter, 'I heard a voice from heaven', has been edited separately by Atkins.

Outstanding among their number are the seven Peniten-
tial Psalms, all without exception good examples of
the expressive and original effects that may be drawn
out of a relatively unpromising medium of only three
voices.   Tomkins avoids mechanism in his imitative
writing by delaying the third entry somewhat, but for
the rest he does what is expected of him: an augmented
triad for 'heavy displeasure' (*Put me not to rebuke*), a
sudden veering to D major at 'Thy great goodness'
(*Have mercy upon me*), and a deep bass voice at the
beginning of *Out of the deep*.

In the verse anthems, or 'Songs to the Organ',
Tomkins has left a solid and impressive monument to
the taste of the times, a taste which he, as a virtuoso
organist, shared to a large degree.   Only in the verse
anthem was it possible for the instrument to become a
vital, creative part of the texture: it stood on a par with
the voices, supporting them in the choruses as well as
it did in the full anthems, but besides this it gave life
and meaning to the solos, duets, and small ensembles
that are so important a feature of the Jacobean verse
anthem.   It would be tedious to cite the frequent expressions of disdain which the verse anthem has inspired in
historians of English church music: the extremely rare
performances of this type of anthem is undoubtedly the
cause, rather than the effect of this disdainful approach
to a unique and eminently worthy art-form.[1]

If one of the advantages of the verse anthem is to be
found in the scope it gives the organist, one of its dis-
advantages is the standard of singing required of the

---

[1] A recent re-appraisal of Tomkins by Bernard Rose (*Proceedings of the
Royal Musical Association*, vol. 82 [1955/6], p. 89) affords welcome evidence of
an unusually enlightened judgement.   See especially p. 100.

soloists. Unless the solo and ensemble passages, as opposed to the choruses, are sung with exceptional poise and accuracy, the entire effect of the music is lost. Given first-rate soloists, and an organist with a discreet flair for pre-Restoration style, the verse anthem becomes a vehicle for the best kind of individual musical appeal. Yet it does not attempt to supplant polyphony by an overdose of monody, as some of its continental contemporaries did; nor does it oust the chorus in order to bathe the soloist in garish illumination. The verse anthem enfolds within its wide compass many of the most outstanding features of the music current during the previous century, but there is no secret in the fact that its most successful advocates were three men who by their position in the Chapel Royal were able to achieve performances very near to perfection — Byrd, Gibbons, and Tomkins.

It seems that of these three masters, Tomkins was decidedly the most prolific, with forty-one verse anthems, and also the most determined in seeing to it that the greater feast-days should be celebrated by music in this style. The Collects in particular contain much of his finest music. His setting of the Collect for Christmas makes apt use of rising melodic sequences and the overlapping and exchange of phrases between solo voices; brilliant too is the brief use of a double choir effect in the chorus passages. All Saints has several similar passages, and is rounded off by a splendid eight-part 'Amen'. A flowing and impressive bass solo tells of St. Mark, though one of the longest verses must be the five-part opening of the Collect for the Holy Innocents. The five voices are hardly ever used together, thus proving one of the main structural features of the verse anthem: it was fundamentally a display of contrasts in register and timbre. In this same anthem Tomkins demonstrates his skill in building up the listener's interest:

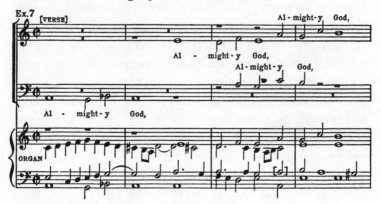

Several of Gibbons's verse anthems are intended to be accompanied by a consort of viols, and there are two by Tomkins (*Above the stars* and *Thou art my king O God*) for which string parts are extant. They were almost certainly written for the Chapel Royal, where such extra musical resources could be found from amongst the players at court. *Behold I bring you glad tidings*, a Christmas anthem of considerable stature, may also qualify for a London rather than a Worcester origin, for its single solo verse is followed by a ten-part chorus which would severely tax the powers of all but a large and entirely professional choir.

Not all of the chorus sections are of such power and complexity. The main function of the shorter choruses is to repeat and confirm the words uttered by the soloist, music as well as text being repeated in some instances: *Above the stars*; *O Lord let me know mine end*; *Praise the Lord O ye servants*. Less usually the very first phrase is repeated immediately after the soloist has stated it, as in *Hear my prayer*:

My shepherd is the living Lord, described as 'Psalm 23 of the ordinary metre',[1] employs two different techniques in its two short choruses. The first does not repeat the words of the soloist, but instead goes on with the psalm text, leading into the next verse section. The final chorus, however, does restate both text and musical motives of the preceding duet.

One particular verse anthem is sometimes indexed under the incipit 'My help cometh from the Lord', these being the first words sung by the solo counter-tenor.

---

[1] A reference to the then still popular psalter of Sternhold and Hopkins.

The entire anthem is to be introduced by the intoning of verse 1 of Psalm 121, *I will lift up mine eyes*. There is a typical example here of the subjugation of phrase by word, when a solo bass voice in its deepest and darkest register sings 'The Lord shall preserve thee from evil'. Similarly striking is the bass solo which begins *Leave O my soul*, whose text (like that of *Above the stars* and *Not in the merits*) is in verse of unknown authorship:

Irregular treatment of verse and chorus relationship is found from time to time, and this suggests that Tomkins was unwilling to follow any hard-and-fast plan, other than the understood method of beginning with a verse and ending with a chorus. In *O pray for the peace of Jerusalem* the first chorus echoes the verse in the accepted manner, then a bass verse repeats the text once more before new material is reached. This rhetorical repetition is not of the kind that irritates critics: their strictures apparently refer to the repetition of a phrase,

or part of a phrase, at the end of a section.[1]   It is perfectly
true that Tomkins frequently does this, but he is in
excellent company because Byrd, Gibbons, and Weelkes
also provide plentiful examples of the same alleged fault.

Several of the verse anthems are intended for feast-
days but are not based on Collects. The Easter anthem,
Christ rising again from the dead, is one of the most successful of these, and arrests the attention by its unusual
opening phrase, its florid organ part, and the delightful
tripla for the second section, 'Christ is risen':

Ex.10 [VERSE]

The text of the anthem for St. Stephen's Day is taken
from the First Lesson, the contrast between narrative
and speech being heightened by contrast of chorus and
verse. No less than six verse soloists are heard, in varied,

[1] Fellowes, *English Cathedral Music,* p. 91.

almost kaleidoscopic combinations of register. St.
George's Day demanded no special text, composers being
left to choose their own in collaboration with their ecclesiastical superiors.[1] Tomkins chose *Who is this that cometh
out of the wilderness* (The Song of Solomon iii, 6) and
clearly enjoyed setting this unusual text to music.

The wide variety of procedures and musical ideas in
these anthems, together with the high degree of skill
apparent in the very best of them should be more than
sufficient a recommendation to those who now have the
means to perform them. As Tudway once said, they are
indeed

very elaborate and artful pieces, and the most deserving to be
recorded and had in everlasting remembrance.[2]

Even more significant than Tudway's judgement,
although endorsing it, is a modern testimonial to the
greatness of Tomkins's music. It comes from the pen
of Tomkins's successor in the office of Organist and
Choirmaster at Worcester Cathedral:

Wherein lies the greatness of Thomas Tomkins's art? To
some extent it resides in the shape and beauty of his melodic lines,
and in his contrapuntal ingenuity. But more especially his genius
is to be found in the unusually bold and rich harmonic progressions,
achieved by free use of passing and anticipatory notes, chromatic
intervals, and frequent false relations. Such works as *A Sad
Pavan: for these distracted times* and *When David heard that
Absalom was slain* are unsurpassed for poignancy of musical
expression.[3]

[1] George Wither, in *The Hymns and Songs of the Church* (1623), p. 193,
describes St. George's Day as follows: 'This may be the called the Court
Holy-Day, for with us it is solemnized upon command, in the court royal of
the Majesty of Great Britain only, or in the families of those Knights of the
Order, who are constrained to be absent from the solemnity there held, which
is usually on the day anciently dedicated to St. George the Martyr.'

[2] British Museum, Harley MS 7339, f. 66.

[3] Kindly communicated by Mr. David Willcocks, M.C.

SONGS OF 3. 4. 5. AND 6. PARTS

In his songs there is melody and accent, as well as pure harmony
and ingenious contrivance.

CHARLES BURNEY, *General History of Music* (1776).

ALTHOUGH Thomas Tomkins began his professional career in music when the composing and
singing of madrigals was nearly at the height of its
popularity, he did not venture into the field of publication
until 1622, when much of the enthusiasm for this kind
of musical entertainment had given place to an extensive
cultivation of the lute-song repertory. He never wrote
lute songs or lute solos, but he admired the skill of
Dowland and Danyel, dedicating to them two of the
songs in his late but outstanding collection. If he had
admiration for the new trends in Jacobean music, he was
content to show it without attempting to copy those
trends or to break faith with his own deep-seated reverence for the traditions he had learned from his master,
William Byrd. Thus his published book of *Songs* (as he
called them, in common with Vautor, who also avoided
the term 'madrigal') appears as a late example of the
madrigalian idiom, whether viewed by his contemporaries or by critics of the present century.

Burney scored the first one of the set [1] but did not

---

[1] British Museum, Add. MS 11587; there are also five keyboard reductions,
probably by Tomkins himself, in Add. MS 29996 (*O let me live for true love;
O let me die for true love; Oyez! has any found a lad?; Weep no more, thou
sorry boy; Yet again, as soon revived*) and one incomplete keyboard version —
not by Tomkins — in Paris, Bibliothèque du Conservatoire, Rés. 1186.

apparently persevere to the extent that Vincent Novello did. In 1844, Novello scored twenty-three of the total number of twenty-eight,[1] though nothing was made available to the public until Barclay Squire edited two of the *Songs*[2] and Fellowes issued the entire set, together with the one madrigal in *The Triumphs of Oriana*, in 1922, just three centuries after the original publication. Late though they came in the stream of madrigal books published during the latter part of Elizabeth's reign and the reign of James I, these *Songs* enjoyed a success that was immediate enough to warrant a further printing. It is doubtful, however, that the second printing was made in the same year, as Fellowes and others have assumed.

Of the two editions known, one is dated 1622 while the other replaces this date with a rule and the words *Cum privilegio*. The undated edition cannot have been printed before 1622 since it was not until May of that year that William Heather, referred to as Dr. Heather in the dedication to *Music Divine*, actually took his degree of Doctor of Music at Oxford. It could have been printed later than 1622, since the type was frequently stored in case of need, and the inference of the term *Cum privilegio* points to a desire for prestige as well as restocking. The privilege to print music came, of course, from royal sources; and the renewal of privilege when a new king came to the throne may well have been the occasion for rejoicing. It is certainly not unlikely that such a renewal would prompt Matthew Lownes, John Browne, and Thomas Snodham to reissue some of their earlier publications with the two words *Cum privilegio*, so much sought after, in place of the date. In the case of Tomkins's *Songs*, there would be an added reason for a

---

[1] R.C.M. MS 616.　　　　[2] *Ausgewählte Madrigale*.

reissue of this kind, for the death of Orlando Gibbons
in 1625 had brought Tomkins to the forefront of musical
life in London, and his music for the funeral of James I
and the coronation of Charles I added very considerably
to this reputation. It is therefore quite possible that the
undated edition was printed in the first year of the reign
of Charles I, both as a tribute to Tomkins, and by way of
a discreet celebration of the renewal of privilege to print
music.

Unfortunately for Tomkins, the historical importance
of his *Songs* has often been stressed to the detriment of
their purely musical appeal, which (as any madrigal
group can confirm) is very considerable. Even a rapid
reading of the entire book is more than enough to con-
vince singers and listeners of the high standard of the
Songs, the best of them reaching a summit of musical
beauty that can only be matched by the finest creations
of Weelkes, Gibbons, and Wilbye. One of the first to
recognize this high quality was E. H. Fellowes, who
refers to the *Songs* as

the last volume of first-rate importance in the great series of
English madrigals. . . . It is consequently very remarkable that
Tomkins's music should have experienced such complete neglect,
as has been the case, ever since the popularity of madrigal-singing
declined in his own lifetime. Except for one or two recent reprints,
none of the work of this very notable English musician is known
to his own countrymen, and it is not improbable that a large
number of musicians of the present day have never even heard of
his name.[1]

A decade later, this opinion was echoed by Stainton
de B. Taylor:

The hand of the master-craftsman is always apparent, as well
as the heart of the sensitive musician, and the lofty habit of mind
of the scholar and church dignitary.[2]

[1] *The English Madrigal Composers*, p. 293.   [2] *Thomas Tomkins*, p. 4.

Even in the madrigal that Tomkins contributed to *The Triumphs of Oriana* there is mastery of an unusual strength for a young composer not yet thirty. He accepts graciously and wittily the pictorial conventions of the time, investing *The fauns and satyrs* with a rustic freshness and simplicity that he never quite recaptured in his later works.[1] The quasi-canonic chordal passage babbles 'of fresh cool brooks' with as much persuasiveness as the finely contrasted section following tells of 'those of woods and mountains', three lower voices being echoed by three upper ones in traditional though touching fashion. The altus has the pleasure of singing the highest part of the three lower voices, and the lowest part of the ready-made trio aloft. When the demi-gods are mentioned, there is a subtle reminder of their half-way status in the half-tone step heard in all three voices:

Although there is nothing at all out of the ordinary in Tomkins's harmonic palette, key-colour and cadential contrast are obviously part of a careful plan. The envoi is allowed to begin in the darker region of the subdominant, so that gradually it can move towards the brightness of the home key. As the music travels pointedly, though without rigidity, from C to G its texture undergoes a corresponding change from epigrammatic homophony to the long, flowing lines of the final cadence, where fair Oriana, supported by a plinth-like dominant pedal, makes her gracious bow of acknowledgement.

It was a creditable beginning for a young man, but

[1] This madrigal was formerly thought to be the work of Thomas Tomkins senior.

since he was a modest man and saw himself surrounded by madrigalists of tremendous gifts, he produced no further examples in this style until his friend Thomas Myriell invited contributions to *Tristitiae Remedium*, an anthology compiled during the years immediately preceding 1616, when it was apparently completed. Tomkins wrote six compositions for Myriell, and three of these appeared later in the *Songs*. Assuming that his B.Mus. degree, his work at Worcester, and his conferences with Dallam about the new organ together accounted for the greater part of his leisure during the years 1602–13, it is likely that these six works were written between 1613 and 1616. The idea of Myriell's collection, a *mélange* of serious anthems, delightful madrigals, and novelties such as the *London Cries* of Orlando Gibbons, may have inspired Tomkins to compile his own anthology as well as to plan it with variety in mind. Thus there are four sacred songs among the total of twenty-eight, calling to mind the principle followed by so many editors and publishers of the Renaissance: let there be secular music by all means, provided that a motet, grace, or anthem round off the collection and serve to sanctify the contents. Tomkins was a little anxious about this, for he mentions in his dedication to the Earl of Pembroke 'the lightness of some of the words . . . an old (but ill) custom, which I wish were abrogated'.

As with the madrigal-books of Byrd, Weelkes, Wilbye, and Ward, that of Tomkins includes music for any number of voices from three to six. Because of its sonority as well as its variety, five-part harmony still remained the prime favourite of composers during the early part of the seventeenth century, and Tomkins sets the largest group of his *Songs* for five voices. Together with these ten, there are six each of three-part, four-part, and six-part *Songs*, making a well-balanced group with adequate contrast in style and type.

The *Songs* set out for cantus, altus, and bassus show considerable ingenuity as well as remarkable contrapuntal resource: the individuality of treatment is scarcely less notable a feature of their design, and (unlike some of Ward's three-part madrigals) they can hold their own against the more elaborate texture of the other groups. The text of *Our hasty life* is particularly apt for Thomas Tomkins senior, who was then in his late seventies. It will be noticed that the dedication of the first song to his father is nicely matched by the dedication of the last one to his son. For Thomas, family life embraced all things, even a book of musical compositions. The harmonic scheme of this first madrigal of the set is simple but effective, especially in the middle section where the imitative passage — 'before we know what we have lost' — becomes a genuine sequence and touches upon A minor and G major on its way to the cadence. Although Tomkins never plays off two voices against two, using a similar technique to the three-versus-three trick in five-part texture, he does vary the sound by using two voices to echo one. At 'hours into days' the structure of the opening point is mirrored by the rhythmically identical 'years make a life', while at the end of the peroration ('when we are waxed old') there is a similar device, more taut than before, as a final cadence deserves.

No more will I thy love importune shares with two of the following three-part songs an imitative scheme at the very beginning which sets off a held note against two canonically mobile voices.[1] The phrase set to

---

[1] Cf. numbers 4 and 5 of the set.

'importune' sets up a graphic chain of treading upon heels, but Tomkins shows that he is more than a *glossateur* in his deft harmonic scheme for 'or pity use':

The latter third of the song is entirely devoted, as is so often the case, to an extended setting of the last line of the six-line lyric. It is the last line that gives the twist to the lyric, and it is therefore understandable that more time and effort should be expended upon it. 'Since I can never hope, I never may desire' grows smoothly, though inexorably, from an initial point handled in a manner that is typical of the later madrigalists in general and of Tomkins in particular: the first imitation is immediate, the second delayed and slightly altered. This feeling for asymmetrical patterns betrays a baroque attitude that may not always be allied to a baroque style. Coming from Tomkins, a traditional composer by design, and a transitional one by accident, this is not surprising. Other traits belonging to the same common cause will be noticed as time goes on.

Sure there is no God of Love, for Humphrey Withy,[1] one of the composer's Worcester friends, is more than usually interesting from a metrical point of view. Although the standard time-signature ₵ is employed in all three voices, the true metre is triple, with frequent hemiolas. Beginning with the first note of the bassus, it would be

---

[1] Not 'Witby', as in *The English Madrigal School*, xviii, 10.

possible to bar the song in $\frac{3}{2}$ $\frac{6}{4}$ time, thus preserving the natural rhythmic aspects of many of the individual phrases. The alternation between chordal and contrapuntal manner coincides, remarkably enough, with the progress of the lyric from one line to the next. The form of the verse itself, but not its rhyme scheme, is therefore brought out and enhanced by the texture of the music.

Nicholas Tomkins, who died a bachelor, was the recipient of the fourth song:

> Fond men, that do so highly prize
> A woman's forehead, lips and eyes,
> And look not to the better part
> What virtues dwelleth in the heart;
> Such kind of loving showeth plain,
> You please the sense and not the brain.

The words 'that do so highly prize' are consistently set to an ascending phrase, whilst the 'better part' emerges as a busy and complex piece of polyphony. Once again the last line of the poem receives the lion's share of the music, a final envoi descanting gaily and unrepentantly above a discreet dominant pedal.

How great delight paraphrases a text by Guarini,[1] which was set by Monteverdi in his seventh book of madrigals, first published in 1619. As *Con che soavità*, the madrigal is well known as a particularly fine example of concertato style: a solitary voice is richly and elaborately accompanied by three interdependent instrumental groups. In view of the appearance of Monteverdi's book some three years before the *Songs* of 1622, it is possible that Tomkins knew *Con che soavità* and admired

---

[1] *Delle opere* . . . vol. II, Madrigali, p. lxx. Monteverdi's setting of this text appears in Malipiero's edition of the *Complete Works*, vii, 137.

its pioneering mastery without wishing to emulate it; he made use, however, of a translation of part of its text and set the words for three solo voices unaccompanied, rather than for one solo voice accompanied by three groups of instruments. Tomkins permits homophony to underline the text now and then, varying the texture slightly for the sake of a sensuous little gruppetto on 'feel (them kiss)', and extending the sonority of a simple cadence at 'wonders'. The gruppetto first heard in connection with the word 'feel' recurs at 'kisses', but only in the two upper voices. In the bassus, there is a slowly moving line which acts fairly consistently as the bass part of the triads implied, except at the final cadence, where imitation occurs.[1]

The last of the three-part songs, *Love, cease tormenting*, like the previous one, is dedicated to a colleague of Tomkins in the Chapel Royal. William Cross and Thomas Day may well have been pleased with these short but charming compositions. There are poignant suspensions for the word 'tormenting', but nothing extraordinary happens at the first statement of 'cruel'. A change of mood and movement accompanies a repeat of the phrase 'pitiless and cruel', and this is the signal for expressive clashes involving the interval of the diminished fourth. Considered as a group, these six songs are pleasantly varied in text and texture, and they tend to show in a small way certain of the most important characteristics of Tomkins's style. His grasp of harmonic resource and his mastery of contrapuntal writing are apparent throughout these half-dozen madrigalistic miniatures,

[1] The text, as given in *The English Madrigal School*, xviii, 23, seems to be corrupt: 'or grant her speaking words' (lowest voice) should read 'and grant her kissing words'. Similarly, on page 22, the last four words of this voice-part should read 'and grant her kissing'.

for in spite of the modest designation of 'song' they manifest all that is most highly prized in the technique of madrigal composition.

The first two of the group of four-part *Songs* are linked together by their texts, their style, and their dedicatees. There is something touching about the way in which Tomkins quotes the well-known opening phrase of Dowland's *Lachrymae* in the uppermost voice of *O let me live for true love*. Countering this genial plagiarism with congenial persiflage, he brings to an abrupt end this tearful exclamation and introduces a flippant *fa-la*. This pattern is repeated, and gives way to a homophonic section in which the phrase 'yet let me live no longer' takes on an air of urgency from the breath of a tripla figure. The last and most extended of the *fa-la* sections makes considerable use of triple metre, which adds to the contrast between these light-hearted passages and the mock-serious, heavy rhythm of the *Lachrymae* borrowings. Unlike Barley, Byrd, Farnaby, and Morley, who all borrowed Dowland's music and used it in their publications, Tomkins found in it material for gentle satire as well as genuine tribute.

If Dowland was the greatest of the English lutenists, John Danyel was a worthy runner-up and a striking and original composer in his own right. The song dedicated to Danyel has for its text the second part of the lyric used in the song dedicated to Dowland: *O let me die for true love*. The opening phrase is also derived from a melodic fragment in the previous piece, but the *Lachrymae* theme does not appear until the words *O let me die for true love*, immediately after the first *fa-la*. The persiflage persists, and a tripla figure, matching that of the previous song, occurs at the phrase 'let not hope or old time come to end my woe'. This time the final *fa-la* has a more four-square feeling about it, so that the two songs, performed in succession, demonstrate artistic cohesion and contrast to a high degree.

Oyez! has any found a lad? makes use of the then popular device of basing a text upon the jargon of the town crier, who appears in the *Cries of London* by Dering and Gibbons as a kind of stock character, hearty to the extent of being somewhat coarse. Tomkins sublimates his town crier in a text whose Marinistic conceits of Cupid would have greatly pleased the Italianate Coperario, to whom the song is inscribed. The harmony becomes momentarily purple when this colour is cited as an attribute of Cupid's wings, and a little later it is removed altogether for a short space whilst bare monophony stresses 'in naked beauty', which uses exactly the same melodic figure as 'with bare gifts' in *The Fauns and Satyrs*.[1] Word-painting is found when the words 'lieth' and 'flieth' occur, the latter giving rise to melismatic parabolas, vivid in expression and plausible in contour.

The second half of the four-part group follows the same pattern as the first half: there are two paired songs, followed by an isolated one. The paired ones, dedicated to his brothers Peregrine and Robert, are based on two verses which constitute a single lyric. *Weep no more thou sorry boy* adds to the pathos of its opening phrase by avoiding too firm a tonality, and Tomkins's acquaintance with the practice of Italian madrigalists is shown by his portrayal of 'sighs' as crotchet rests (*sospiri*),[2] which create a hocketing effect between the upper voice and

---

[1] *The English Madrigal School*, xviii, 215.

[2] Cf. Monteverdi, *Complete Works*, viii, 287: 'un gran sospir dal cor'. Bontoux, in *La Chanson en Angleterre*, p. 644, comments on the delicacy of expression in Tomkins's song.

the three lower ones. The fickleness of love is nicely depicted by Gesualdo-like chordal juxtapositions at 'laughs and weeps':

Ex. 3

Similarly, 'dancing' gives rise to a fleeting tripla; 'angry eye' a harmonic jolt which far transcends the bounds of *Augenmusik*, and brings with it a false relation or two for good measure. The lover, thus rebuked, sits down in a recurring and unmistakable octave drop, and true to certain traditions takes an unconscionable time a-dying.

Yet again, as soon revived is an admirable sequel, and (like its prototype) begins with a statement of the opening line or title by the three upper voices, repeating it when the bassus joins in. Joy and grief, aptly portrayed, lead to the phrase 'change there is of joy', at which the metre obediently changes to triple time, returning as suddenly at the word 'sadness', long held on a soulful chord of A-flat. There is a bold and expressive touch when a cadence on 'gladness', purposely deprived of its third, leads to a broad hint of E minor at the words 'then weep no more, thou sorry boy', recalling the opening line of the first verse. With weeping joy, sighing and dying, dancing and singing, the song moves towards its close, evoking shades of Monteverdi's *Zefiro torna*,[1] with its contrasting music for 'hor piango, hor canto'. But Tomkins's master-stroke is left to the very end, when

[1] Monteverdi, ix, 9.

crocodile tears are suggested by ululating downward sequences and an optimistic ending in D major.

The group is rounded out by another song dedicated to one of Thomas's brothers, this time Giles, who was destined to become organist of King's College, Cambridge, and Salisbury Cathedral. *Was ever wretch tormented* is a conventional enough love-lyric, yet rich in contrasting words that call up powerful musical images. Not without very good reason did Tomkins choose a relatively low tessitura for the voices: their dark colours prove to be effective and compelling in the middle section of the song. At the outset, the three lower voices reach out tortuously and expressively for a cadence on 'tormented':

Significantly, three out of the four voices sing their highest note at the mention of 'heaven', and later there is a deep and fiendish ostinato for 'hellish firing'. There is still a strong proclivity for word-painting in its most individual form, as opposed to a consistent emotional mood, for the sake of relief and change: the ascending runs on 'flames' and the infectious gaiety of 'delighted' are the only rays of light in this sad and solemn portrayal of 'pinish grief and anguish'.

Seven of the ten songs for five voices are written in the style of the ballett, yet this group is far from being wholly light and bucolic. The first of the sacred songs, *When David heard*, appears here amidst the richness and variety of five-part vocal colour, and it is the only one of the group to depart from the otherwise standard practice of having the two uppermost voices of equal and even tessitura. *To the shady woods* (possibly a pun on the name of Robert Chetwode, its dedicatee) is a short but charming song in which Tomkins begins at once to make use of the possibilities of voice-exchange afforded by the cantus and quintus. The two *fa-las*, one in duple and the other in triple metre, offer rhythmical as well as thematic contrast, and do much to dispel the notion that these simple refrains were no more than mechanically composed codettas of little importance. The tripla section at the end is introduced, in the original part-books, by no less than four different mensuration signs: against the probability that the printer was feeling whimsical may be set the more likely explanation that such signs were no longer called for at the time when the *Songs* were published. It is true that one or two archaic time-signatures continued until the end of the seventeenth century, but there is no evidence to show that printers were keen to keep them in stock.

Too much I once lamented is a finely contrived song, and one that surely made Byrd (to whom it is inscribed) proud of his pupil. The expected suspensions and harmonic twists accompany the opening line and its successor, 'while love my heart tormented', but the gloom is dispelled by a fascinating *fa-la* which rises in two-bar sequences, changing the texture as it goes. There is much expressive and unusual melodic beauty in the lines that carry 'alas and ay me', but once again the sorrowful mood is done away with by neat homophony and a vivacious *fa-la* whose essence lies in its pairing of voices.

Nathaniel Giles, whose exercise in proportional

notation was reprinted by Hawkins,[1] could hardly fail
to be amused by the song dedicated to him: *Come
shepherds sing with me*. The verse form is treated in
cavalier fashion so that the second line, which begins with
the word 'thrice' can change to a tripla, while three
voices remain singing as far as the *fa-la*. The falseness
of love is suggested by shifting syncopations, beneath
which the bassus firmly resolves 'to love false love no
more' in a series of long, held notes. The last *fa-la* is
one of the longest Tomkins wrote, yet it is splendidly
organized, with texture changing from groups of three
and four voices until the final chorus from all five, and
well-balanced modulation leading through G minor and
B flat back to the home key of F.

Cloris, whenas I woo (for Orlando Gibbons) uses deft
and effervescent counterpoint to suggest the maid's
refusal, the 'no no no' corresponding to a *fa-la* refrain,
and occupying the same place in both lyric and music.
The second refrain is especially interesting for its use of
ascending sequential phrases over a chromatic altus,
which reiterates 'no' until all join in and the scheme is
repeated, this time with the bass ascending in diatonic
but none the less forceful negatives.

See, see the shepherd's queen was dedicated to John
Stevens, one of the composer's colleagues in the Chapel
Royal. Its text is that of an extended ballet, with three
couplets each followed by a *fa-la* refrain. This time, even
Tomkins's ingenuity is severely taxed to find adequate
variety in the refrain sections, which occupy about two-
thirds of the total time of performance. He emerges
from this artistic ordeal with flags flying: the first *fa-la*
is deliberately conventional, so that when the second is

[1] *A General History . . .*, iii, 462.

heard, with its vivacious solo roulades, interest and excitement grow apace. The third and longest refrain returns to the epigrammatic, paired phrases of the first, but with certain differences: a long and slowly descending bass line seems to bind together the more quickly moving upper parts, while the final cadence is reached by way of an upward surging sequence of insistent *fa-las*, leading back to the key of G major. The couplets themselves, especially 'then dance we on a row', have characteristically subtle rhythmic schemes, and make up for their shortness by their full and sonorous texture.[1]

There is a possible link between the lyric of *Phyllis, now cease to move me* (for Mr. Henry Molle of Worcester) and the previous one beginning *Come, shepherds, sing with me*, which ends

> From hence we all have swore
> To love false Love no more.

The second, and last couplet of *Phyllis* seems to echo these lines, though to be sure the oath is singular rather than plural:

> Content thee! I have swore
> To love false Love no more.

Four upper voices administer the dissuasive understatement with which the song begins, and their declamation is consistent in its natural and easy flow; there is

---

[1] The music is used also for the *Sanctus* in *Musica Deo Sacra.*

something of speech-rhythm here, and the exaggeration
(if it is present at all) is just that of a testy rebuke.

The first *fa-la* is of the sequential type, where rising
repetition gains momentum from the overlapping of the
two equal upper voices. True to the accepted scheme of
the ballett (of which this is the last of a continuous group
of six) the second couplet is regaled with lilting homophony, and as soon thrust aside for a refrain compounded
of bold melodic figures and subtle rhythms. On its
first and second appearance, the *fa-la* phrase well exceeds
the octave; paired, it keeps within bounds but is doubly
exciting. So too is the tenor part, with its delightful
symmetry and syncopation:

Ex. 6

TENOR

Fa la la la la la la,   Fa la,   la, Fa la la la la, Fa la   Fa [la]

However moving or beautiful the settings of David's
lament by East and Weelkes, there is one English
composition on this wonderful theme that can hold its
own, in sheer poetry and dramatic effect, against the
settings by Josquin des Prez, Jacob Handl, and Heinrich
Schütz. It is Thomas Tomkins whose 'exquisite invention, wit, and art' (to quote from Charles Butler) [1]
endowed this lament with such feeling and expression.
His mastery of madrigalian idiom stands him in good
stead when these same principles are applied, in a re-
served and reverent way, to the well-known text from
2 Samuel xviii, 33. Thomas Myriell, to whom the work
was dedicated, and who included it in his musical
anthology *Tristitiae Remedium*, must have been an
especially good friend of Thomas Tomkins to deserve
so fine a gift.

[1] This appraisal is quoted in full on p. 36.

The work falls roughly into two halves: the narration
and the lament. *When David heard that Absalom was
slain* begins as if it were a four-part composition for
cantus, quintus, altus, and tenor, and the voices rarely
exceed the total compass of a twelfth as they sing, with
hushed expectancy, of David's grief. Even when the
tenor rises to an octave G at 'he went up to his chamber'
there is no impression of a lack of restraint in word-
painting: if such a phrase occurred in a song, it would
be set to some gay scalic ascent. Here, the clean but
audible change of octave does all that is required of it.
The near-sequential lines of the upper voices ('and wept')
achieve their effect too, without an extravagant display
of chromatic emotion, and the quasi-apostrophic half-
close at the end of the section prepares the way eloquently
for the high, ringing, and solitary tenor note on which the
lament begins.

From this point onwards the polyphony unfurls its
sad beauty with a mastery that defies description. To
the ever-shifting contrasts of vocal colour Tomkins adds
contrasting motives to the same word, the key-word of
the lament:

There is a shift, this time of harmonic emphasis, on the
phrase 'would God I had died for thee', which seems to express the ever-changing, ever-renewing aspects of David's
sorrow. Perhaps the most wonderful touch of all is the

way in which Tomkins seems to bring in a note of quiet
resignation as the descending, cambiata-like point for
'Absalom, my son' gives place to an ascending figure,
set to the same words, and enclosed as it were in the
comforting embrace of a dominant pedal and an inverted
tonic pedal. As devices in the successful building up of
a musical peroration, these are simple, even commonplace: used with the skill and judgement that Tomkins
lavishes upon them, they take on a character that is
nothing if not ethereal.

The title of *Phyllis, yet see him dying* clearly recalled
Phyllis, now cease to move me, for both songs begin with
exactly similar rhythm and initial change of chord.
Beyond this, there is nothing in common, for the verse
forms differ, and there is no *fa-la* refrain in this charming
song inscribed to Nicholas Carlton, a fellow-madrigalist
and near neighbour of Tomkins. The texture, accentua-
tion, and spirit of the music are apt to change (as in certain
of the previous songs) as soon as a new line of the lyric
is reached, but if there is a touch of the mechanical here
it is effectively dispelled by certain irregularities that
cannot fail to strike the ear. The first really noticeable
one is the augmented triad, on a strong beat, where the
word 'dying' occurs for the second time. Although this
chord was not unknown to Elizabethan and Jacobean
writers, it was sufficiently rare to produce that *nouveau
frisson* which Tomkins certainly intended. A further
irregularity is heard at the last mention of the word
'hateful', when the cantus declines to allow its seventh
(G) to resolve downwards in normal fashion, moving up
instead to a B flat which creates a sharp though momentary dissonance with the A of the quintus. Perhaps the
boldest stroke in the entire song is the reappearance of

the augmented triad, followed briskly by a false relation, at 'thine eyes have slain':

As in many other songs of this type, there is an extended and optimistic codetta, rich in word-painting and the crossing and pairing of voices.

The last of the five-part balletts is dedicated to the poet and divine, Phineas Fletcher, who had been such a good friend of John Tomkins during their Cambridge days. *Fusca, in thy starry eyes,* begins conventionally enough with altus alone calling out the lady's name; but soon there is a tripla, set to the words 'Love in black still mourning dies'. There is, of course, no reason at all for Love to die in a lilting triple metre. Had there been allusion to 'change' or 'dance' as in *Yet again, as soon revived,* the new time and tempo would be easy to understand: here the operative word is the innocent-looking epithet 'black'. In the original edition, in fact, the phrase is set to black notation, which was still occasionally used by Elizabethan composers for *proportio sesquialtera,* or three notes in the time of two. Almost equally remarkable at this point is the harmonic progression of three, then four voices: practically every chord is in its root position, and the effect is quite as odd as the *Augenmusik* itself. In the second couplet, the mock pathos of 'so many slain' leads quickly and naturally to the capricious rhythms of 'thou hast loved none again' and the coquettish syncopations of the final *fa-la.*

Adieu, ye city-prisoning towers, for Mr. William White of Durham, is a delightful eulogy of country life, with a brilliant portrayal of budding trees, musically related birds singing upon hedges, and a hocket-like passage to illustrate their chirping. Cantus and quintus overlap enthusiastically at 'delay not', and although there is delaying, even dallying, at the cadence which follows, the coaxing, cajoling tripla for 'come, come, sweet love' is as gracious an invitation as any since the time of 'veni, dilecti me' in Dunstable's *Quam pulchra es*.[1]

The addition of a sixth voice (sextus) in the last six songs does not give rise to a texture that is noticeably more dense or more rich, though it certainly becomes more varied. Tomkins uses real six-part writing very rarely in *When I observe those beauty's wonderments*, written for his Chapel Royal colleague Mr. Thomas Warwick. There is a brief example of full sonority at the last repetition of 'how do you mourn' and a slightly longer one when the tenor sings, for the last time, 'open her deaf ears or close mine eyes'. For the rest, Tomkins is content to play with his vocal colours in kaleidoscopic fashion, blending and changing them as the spirit moves him, and less attentive than usual to the demands of the text. The pairing or otherwise associating of two equal middle voices (altus and quintus) as well as two equal upper voices (cantus and sextus) tempts many a fruitful point of imitation: homophony is here subservient to the inventive flexibility of Tomkins's superlative counterpoint.

In *Music Divine*, perhaps a compliment to Dr. Heather on the receipt of his degree from Oxford, there is more six-part writing than in the previous song. Indeed, it is called for in such phrases as 'where tuneful

[1] Cf. *Musica Britannica*, viii, 112.

concords sweetly do agree', and in the righteous indignation of the final line 'to call that love which is indeed but
lust'. What must have pleased the good Doctor even
more than these, even more than the joyful octave leaps
on the last word of 'proceeding from above', were the
daring cambiata chains set to the word 'harmony'. Now
alone, now in pairs, the voices attempt these festoons of
minute and scintillating discords with genuine verve, here
and there anticipating a chord by adhering firmly to the
descending melodic sequence: B flat below a chord of F,
C minor below G major.

Oft did I marle, dedicated to John Ward, whose book
of madrigals had preceded Tomkins's *Songs* by some
nine years, is one of the compositions included in Myriell's
anthology,[1] and may be dated before 1616. The title is
announced by one voice, then by three, and by four,
alternating in pairs. Apt roulades suggesting 'water and
fire' disappear at the words 'did well together', when the
harmonious ensemble of the elements is expressed through
the medium of all six voices in chordal style. The
succeeding phrase, 'seeing 'tis known in contraries'

invites the contrast of texture that Tomkins deftly

---

[1] The error in the printed part-books mentioned by Fellowes (*The English Madrigal Schoo,l* xviii, 166) is confirmed by the manuscript copy in *Tristitiae Remedium*.

supplies, with a heightening of effect brought about by
the contrary rhythm of a hemiola.

A corresponding example of word-painting in vivid
perspective is heard immediately after this, when three
or more voices sing 'each seeks the hurt and spoil of
either' in actively overlapping downward scales, whilst
a slowly-moving motive in semibreves gradually creeps
upwards. Tomkins, obviously enamoured of the sound,
repeats the idea three times before moving on to the
next line of the lyric, which (as harbinger of the final
couplet) takes up a sizeable portion of the composition
as a whole, in the same way as in the four-part and five-
part songs.

The three sacred songs, according to Fellowes, 'do
not quite reach the same standard as the rest of the
volume'[1] an opinion which is echoed, rather forcefully
in the case of *It is my well-beloved's voice*, by Stainton
de B. Taylor, who finds it 'one of the least satisfactory
of the set'.[2] Taylor shows a more generous appreciation
of *Woe is me*, whose texture he likens to that of a six-
part fancy for the viols. In view of Charles Butler's
account of the performance of *When David heard*, it is
not difficult to concede that a similar manner of performance would be apt for the other sacred songs. The collections by Leighton, Amner, and Tailour[3] encouraged
instrumental participation, and this may well have been
the rule rather than the exception, even though title-
pages tend to be uncommunicative.

Woe is me, based on a verse from Psalm cxx, was
written for John Tomkins, who had been appointed

---

[1] *The English Madrigal Composers*, p. 295.   [2] *Thomas Tomkins*, p. 6.
[3] Leighton, *The teares or lamentacions of a sorrowfull soule*, (1614); Amner,
Sacred hymnes of 3.4.5. and 6. parts (1625); Tailour, *Sacred hymnes* (1615).

organist of St. Paul's Cathedral only a year or so before
the publication of the *Songs*. The text was a strange
one to choose for a younger brother, unless it may be
taken as an expression of regret at being domiciled far
away in Worcester:

Woe is me! that I am constrained to dwell with Mesech;
and to have my habitation among the tents of Kedar.

In 1620, the year after John's appointment, Thomas
was made a Gentleman of the Chapel Royal, and the
two brothers were thereafter able to keep a little more
closely in touch. If the text does contain a shade of
personal feeling, then it is likely that the date of composition was 1619. Most notable among the sombre features
of this work, where the tessitura of all voices is low and
dark, are the discords of the opening section, as altus
and cantus sing the word 'woe'. The individual parts
show little disposition to be active until after the short,
tripla-like passage 'and to have my habitation': when this
portion of the text is repeated, there is more animation
and variety of rhythm. The coda is given up to the tents
of Kedar, at first sparsely pitched, and then slowly more
and more crowded, as the texture expands from three to
six voices.

Dedicated very suitably to a learned Doctor of
Divinity, Theophilus Aylmer, *It is my well-beloved's
voice* draws for its text upon The Song of Solomon ii, 8.
The version of the text is a metrical paraphrase of the
psalm verse, and affords many opportunities for brilliant
word-painting. Aptly enough, the voice of the well-
beloved is first heard in the upper register, as if from
a distance. As he approaches, the lower frequencies
become more and more audible, and the pulsating heart-
beat is characterized by a subtle, though ever-present

hemiola.   Lively rhythmic figures help to animate the final section, which sings of hopping and skipping, of hills and mountains, making uninhibited use of every known pictorial device in the musical vocabulary.   Yet, conventional as this setting may be, it has a key-scheme which is almost modern in its approach to the question of tonal balance.   After the dominant is reached, and its own dominant avoided by an interrupted cadence, there is a momentary return to the tonic; then the same pattern unfolds, but this time there is no interrupted cadence to ward off the brightness and sparkle of A major.   The tables are quickly turned, however, and the darker tones of the subdominant emerge to balance the former brightness, leading the way to a well-prepared and satisfying cadence on G.

Turn unto the Lord, for Nathaniel, son of Thomas, takes its text from Joel ii, 13, and Psalm c, 4.   Nearly half of the composition is given up to a descriptive interweaving of the phrase 'from generation to generation'; this type of polyphony pervades the opening portion also, giving the impression of a Latin motet texture rather than that of an English anthem.   The general sentiment of the text is honoured here, and only occasionally are there found slight hints of musical imagery, as when the word 'turn' gives rise to contrary motion, or 'everlasting' has the effect of avoiding clear-cut cadences.   It is a noble ending to a book of songs whose excellence cannot be over-rated.

MUSIC FOR KEYBOARD
INSTRUMENTS

If he be musical, and can bear a part in a consort, though never so
meanly, they will prefer him before Tomkins the organist and
Dowland the lutenist.

THOMAS NASH, *Quaternio* (1633).

DOWLAND is John without a doubt, for his son
Robert never achieved great eminence as a performer; but Tomkins is not quite certainly Thomas.
John and Giles, half-brothers of Thomas, were both
highly respected for their talents and extremely well
known in the musical profession, the former by reason
of his fame as organist of St. Paul's, and the latter by
reason of his notoriety achieved during the *affaire* Holmes
at Salisbury. In the very same year that Nash published
his *Quaternio*, both John and Giles were appointed joint
organists 'to wait on His Majesty in his Scottish journey',[1]
and thus managed to come before the eyes of more than
one public.

Thomas nevertheless has a reasonable claim of his
own, as the rightful subject of Nash's forward-looking
though back-handed compliment. Nash, like Thomas
Tomkins, was both an Oxford graduate and a staunch
Royalist; moreover, he owned property in Worcestershire,[2]

[1] May, 1633, though the warrant was signed during the previous year.
The King's Musick, p. 84.

[2] At Mildenham Mills, near Claines. Nash is not to be confused with his
more illustrious namesake, the dramatist and poet.

where Thomas's renown as cathedral organist for thirty-six years was at its height. Nash would have known him in London as well as in Worcester, for the appointment as organist of the Chapel Royal dated from 1621. When it is a question of organ music, rather than organ-playing, Thomas takes pride of place over his brothers through the sheer bulk of his writing for the instrument. Some fifteen solo pieces are known,[1] apart from the often elaborately worked out organ accompaniments to the forty-one verse anthems in *Musica Deo Sacra*. Without doubt he penned far more than this during his sixty-year tenure of the office of organist at Worcester Cathedral, since every service at which the organ played would require two or more voluntaries or 'still verses' as they were sometimes called.[2] Much of this material was as improvisatory in character as it is in our own day, yet it is certain that the methodical Thomas would have wished to preserve the best of it for his immediate successors' use in particular, if not for posterity in general.

Besides the organ music, there are more than fifty pieces apparently written for the virginals, harpsichord, or clavichord. It is not known which of these instruments Thomas owned, for there are no references to them during his lifetime, and no trace of them after his death. The possibility of their being named in his will is ruled out by the fact that no will was ever made: instead an administration was granted to his nephew John in 1659,

[1] See *Musica Britannica*, v, xvi, for a note on the instruments. The pieces with Latin titles do not, of course, necessarily imply the use of an organ; e.g. *Clarifica me pater*.

[2] There are several mentions of a still verse (a quiet organ voluntary) in the Bishop of Durham's form for the consecration of the chapel at Auckland Castle on St. Peter's Day, June 29, 1655. (Lambeth, Archbishop's Library, Gibson MS 929, No. 85. Printed in J. Wickham Legg, *English Orders for Consecrating Churches*, p. 224. *Henry Bradshaw Society*, xli.)

and this document gives no specific details of personal property.[1] Generations of Tudor choirboys had learned their elementary keyboard technique on the clavichord, and Thomas (whose duties included the teaching of choirboys) must have owned a clavichord if only for that purpose. His comfortable though by no means affluent financial circumstances may well have permitted him the luxury of a pair of virginals, or even of a small harpsichord, for it is these two instruments whose characteristics are suggested by the greater part of his extant keyboard music.

His acquaintance with English keyboard music was both profound and practical, for he was the fortunate possessor of a large volume of organ music whose earliest compositions date from the middle years of Henry VIII's reign.[2] The composers named are sometimes well-known figures like John Redford and Philip ap Rhys of St. Paul's, John Thorne of York, and Thomas Preston of Windsor; men of lesser musical stature, such as Kyrton, Strowger, and Wynslade, help to fill out the contents of these early pages, and Thomas has seen fit to annotate them from time to time in generous and commendatory fashion. Of an anonymous setting of *Salvum fac* (f. 24v) he writes 'an excellent verse', possibly to show his approval of the neatly turned passage in 3.1 proportion. An anonymous set of verses for *Magnificat* (f. 26) brings forth such comments as 'a good verse

[1] Prerogative Court of Canterbury, A.A. 1659, f. 54.

[2] London, British Museum, Add. MS 29996. For a description see Hughes-Hughes, *Catalogue of Manuscript Music in the British Museum*, London (1906), iii, 80, 85. Also Henry Davey, *Die ältesten Musik-Handschriften auf englischen Bibliotheken*, in *Monatshefte für Musikgeschichte*, xxxiv (1902), 33. The *Pretty Ways: for Young Beginners to Look On*, although in Tomkins's hand, are almost certainly not by him. See H. M. Miller, *Pretty Wayes . . .* in *The Musical Quarterly*, xxxiii (1947), 543.

. . . 3 to the semibreve', whilst the margin offers him room to re-copy a short musical passage which was poorly written out by the original scribe. 'Note this', writes Thomas of an oddly juxtaposed pair of parts, in black and white notation respectively, on f. 34v.

Even more frequent and voluble are his remarks in the section of the manuscript containing an incomplete cycle of alternatim hymns for the church year. He appears to have found these splendidly written but unfortunately anonymous works particularly congenial, recognizing at once that they are mostly based not upon the hymn melody itself, but 'upon the faburden of these plain-songs'. The faburden, as he knew from his lessons with William Byrd, was formed by adding a freely decorative part a sixth (or sometimes an octave) below the hymn melody. Although there are no examples of the use of this technique in those of his keyboard works based on a liturgical cantus firmus, he was clearly able to see and appreciate its use in the music of others. Sometimes his remarks reveal the wary eye of a musician much practised in dealing with corrupt and badly-copied manuscripts: 'the cliff changes' (f. 158v); 'tripla to the semibreve' (f. 159v); 'a crotchet rest' (f. 177v). Most often, however, he is content simply to write 'good', or an occasional superlative like 'a good old indeed, very good' (f. 165) or 'a dainty fine verse' (f. 176v). He loves to light upon canons in middle voice-parts, writing regularly on these occasions 'two parts in one in the fourth' and is only very rarely mystified by a strange proportional sign, such as the ƆC on f. 177: 'note this mark receives 3 to the minim and six quavers but I know not the reason for it'.

All this is evidence of an enquiring mind and a well-exercised critical faculty, and it also shows Thomas as a great respecter of tradition, in spite of the fact that fundamental changes in liturgy divided his world of organ music from that of his early Tudor predecessors. Nevertheless, certain of the plain-songs used liturgically by Redford and his contemporaries survived the reformation by becoming secular, notably the short antiphon *Miserere mihi Domine* and the long offertory *Felix namque*. Neither too long nor too short (like Cherubini's definition of the ideal fugue subject) was *In nomine*, otherwise known as *Gloria tibi Trinitas*; but this was never set by the early organists since its origin was not strictly liturgical, but rather a short section from a polyphonic setting of the Ordinary of the Mass by John Taverner.[1] Tallis, Byrd, Bull, and Thomas Tomkins all set one or more of these plain-songs more than once, the usual motives being sheer virtuosity and rhythmic inventiveness.

The later sections of Thomas's organ book consist of music by his own contemporaries — Byrd, Nicholas Carlton, Gibbons, Ferrabosco, Farmer and Morley — in his own hand. There is even a piece by his brother John, suitably enough a set of variations on *John come kiss me now*. By no means all the music in this section qualifies as solo keyboard music, for there are a number of straightforward keyboard scores of madrigals and balletts, including some of his own from the *Songs* of 1622. Important as this holograph is, it cannot match the fascinating and fundamental importance of the manuscript in the Paris Conservatoire.[2]

Once the eighth of a set of manuscript music-books in Thomas's own library at Worcester, this volume

[1] See Gustave Reese, *The Origin of the English In nomine*, in *Journal of the American Musicological Society*, ii (1949), 7.

[2] Réserve 1122, listed by van den Borren and others under its accession number: 18547.

reached Paris by way of Oxford and London only after some two hundred years had elapsed. It belongs to the most mature period of its composer and compiler, who (although he included works by Byrd and Bull) devoted the greater part of the available space to his own works. Many of the pieces are accurately dated, the earliest being the *Fancy* (September 9, 1646) and the latest *The Perpetual Round* (September 7-8, 1654). If we are to accept the general view that these dates refer to composition and not to copying — and there are historical facts to show that this view is correct — this late flowering of Thomas's genius provides a steady coverage for the period stretching from the second siege of Worcester to the removal of Thomas and his newly married son Nathaniel into the manor of Martin Hussingtree.

There is every indication that Thomas intended his last collection of music to be a fair copy rather than a sketch-book; yet as the pages are turned, it becomes increasingly clear that the aged composer gave up his early resolve, supplanting it with a desire to create and re-create, to polish and re-polish, however bewildered the reader becomes, and however bleary his eye. The book is thus a human document as well as a musical one, for it displays the agile and resourceful workings of Thomas's mind, his considerably less agile penmanship, and his determination to say in forthright musical terms what he thought and believed to be the best in works of that kind. As we have seen, he left no will; but he left this matchless musical testament whose content will probably do more to spread his renown than all the anthems in *Musica Deo Sacra*.

The history of the manuscript is remarkable in itself, embracing the names of famous collectors of early music

both in France and in England. Strangely enough, its
first short journey from Worcester to Oxford has so far
proved most difficult to trace, because Nathaniel is
generally assumed to have taken charge of Thomas's
property. The discovery of the administration[1] naming
John, Thomas's nephew and the son of John Tomkins
of St. Paul's, has clarified matters considerably. It was
through this nephew, born in 1631, that the male line
of the Tomkins family was continued until the late
eighteenth century, when the name was changed to
Berkeley. Among the last of the family to bear the name
Tomkins was a great-grandson of nephew John: the
Reverend Richard Tomkins, who went up to New
College, Oxford, in 1742, when he was 21 years old,
and took his B.A. degree four years later. During his
residence at Oxford, a young man named Thomas Bever,
of Stratfield Mortimer in Berkshire, arrived as a gentleman scholar of Oriel College. It is not impossible that
the manuscript changed hands between 1744 and 1746,
for Bever began to collect rare and valuable books at an
early stage in his subsequently illustrious career. He
became a D.C.L., a Fellow of All Souls, Judge of the
Cinque Ports and Chancellor of Lincoln and Bangor, and
by the time of his death in 1791 he had assembled a fine
and valuable library, including many rare musical items.

Bever left the greater part of his library to a lay
vicar of Westminster Abbey named John Hindle, but
Hindle died within five years of this bequest and the
library was put up for sale in 1798. According to a
contemporary report,[2] the library

---

[1] Thomas died intestate. The administration was drawn up three years
after his death.

[2] *The Gentleman's Magazine and Historical Chronicle*, vol. 68 (1798),
p. 715.

contained, among many other curious articles, the complete works of Luca Marenzio, Orlando di Lasso, Morley, Weelkes, Wilbye, Bennet, Purcell and other eminent composers of the late 16th and 17th centuries; . . . the whole in fine preservation obtained and purchased with great judgment and indefatigable pains, at considerable expense during a long course of years by Dr. Bever. The several articles fetched very high prices.

Annotations in the manuscript by known and unknown hands of the early nineteenth century indicate that the volume changed hands more than once before making its final journey. There is reason to believe that a certain J. Finley Foster was one of the owners, and that later on it became part of the library of Edward Jones, some of whose manuscripts were sold by Sotheby in 1825. Item 441 of the Jones sale catalogue reads as follows:

Virginal books: containing the Compositions of Orlando Gibbons, Dr. Blow, Farinelli, W. Byrd, Dr. Bull, Tallis and others, on six-line staves. 6 vol. 1635-95.

The composers named here almost match those of another virginal book now in the Paris Conservatoire,[1] with the sole exception of Byrd. This indicates that the rough catalogue description does not refer to any one of the six books, but was made by somebody who thumbed quickly through the volumes and picked out composers' names at random. Music by Byrd and Bull appears in the Thomas Tomkins autograph, as we have seen, and these two names may well have been taken from this very volume. The six manuscripts were bought by a bookseller named Thomas Thorpe, and it was he who ultimately sold four of them to M. and Mme Farrenc of Paris.

Farrenc's references to these treasures in his introductions to volumes 1 and 6 of *Le Trésor des pianistes*

---

[1] Réserve 1186 bis (accession number: 18570).

are well known. He tells of his acquisition of two virginal books, and later of several very valuable ones bought in London. But no music from the Tomkins volume is printed, nor is any specific mention made of it. The fact that it *was* among those valuable manuscripts is conclusively proved by the article on Thomas Tomkins in the famous dictionary of Fétis,[1] published in 1864:

> M. Farrenc possesses an original manuscript of pieces by Thomas Tomkins for harpsichord and organ; the last of these pieces bears the date 1654.

When Mme Farrenc died in 1875, the manuscripts were presented to the library of the Conservatoire, and they remained there unobserved until the first decade of the next century.

They were duly examined and mentioned by their accession numbers — but not studied in detail — by Charles van den Borren, who was then in course of writing a valuable and pioneering book on English keyboard music.[2] Thanks to the interest shown by van den Borren, the librarian of the Conservatoire was able to send a brief description of them, together with some tracings of signatures and scribbles, to Sir Ivor Atkins, whose indispensable account of Worcester organists was being prepared for the Worcestershire Historical Society.[3] In acknowledging the help of Mlle Pereyra, the librarian, Sir Ivor called attention to the fact that a complete description was not then possible, as the Tomkins autograph, together with other valuable items, had been removed to a place far from the destructive hazards of war.

[1] *Biographie universelle des musiciens* (1860–65).
[2] *The Sources of Keyboard Music in England* (1914).
[3] *The Early Occupants of the Office of Organist and Master of the Choristers . . .*, pp. 37-78. *Worcestershire Historical Society* (1918).

By 1926 a very thorough series of articles by Mlle Pereyra began to appear in the *Revue de Musicologie*,[1] and they dealt with three of the Paris manuscripts of virginal music, but not with the Tomkins autograph. At about the same time Margaret Glyn was assembling materials for her book on virginal music,[2] and E. H. Fellowes was similarly engaged in his work on William Byrd. Both of these authors had either seen the manuscript itself, or photostats of it, but it was not until Stephen Tuttle of Harvard came to study it in detail that the true worth of both music and annotations came to be known. Thus, almost three centuries after the death of the composer, Stephen Tuttle's edition of the keyboard works (most of which are found in the Paris manuscript) came before the general public.

The letter H appears not only outside but also inside the front cover of the volume, and the significance of this letter is explained by a list of books on page i. Through the scribbled mass of Tomkins names — John, Thomas, Sylvanus, and Nathaniel — the following list can be seen:

MR. THOMAS TOMKINS HIS BOOK

A	4to	Thomas Farington Tomkins	1600
B	4to	russet leather	1620
C	4to	Jo. Tomk. wth ye K. arms	1630
D	folio	J T . T T	1645
E	folio	Thomas Tomkins autograph on to June 9.	1656
F	fol.	Rich. Brown and N T. hand	
G	a lesser fol.	Rich. Brownes hand	
H		T	1646

[1] 1926, p. 204; 1927, pp. 36, 205; 1928, p. 235; 1929, p. 32; 1931, p. 22; 1932, p. 86; 1933, p. 24.

[2] *About Elizabethan Virginal Music and its Composers.* (1924; revised edition, 1934.)

Against the last date, which coincides with that of the *Fancy* already mentioned, some comparatively recent annotator has written 'to 19 July 1654', although there are three items dated slightly later than this. The reason for some of the other dates in this list is not always clear, since the first four seem arbitrarily chosen (unless the word 'composed' written just to the left of, and above 1600 is taken at its face value) and the fifth corresponds exactly with the date of Thomas's burial. They may have been added to show that the volumes stood in chronological as well as alphabetical order.

Sadly enough, no volumes bearing on their cover the letters A to G have ever been found, and it must therefore be assumed that the greater part of this fine collection of early manuscripts is lost beyond recall. It does seem likely, however, that Add. MS 29996, with its extensive annotations by Thomas, and so many of his compositions, remains a strong candidate for inclusion in this gamut of music-books. There is no sign of a letter on its cover now, although an earlier binding or loose cover may have afforded the necessary evidence. Perhaps it is what Thomas refers to as the 'redish clasped book', since one of the pieces said to be found there, and confirmed by a written-out theme,[1] does in fact appear in Add. MS 29996: it is the *Ground* dedicated to Arthur Philips.

Thomas also refers to an '(Old) Black Clasped Book' and to a 'Red Old Book'; but there is no possibility of proving their identity, because no list of pieces occurring in these two books corresponds with any known keyboard manuscript now extant. The 'Lessons of worth' on page ii of the autograph volume gives many titles

[1] Rés. 1122, p. ii.

that are now unknown or uncertain,[1] but the list is of great value not only for giving us an insight into Thomas's musical taste (he mentions only Bull, Byrd, Carlton, Gibbons, Tallis, and brother John) but also because at least one item — *Robin Hood* — is named there as a work of Thomas, whereas the only piece of music with this title appears anonymously in Will Forster's Virginal Book. It has thus been assumed that this unclaimed *Robin Hood* is indeed by Thomas, and is included as such in the complete edition of keyboard music.

The autograph volume in Paris is remarkable for the amount and frequency of letter-figure combinations written usually at the beginning of the music. The *Pavan of 3 parts* has for example 'F.169 Ib.57 / E.252 f.57'. *Fortune my foe* bears the legend 'Ib.214 c.21 F 243'. These references appear to have been placed in a conspicuous position in order to show the player where another version may be found, and it is quite possible that the letters refer to the volumes marked A–G, and the numbers to pages in the volumes. Tomkins uses the letters B–G in these letter-figure combinations, and even overshoots the gamut on two occasions with a mention of K. If the numbers do refer to pages, it is clear that some of the volumes must have been very extensive collections, for the numbers go as high as 385 in one instance and 472 in another. All the more reason, therefore, to bewail the loss of the other volumes in the set.

The orderly way in which Thomas would set about a task is concisely shown on page 186 of the autograph, in which he refers to the third volume in the collection, marked 'C 4to Jo. Tomk. wth ye K. arms'. He writes:

---

[1] Details of these are given in *Musica Britannica*, v, 157, 158.

'I could wish that the great book which was my brother John's should be fair and carefully pricked with so judicious a hand and eye that the player may venture upon them with comfort: which he may easily do: if the notes be distinctly valued with the semibreve or minim: and not too closely huddled up together. My son's judgement may give better directions than these weak expressions: but this by the way'. Then follows a list of chosen pieces; some of them, like Bull's *Walsingham Variations*, Tallis's *Offertory* (one of the two great settings of *Felix namque*) and Byrd's *Fantasy in gamut* are well known even to-day, whilst others, such as Carlton's *Fading* (apparently an Irish tune) and Bull's *Offertories* cannot now be identified.[1] In conclusion, Thomas adds: 'They [the six compositions immediately preceding] being in the key of gamut to be suited and sorted together. And whatever fancies or selected voluntaries of worth: to be placed in their own native keys not mingling or mangling them together with other of a contrary key: but put in their right places'.

The re-copying of C in accordance with Thomas's instructions, whether or not they were amplified or confirmed by his son Nathaniel, seems never to have been carried out. But the instructions remain as a vivid memento of the aged organist's mind and character, just as a random remark on page ii of the same autograph gives us insight into his critical opinions. Two compositions of Bull (the *Quadran pavan in gamut* and the *Ut re mi fa sol la*) are described respectively as 'Excellent for the hand' and 'For the hand', whereas Byrd's *Quadran pavan and*

---

[1] Neither of the two richest sources of Bull's keyboard music (Paris Conservatoire, Rés. 1185; London, British Museum, Add. MS 23623) contains an offertory so named, though many of the items would qualify from a practical rather than a strictly liturgical point of view.

galliard is 'Excellent for the matter'. In a further note the rival claims of technique and expression are joined by a third quality, for Thomas recommends two of Byrd's works 'for substance' which they undoubtedly possessed, if the *Ut re mi* on the very first page of the Paris manuscript is a typical example.

*   *   *   *   *

In the following discussion of the keyboard music, the grouping and numbering is that of Stephen Tuttle's monumental edition.

Although the two *Preludes* are not markedly different from numerous examples of this style in *Parthenia* and in contemporary manuscript collections, their grandiose and heavily órnamented proportions stamp them as the work of a man who could, on occasion, say very little in an imposing and often brilliant manner. The function of a *Prelude* was twofold: to allow the player time and opportunity to warm up to his task, and to set the prevailing key of the music to follow. In this respect, Tomkins had the same attitude of mind as Couperin and Bach, even if his figuration and his fingering were both unlike theirs. In its first form, *Prelude* (1) could serve as an introduction to *Robin Hood* (63); whilst its alternative ending (to which we are referred by the composer himself in a note *vide* 146 — the page concerned in the Paris autograph) leads to a close in D, and a suitable link with, for example, *Barafostus' Dream* (62). A cadence on a major chord, and a fresh start with the same chord in its minor form, was a typical feature of much Renaissance music, and it works well not only in the combination just cited (1 + 2, 62) but also in the juxtaposition of the *Prelude* (3) with *Fortune my foe* (61) or

What if a day (64). The eight settings of *In nomine* (six really, if we exclude alternative versions of two pieces) would of course be equally suitable, since the cantus firmus is always used a fifth above its normal pitch, beginning and ending on A. No *Prelude*, therefore, is a disembodied and meaningless object if it is employed in a practical, companionable manner, and this manner is surely near to the intention of the composer, even though he may not have expressly associated other works with his *Preludes*. There is evidence, nevertheless, that Tomkins aimed at a higher degree of internal cohesion in the *Prelude in A* (3), for a motive heard soon after the preliminary flourish occurs again before the final cadential cascade, recognizably, and doubtless intentionally.

Clarifica me pater[1] is an example of a little-known secularized plain-song being used well over a century past the time when it ceased to have any liturgical significance. Why Tomkins used it is a small mystery, for he did not even know its correct title, and can hardly have had access to an Antiphoner containing the original chant. He calls it *Glorifica me*, copying an earlier source of keyboard music that was either corrupt already or not clearly written. There are three pieces by Tallis, in the *Mulliner Book*,[2] based on this plain-song; but all three are untitled. Byrd has two settings in the *Fitzwilliam Virginal Book*,[3] and although these have a title — *Miserere* — it is not the correct one. Scribes who interchanged

---

[1] According to the Use of Sarum, this antiphon was sung on the sixth Sunday of Lent and the Vigil of the Ascension. See *Antiphonale Sarisburiense*, plates 201, 266.

[2] *Musica Britannica*, i (1951), Nos. 99, 101, 104; *Commentary* (1952), p. 38.

[3] Vol. ii, 230, 232, of the edition by Fuller Maitland and Barclay Squire. Also Byrd, *Complete Works*, ed. Fellowes, xx, 137, 140.

with impunity *In nomine* and *Gloria tibi Trinitas* probably thought that the same could be done with *Clarifica me pater* and *Miserere*. But Tomkins, a pupil of Byrd, may well have seen the originals when studying with him, mis-spelling the title through his unfamiliarity with the Catholic liturgy. Since this setting (dated September, 1650) is non-liturgical, it was doubtless intended for virginals or harpsichord just as much as the *In nomine* pieces were. Like these, *Clarifica me pater* shows the composer's preference for the transposed form of a Dorian cantus firmus.

The *In nomine* pieces were all written between 1647 and 1652, and thus represent a late phase of an already latter-day aspect of the composer's art. He apparently found it difficult at first to return to this admirable but archaic style of composition, although he had made some previous essays in the same form for a consort of three viols. The first keyboard setting (5) begins boldly enough with a strong dactylic figure entirely typical of Tomkins, and proceeds by way of a lyrical, two-notes-against-three section to a display of uninhibited virtuosity. No less than six alternative endings were provided, though the first of these has been cancelled by the composer himself. The third ending, which forms the principal text of (6), gives this item its longest form, whereby the cantus firmus is used for only two-thirds of the composition, the remaining one-third acting as an enormously extended coda. It is true that the other settings of *In nomine* own a more than usually generous residuum after the point at which the plain-song comes to a cadence on A; but this third ending of (6) outstrips them all in length and complexity.

A new departure may be seen in the very first bars

of (7) which present a foretaste of the first three notes (A C A) of the cantus firmus, in an ornate and flowing triple time. The fourth entry of the point is the cantus firmus itself, in the bass, duly decorated in accordance with the preceding voices; so that we here have an example of an infectious and interesting rhythmic scheme successfully disturbing the solemn progress of the cantus firmus for some little time. The points and figurations are varied in expert fashion, much use being made of repeated notes of identical pitch:

Ex. 1

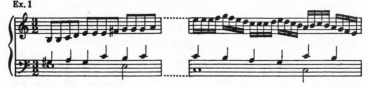

The rhythmic contours, basic time, and opening style of (8) recall those of (7) written during the previous month, but now there is a stronger contrapuntal feeling, and an increasing reliance on tightly woven imitation. All this gives rise to an impression of elegant intellectual brilliance, as if Tomkins had already begun to master the subtleties of this kind of keyboard writing. The coda is distinguished by a display of figuration in thirds and sixths, ultimately relaxing into an expressive cadence on a tonic pedal.

The cantus firmus suggests the first point of imitation in (9), others of independent origin following in smooth succession. A short yet effective setting, it makes good use of sequential material in its closing bars, and preserves a good sense of balance between the elements of ingenuity and display. Much longer, and much more difficult for the player is (10) and its variant (11), both being remarkable for a last-minute pull in tonality towards

D, and an opening point that covers two octaves in a rolling, sweeping descent:

Ex.2

At certain points in the body of the piece, the figuration is not greatly different from the kind of thing one finds in music written a century previously; Thomas Preston's *Felix namque*[1] is a typical specimen of what could be done by an earlier generation of keyboard virtuosi. As Tomkins once owned the manuscript containing this piece, it is possible that he had played it through and found its figuration worth developing.

The last *In nomine* (12) has its imitative figures in a relatively high tessitura, for the cantus firmus remains in the bass and supports the counterpoint, now staid, now decorative, in the upper parts. Just before the plainsong theme reaches its close, an imitative duet almost reaches the status of a fully-fledged canon at the octave, but it is soon deflected into a brilliant cadential flourish. The settings of *In nomine*, taken as a group, certainly present music that is at the same time academic in its insistence on strong contrapuntal interest and virtuosic in its demands upon the player. It is in striking a balance between the two elements that Tomkins succeeds as a writer of keyboard pieces in this genre.

Technically speaking, the eight *Miserere* settings are very similar to the *In nomine* pieces. They are shorter, because the cantus firmus itself is shorter than that of

[1] Printed in *Altenglische Orgelmusik*, Bärenreiter-Ausgabe 385, Kassel, 1954.

In nomine, but the prevailing texture is generally of three parts, excepting for certain final sections (14, 18, 20) and the position of the cantus firmus is varied between treble, alto and bass. The first four settings (13-16) use an opening point based on the descending motive C B A G, while the other four (17-20) lean heavily upon an ascending point, usually G A B C or a variant or transposition. The slight significance of these melodic similarities is, however, quite overshadowed by certain other factors of form. *Miserere* (18) repeats the plainsong twice, first in the treble, then the tenor; while *Miserere* (16) presents it three times, in tenor, treble, and tenor respectively. The appearance of a liturgical tenor in double or triple cursus was an accepted feature of motets and Masses of the *ars nova* and the Renaissance, and it is by no means entirely unknown in the field of keyboard music. The Exeter organist, John Lugge, composed an *In nomine* with double cursus [1] and there are earlier examples by Bull in one of the Paris manuscripts of virginal music.[2] Tomkins is thus in good company, even if he cannot be dubbed an innovator.

His really new contribution to the *Miserere* situation was, oddly enough, a resuscitation of an old principle. From his perusal of Add. MS 29996, he knew that settings of *Miserere* were grouped together by the early Tudor organist in suites of three or four, and this principle he endeavoured to follow when compiling his own anthology. At various points in the manuscript he has written the figures 1, 2, 3 and 4 among the *Miserere* settings, and if they are grouped in this fashion the first of these suites consists of (17), (13), and (18). Since the last of these is

---

[1] Oxford, Christ Church Library, MS 49.
[2] Rés. 1185, pp. 134, 156.

a double cursus piece, there is formed a group of four *Miserere* settings after the pattern of those on the very first pages of Add. MS 29996. There, the purpose was a liturgical one, for according to the Sarum rite either three or four psalms were sung at Compline, and the organist had to be prepared to play a short keyboard version of the antiphon after each psalm. It may perhaps be not too far-fetched to consider others among the Tomkins *Miserere* pieces as likely to form a group: those on pages 162–3 of the original manuscript (14), (19), and (20), and the tripartite setting which is in itself a suite (16).

The influence of the liturgical element, however distant in point of time, must always be seriously considered in the keyboard music of Tomkins. The *Offertory* (21), misread by some earlier scholars as *Affection*, recalls in its scope the tremendously long and involved pieces that Tomkins knew from the volume containing *Miserere* settings. These long settings of plain-chants for the offertory were usually based on *Felix namque*, although other chants were used from time to time before the Reformation. Tallis wrote his two settings of *Felix namque* during the reign of Elizabeth, and it was largely due to him that the form became secularized whilst still retaining its former title, even though this might be corrupted into *Felix nunquam* and the like.

The Henrician organists almost invariably set that part of the chant beginning at the word *namque*, in order to allow the celebrant to intone the word *Felix*. Tallis, however, set this intonation, and even suggested by repeat marks that it should be played through twice. But this is not all: the final stage in this liturgical *reductio ad absurdum* was to come from Tomkins, who ignores the

entire body of the chant but sets instead the intonation,
using it as a ground throughout the piece. A comparison
of Tomkins's theme and the original plain-chant for
Felix demonstrates the close relationship between the
two:

This composition is thus an elaborate set of variations
on a ground that freely paraphrases the Sarum plain-song
for the word *Felix*. The ground is not simply a bass;
it moves freely throughout the texture without any pre-
arranged plan or system of tonality. There are some
fifty-five appearances of the ground, in treble, tenor, and
bass, and all these appearances except one begin and end
on A. A momentary transposition to D takes place at
bar 277, but the principal tonality is quickly restored.

At certain cadences of the *Offertory* pauses have been
placed, and their exact function has from time to time
been questioned. Although dated 1637, it is certain
that the work was composed in short sections over a
considerable period of time, and the date given by the
Bodleian manuscript may refer to the year in which the
entire set of variations was completed. Once this is
assumed to be correct, the pauses can be regarded as
indications of the progress of the work at different
times: again and again Tomkins returned to his task,
adding new sections and fresh pauses as the music pro-
ceeded. Purely practical considerations suggest a somewhat different, though not entirely opposed viewpoint;
and that is to accept the *Offertory* as an effective and use-

The ending of the *Offertory*, signed ‘ Mr. Thomas Tomkins:
organist of His Majesty’s Chapel, 1637 ’. Two short pieces
‘ for Edward ’—Edward Thornbrough, Archdeacon of
Worcester

Bodleian Library, Oxford. Ms [*Mus. Sch.*] C. 93, f. 80

ful accompaniment to the collection of alms after the offertory sentences at Matins or Communion. The use of the organ at this point in the service is borne out by a description [1] of *The Princely Coming of Her Majesty to the Holy Communion at Easter*, in 1593:

Then Her Majesty's royal person came most cheerfully, having as noble supporters the Right Honourable the Earl of Essex, Master of Her Majesty's Horse, on the right hand, and the Right Honourable the Lord Admiral on the left hand, the Lord Chamberlain to Her Majesty (also next before Her Majesty) attendant all the while. Dr. Bull was at the organ playing the offertory.

The internal pauses written over certain cadences might then serve to regulate the length of the composition, which had of course to depend upon the amount of time available to the organist at that point in the service.

Of the twelve examples of *Fancy*, *Voluntary*, and *Verse* (22-33) the title, character, and style of the *Fancies* point to secular use, just as the *Voluntaries* and *Verses* suggest a close link with the organ music used for the Anglican liturgy. Some of the earliest examples of the *Fancy* and the *Voluntary* occur in the *Mulliner Book*, a compilation of keyboard music which was completed shortly before Tomkins was born. As he grew up, he heard these comparatively new and free forms in mansions and cathedrals, and later composed them himself.

The texture of four of the *Fancies* (22, 23, 25, and 29) often recalls the clarity of string-writing, though there is enough freedom in the contrapuntal element — usually in four parts — to give the keyboard player a feeling of ease and the right idiom. Sometimes the point is maintained for only half the total length of the piece

---

[1] Rimbault: *The Old Cheque Book . . . of the Chapel Royal,* p. 150.

(22, 25), rarely for the whole (23); whilst an even slighter degree of thematic insistence is found in the A minor *Fancy* (29) with its opening phrase so reminiscent of the French chanson type.

In writing his *Fancy: for two to play* (32) Tomkins was probably less concerned with writing eight-part, or even six-part harmony, than with exploring the sonorities of the virginals.[1]   Even in some of the polyphonic duet sections there are often no more than four real parts, yet the sound is so vastly different from that produced by only one player because of the more extended tessitura. Antiphonal effects between upper and lower registers are common, yet in some cases a theme is shared between the left hand of the treble player and the right hand of the bass player.   A similar duet, perhaps the source of Tomkins's inspiration, was written by his friend Nicholas Carlton, and this is found in the same manuscript.

The *Fancy: for five viols* (33) is a keyboard para-phrase of a string piece no longer extant.   Much of the detail has inevitably been lost in the process of para-phrase, though as written out by Tomkins the piece is well accommodated to its new medium.   It would be an interesting but difficult task to attempt a reconstruction of the original from the keyboard version, though the result, if successful, would fill a gap in the catalogue of Tomkins's music for strings, for there are no fantasias for five viols among his otherwise representative output. His keyboard version (56) of the *Pavan in A minor* shows a far more satisfactory presentation of idiomatic and effective writing.

Of the three *Voluntaries*, only one (24) bears a date, August 10, 1647, which places the work in the year

[1] See H. M. Miller, *The Earliest Keyboard Duets.*

following the second siege of Worcester, when the cathedral organs were dismantled and services were suspended. Tomkins may have written down this richly contrapuntal *Voluntary* for use when the services were resumed, but that day he never lived to see. It is certainly the most mature of the three, and shows much inventive skill besides a fine sense of structural feeling. The *Voluntary* in A minor (28), although equally long and rich in dexterous keyboard counterpoint, relies a little too much on the opening point, new material being brought in only during the last third of the composition. Once again, however, the modulatory scheme is well planned and there is adequate contrast of key colour. The third *Voluntary* (30) is much shorter than the others, and maintains the point throughout, with deft play on the false relation inherent in the opening phrase:

Ex.4

With the *Verses*, we have yet another triptych of which only one aspect is dated. Again the date in question (August 12, 1650) stands within the period when cathedral services had ceased, so that it may be more expedient to classify this *Verse of 3 parts* (26) as a *Fancy*, under which heading it is entered in the original index to the Paris autograph. There are two main sections and two main points, one grave, the other gay. The *Short Verse* (27) tends on the other hand towards monothematicism, and a unity which is achieved by a clever touch of diminution towards the end:

Ex.5

In his *Substantial Verse: maintaining the point* (31) Tomkins demonstrates his resource in the matter of faithful yet varied presentation of a single theme. True to its title, this *Verse* keeps the point on active service right until the final statement of the last two bars, where it is discreetly hidden in the tenor. Yet there is careful avoidance of epigrammatic and short-winded statements: the contrapuntal flow is regular and possesses more than adequate momentum.

Byrd, Bull, and Tomkins all loved to exercise their musical and technical ingenuity on hexachord variations, a genre of composition which had a comparatively short though brilliant career. There is a set marked expressly *for a beginner* (34) and a lengthy set which might well be marked *for a virtuoso of remarkable stamina* (35). Musically they have nothing at all in common except this six-note figure, ascending then descending, and carrying with it the most extraordinary displays of keyboard virtuosity. Like the *Offertory*, there is ample evidence that the gigantic *Ut re mi* (35) was composed piecemeal, and that Tomkins never succeeded in joining together all the sketches and fragments scattered throughout his manuscript volume. Two of them (36 and 37) may well have been intended as parts or variants of the main setting, the former being an example of the use of triple time in the hexachord itself, rather than in its accompanying counterpoints. Nothing is dated except a fragmentary *Ut re mi* (71) whose conclusion is almost illegible due to the composer's weakening hand. By June 30, 1654, he was in his eighty-second year.

Tomkins liked to transpose his themes to the upper fifth, possibly for greater brilliance, or else in order to suit the compass of his instruments. Just as the *In nomine* pieces are in transposed Dorian, so the *Ut re mi* variations (with the exception of 71) begin and end on G, a fifth above the normal compass of the natural hexachord. Within the vast and varied structure of (35) other hexachords are used: C–A and D–B, and these occur between statements of the main G–E hexachord rather in the manner of episodes in a rondo. In one work (38) Tomkins employs the hexachord in broken thirds, so that the title is *Ut mi re*. After a somewhat mechanical beginning, there flow in one after the other a tremendous variety of figures, many of them apparently designed to exercise unflexible wrists. As transcendental studies of the late Renaissance, these hexachord settings have perhaps more technical than musical value, or as Tomkins would say, excellent for the hand rather than for substance.

Both the pieces called *Ground* are based on seven-note figures. The monotony inherent in a figure such as that heard at the outset of (39) is to some extent avoided by alternate statements in treble and bass, while the care shown by Tomkins in avoiding too frequent cadences can hardly be accidental. The theme of the *Ground* is very similar to that of Farnaby's *Up tails all*, which is found in the same source,[1] but there is no proof of anything more than melodic kinship, since the two composers do not seem to have been particularly close friends. Tomkins's variations are notable for their

---

[1] *Fitzwilliam Virginal Book*, ii, 360.

technical demands, especially at the point where rapid
runs in thirds occur, and later on where intervals in the
theme are filled in and the texture thickens. The other
Ground (40), headed by the name of Arthur Philips,[1] is
hardly less brilliant, and may very well be an occasional
or dedicatory composition. Tomkins was fond of dedicating his music to friends and colleagues, and this is
borne out not only by the *Songs* published in 1622 but
also by the string pieces he wrote for his friend Withy
and the keyboard pieces inscribed to Archdeacon Thornborough.[2] Perhaps this *Ground* was a kind of musical
gift for Philips.

Some of the very finest of Tomkins's keyboard music
is found in the *Pavans* and *Galliards*, of which there are
four paired sets (41–50,) the first being available in two
versions; seven apparently separate *Pavans* (51–57);
and three Galliards which also seem to be independent
works (58–60). It is in this extended group of pieces
that Tomkins makes the greatest use of his very considerable harmonic resource, his instinctive grasp of
formal elements, and his power to move his hearers by
sheer and sincere musicianship. This is not to under-
estimate the difficulty of execution which many of these
pieces present, nor their wealth of ornament and richness
of polyphony. These are available in ample measure,
yet their very brightness is made to seem dim by the
expressive and emotional qualities of the music itself.

It is not coincidental that three of these pieces belong
to the category of music sometimes known as *tombeau*:
that is, in memory of a friend or of some dignitary worthy
of musical tribute. Earl Strafford, a loyalist whose warrant

---

[1] Professor of Music at Oxford, 1639; B.Mus., 1640.
[2] These are discussed more fully on p. 153 and p. 171.

for execution Charles I was forced to sign, was highly respected by many of the high-church party, and it is not surprising to find Tomkins commemorating the Earl's death in the form of a *Pavan* and *Galliard*. The short versions (41 and 42) differ from the long ones (43 and 44) in one major respect: the repeats in the long versions are written out in full and ornamented in noble and fiery fashion. Although written in 1647, some six years after Strafford's execution, this memorial piece is not lacking in solemn and meaningful passion. Archbishop Laud was put to death in 1645, and the city of Worcester was besieged for the second time in the following year: by 1647 Tomkins was ready to pen these touching memorials to Strafford and Laud, little knowing that worse was to come in 1649, when the King himself suffered the extreme penalty.

The *Pavan: Lord Canterbury* (William Laud, Archbishop of Canterbury) is available in only one source, from which the removal of a folio has deprived us of the third strain of this remarkable and moving composition (57). As in the long versions of the *Pavan: Earl Strafford*, the repeats are highly decorative and elegantly contrived. Yet there is a serious beauty in the unadorned first and second strains, the first with its three-note sigh, repeated again and again in notes of higher pitch; the second with its chromatic cry of indignation, rising too, in four distinct statements, just as the first strain did.

The *Sad Pavan: for these distracted times* (53) is dated February 14, 1649, only a few days after the execution of Charles I. Again, there is much tense emotion packed into a little space; and the unornamented repeats together with remarkable symmetry in the melodic structure give an overall impression of conciseness and unity. A skilful use of suspensions and unessential notes brings out the pathos of the first strain, which nevertheless exhibits a symmetry of design by no means unusual in this group of compositions. Treating the first chord as an anacrusis gives the following pattern, in which note-values are reduced by half:

Ex.6

Of the remaining *Pavan* and *Galliard* pairs, only the 1654 group (almost the last works Tomkins wrote) have common thematic material (47 and 48). The subtle rhythm of the *Pavan* is built on a characteristic hemiola pattern:

Ex.7

The *Galliard* is one of the liveliest that Tomkins wrote, and owes much of its appeal to the lilting dotted rhythm of the first strain, the rapid imitation of the second, and the well-placed melodic climax of the third. Written four years previously, the long *Pavan* and *Galliard* (45 and 46) with their varied strains and effective ornamentation prove that Tomkins enjoyed considerable facility at the keyboard in spite of his advanced age. The *Pavan* and *Galliard* (49 and 50) both 'of three parts' may be thought of as an exercise in a more transparent contrapuntal style. There is no feeling that the composer is hampered by his own restrictive practices, however, and the impression given by this well-balanced pair is one of clarity and elegance.

Of the separate *Pavans* not discussed so far there are three of the short variety, and two with fully fledged

A Sad Pavan: for these distracted times, dated February

Bibliothèque du Conservato.

49. Charles I was executed on January 30, 1649

repeats. One of these longer *Pavans* (55) is called 'short' by Tomkins, and short it is by comparison with the great A minor *Pavan* from the *Fitzwilliam Virginal Book* (56). In the two (51 and 52) written within a few days of each other in the month of September, 1647, Tomkins uses one of his favourite scalic figurations, involving rapid upward runs within the compass of a seventh. *Pavans* 54 and 55 are notable for their symmetry of design, especially in the first strains, as well as for their economy of material.

The most famous of the *Pavans* is undoubtedly the one that has been longest known, by reason of its publication many years ago in the *Fitzwilliam Virginal Book*. It was well known, however, even in Tomkins's day, for besides another copy of the keyboard version there are several manuscripts containing string versions, and one printed book [1] which brought it to the notice of continental musicians. The power of the piece lies in its finely contrasted harmonic aspects: the first strain establishes the home key, the second reaches the dominant by traditional though colourful methods, and the third returns to A by way of descending chromatic digressions in the best Italian manner. It is not unusual to find exceptional brilliance (which some have censured [2]) in a work written early in the composer's career, when he was — as it were — fresh from school and anxious to show his skill.

The *Hunting Galliard* (58), if not definitely descriptive, at least portrays some of the excitement and movement of the chase. In the intensity and vigour of its

---

[1] Simpson's *Opusculum neuer Pavanen, Galliarden, Couranten und Volten* (1610).

[2] Van den Borren, *op. cit.*, p. 283, mentions the 'too prominent character of its figuration'.

figuration it is not unlike the music of Bull, for it certainly demands the kind of virtuoso performance that would be out of place in the other two galliards.   The one named after *Lady Folliott* (59) is a short but charming composition, designed perhaps as a tribute to Isabella, daughter of Guthlake Folliott, a chapter clerk of the cathedral. In 1654 Tomkins's son Nathaniel married Isabella, and the three retired to Martin Hussingtree, whose manor house, together with the patronage of the church, Isabella had inherited from her first husband John Haselock.   The variations of the three strains in the last *Galliard* (60) vary between the harmonic and melodic types: there is a constant shift of interest which lends the music a subtle and distinctive quality.

The four sets of variations on popular songs of the sixteenth century are found in four different sources, and they may well belong to different periods of Tomkins's life.   The *Fitzwilliam* set, based on *Barafostus' Dream* (62), must be fairly early, and seems to belong stylistically to the first decade of the seventeenth century.   The tune, sometimes known as *The Shepherd's Joy*, is mentioned in a poetical anthology called *The Golden Garland of Princely Delights*, published in 1622; but it was certainly current at a much earlier date.   There is an anonymous set of variations on this tune in the same manuscript [1] besides a consort piece in Rosseter's publication of 1609. Tomkins wrote his variations in a brilliant and dashing style, with the accent on melodic rather than harmonic interest.

At the other end of the scale lies the very expressive (though by no means easy) set based on *Fortune my foe*

---

[1] *Fitzwilliam Virginal Book*, i, 72. Compare also *Jacobean Consort Music*, No. 95.

(61) which was composed in the summer of 1654 at Martin Hussingtree.   Late as they are, these variations compare favourably with the settings by Byrd, Sweelinck, and Scheidt [1] and they display many characteristic features of Tomkins's decorative style, especially his liking for repeated notes, dactylic figures, and formations of broken sixths.

Robin Hood (63) uses the major version of the tune that appears in a Cambridge lute manuscript [2] and Ravenscroft's *Pammelia* in the minor key.   There are ten variations, of which the sixth is noteworthy for a delightfully syncopated cadence, the seventh and eight for flowing tripla tunes, and the tenth for its canonic flavour.   Much shorter is the set based on *What if a day* (64), a poem by Thomas Campion which was set to music by Alison in *An Hour's Recreation in Music*, published in 1606.   The tune used by Tomkins is not the same as that used by Alison, but it does correspond with the tune which is found in a setting for keyboard by Richard Creighton, and dated October 27, 1636.[3]   It is possible that the variations by Tomkins are much earlier than this, for they are reminiscent of Bull's most brilliant writing, and appear to belong to the same period as *Barafostus' Dream*.   The structure is taut and effective, with each of the three strains varied immediately after its initial appearance, and then a repeat of this pattern involving all the resources of the keyboard virtuoso.

In *Worcester Brawls* (65) the composer pays gracious tribute to the city which sheltered him for more than sixty years.   The term 'brawl' now implies something

---

[1] To be found respectively in *Fitzwilliam Virginal Book*, i, 254; Sweelinck, *Complete Works*, i, 127; Scheidt, *Tabulatura Nova*, in *Denkmäler Deutscher Tonkunst*, i, 126.

[2] University Library, Dd ix, 33.   [3] Rés. 1186, f. 15.

less elegant than the *bransle simple* from which the
English dance was originally derived: Morley, com-
paring it to the alman, says that it 'goeth somewhat
rounder in time . . . otherwise the measure is all one'.[1]
The Perpetual Round (66) is probably Tomkins's last
composition, for it is dated September 7-8, 1654. The
theme of the round rises gently to the fourth above the
opening note; it is then repeated at the new pitch until
the note c' is reached. A third repetition then follows,
and here the pattern perforce comes to an end. If it
were to be continued, the theme would eventually arrive
back at its starting-point; hence it is in a sense perpetual.
The new material which follows the opening point has
similar characteristics, this time descending, and its
accompanying counterpoint — also sequential — eventually moves to the treble and continues the *moto perpetuo*
impression. A division, or variation on this material,
makes considerable use of conventional figuration in
scale-passages and broken thirds.

The *Toy: made at Poole Court* (67) is interesting since
it is the only one of Tomkins's pieces, barring the
Worcester Brawls, to mention a place-name. The composer's ancestors came from Lostwithiel in Cornwall, and
at some time during his life Tomkins must have returned
to the land of his fathers on a short visit or holiday. He
stayed at Poole Court, about sixteen miles from Lostwithiel, and although the Court is no more, the village
of Menheniot still stands. In Elizabethan days the house
was owned by the Trelawny family, but after they left it
the property was allowed to decay, and eventually served
as a poorhouse.[2] By 1730 the house had ceased to exist,

---

[1] *A Plain and Easy Introduction* . . ., ed. Alec Harman (1952), p. 297.
[2] Hitchins, *History of Cornwall*, ii, 464.

and the property was disparked.[1] When Tomkins stayed there, the outlook (to judge by the music) was considerably more cheerful, or at least pleasant enough to inspire this 'light, frivolous, or lively tune' which was the meaning of the word *Toy* in those days.

The mysterious piece (68) from a Christ Church manuscript appears to be founded on a plain-song, but the theme does not possess plain-song characteristics. The initial descent of a major sixth, stepwise, is atypical of any plain-song form; and whilst it is possible that the opening of the melody as given by Tomkins is not the real opening, it is more likely that the melody was simply invented for the piece. The three-part texture, of gradually increasing complexity and innovation, is reminiscent of certain *In nomine* and *Miserere* settings.

One of the most interesting of the pieces printed in the appendix to the keyboard works is the *Toy* (69), inscribed to 'Mr. Curch' in one of the New York Public Library manuscripts.[2] Nothing is known of this dedicatee, nor is it certain that the music is by Tomkins. Under the title of *Almain*, it is associated with the name of Tomkins in a Christ Church source,[3] but the *Fitzwilliam Virginal Book* has the attribution 'Giles Farnaby'. Stylistically, the music resembles that of Farnaby rather than Tomkins, and as far as is known the mysterious Mr. Curch was not among Tomkins's circle of friends.

Edward Thornborough, Archdeacon of Worcester, was among that circle, however, and there are three pieces in a Bodleian manuscript[4] that seem to have been expressly written by Tomkins for his friend. Edward, to whom the first two pieces are inscribed, was collated

---

[1] *The Western Antiquary*, iv (1884/5), 48.   [2] Drexel MS 5612.
[3] MS 1112.   [4] [MS] Mus. Sch. C 93, ff. 80, 81v.

Archdeacon on August 3, 1629, and died in 1645.[1]   He
was the second son of John Thornborough, Bishop of Worcester from 1616 to 1641.   The third piece carries a
more formal inscription: 'For Mr. Arch[deacon] Thornborough' and is undoubtedly in Tomkins's handwriting.
All three pieces have the character of short *Fancies*, and
although they are slight in musical importance and are
not signed by Tomkins (which is perhaps the reason
why they are not included in the collected edition of
keyboard music) the internal evidence of the handwriting
and dedications is sufficient to enable them to qualify as
genuine works of Tomkins.

*   *   *   *   *

Fétis, in his short article on Tomkins, found room for
a rather surprising critical remark which compares the
work of the Englishman with that of a contemporary
German master:

> The pieces for organ and harpsichord in M. Farrenc's manuscript are exact imitations of the style of Samuel Scheidt's *Tabulatura Nova* published in 1624.[2]

If Tomkins imitated anyone, it was William Byrd;
but in modelling his style upon that of his master he
brought certain new characteristics of harmony and
figuration which are often more than enough to prove
the power of his musical personality.   The fact that
he chose to write the bulk of his keyboard music towards
the end of his life, and cannot therefore be placed in a
neat historical pigeon-hole, may be looked upon as a
sign of weakness by certain critics.   But there is no real
reason why a retiring, or indeed retired, organist of the

---

[1] Le Neve, *Fasti Ecclesiae Anglicanae*, iii, 75.

[2] *Biographie universelle, loc. cit.*

Chapel Royal should not compose in a highly traditional manner for his own pleasure and amusement. Even at 60, he had ample technique besides a very wide experience of music, and that is the main reason why so much of his keyboard writing is fresh, idiomatic, and rewarding to the player. In his introduction to the keyboard works of Tomkins, Stephen Tuttle has summed up the position in the following words:

The music of his later years is written in a more conservative style which resembles that of his teacher William Byrd. Here in the years of the mid-century the circle has closed. Tomkins, the last of the school, returns at the end of his life to the style of his master, the first, and perhaps the greatest, of the virginalists.[1]

[1] *Musica Britannica*, v, xiii.

CONSORT MUSIC

> You need not seek outlandish authors, especially for instrumental music; no nation (in my opinion) being equal to the English in that way; as well for their excellent, as their various and numerous consorts, of 3, 4, 5 and 6 parts.
>
> CHRISTOPHER SIMPSON,
> *A Compendium of Practical Music* (1667).

ALTHOUGH the surviving consort music by Thomas Tomkins exceeds thirty individual items, and although this music was composed over a period of more than thirty years,[1] he was never acknowledged by his contemporaries as an outstanding consort writer, nor can it be said that more recent authorities have shown any great enthusiasm for this branch of his art. There was indeed an uneasy tremor nearly seventy years ago, though its effects cannot, in the nature of things, have made a very vigorous or widespread impression:

> His biographers all do justice to Thomas Tomkins . . . but I nowhere find any mention by them of his instrumental compositions. Rimbault does not name him among viol writers, in his notes to Gibbons' 'Fantasies'; and neither Burney, nor Hawkins, nor the writer for Grove's Dictionary, adds any instrumental writing to the list of his known works, whether printed or in manuscript.[2]

Neither Mace nor Simpson mentions Tomkins in his list of consort composers, and later scholar-musicians

---

[1] A pavan *a 5* appeared in Simpson's *Opusculum* of 1610; another (no. 43 in Bodley MS [Mus. Sch.] E 415-8) bears the date 1641.

[2] Armitt, in *The Quarterly Musical Review*, iv (1888), 186.

like Anthony à Wood and Roger North are equally silent, in spite of their love for consort music. This silence was duly copied by Burney, Hawkins, and Rimbault, who were content to leave the situation as they found it: a complete and utter blank.

Whether or not the article in the *Quarterly Musical Review* for 1888 ever came to the notice of Arnold Dolmetsch is a matter for conjecture; but one thing is certain, and that is the appearance of a Tomkins fantasia in the first of the annual Dolmetsch Festivals, held in the year 1925. Inspired either by the almost shocked tone of the *Quarterly Musical Review*, or by his own researches into consort music of the Elizabethan and Stuart eras, this energetic champion of early music and early instruments transcribed works by Tomkins, Locke, Jenkins, and Lawes and had them played in public, possibly for the first time in centuries. The healthy reactions of one critic are altogether noteworthy:

> Already at this half-way stage of the Festival many musicians have come to realize the extreme importance of the period (roughly from 1550 to 1650), when the English fantasy was cultivated. As a result it may reasonably be hoped that the sphere of pure chamber music will be widened to include the concerted music for viols. A fund of wealth, beauty and invention will be discovered there, and we shall regard the complexities of modern music from a new and enlightened standpoint.
>
> We cannot hope to produce contemporary composers of the same calibre as Thomas Tomkins, Matthew Lock, John Jenkins, and William Lawes, but we can fall back on their amplitude and immense calm for a while, and begin the battle afresh with something of their courage, and, above all, something of their clarity.[1]

Until the last decade, hardly any consort music by Tomkins was published, and even now less than a third

---

[1] *The Daily Telegraph*, August 31, 1925.

of his extant music in this style can be said to come within the easy grasp of the public. Critical opinions are, however, being gradually revised: there is a hint of Tomkins's excellence in this brief phrase from a lecture on Jacobean consort music:

> With the exception of Ward, Gibbons and Tomkins, none of the madrigalists distinguished themselves as composers of consort music. . . .[1]

One of the greatest authorities on English baroque music finds the consort music of Tomkins rather uneven in quality, though he affirms that it is

> real viol music, and not (as for example the excellent Ward) merely good counterpoint conceived really in the vocal mood.[2]

This is a splendid tribute to Tomkins, for his main interest was in the music of the Church, and he had constantly before him the ideals and methods of the great Elizabethan composers of vocal music. The first music for instrumental consorts in the second half of the sixteenth century stemmed from vocal sources, either sacred (the *In nomine* derived from a four-part section in the *Benedictus* of Taverner's *Missa Gloria tibi Trinitas*) or secular:

> But thus far is material, the earlier consorts were composed for 3, 4, and more parts, for songs in Italian or Latin out of the Psalms, of which I have seen divers, and mostly in print, with the names of the *patroni* inscribed. And in England when composers were scarce, these songs were copied off, without the words, and for variety used as instrumental consorts, with the first words of the song for a title.[3]

In addition to the songs in Italian, North might well have mentioned the numerous French chansons that

[1] Thurston Dart, *Jacobean Consort Music*, p. 68.
[2] Communication to the author from Mr. Robert Donington.
[3] North, *Memoirs of Music*, p. 73.

were used as consort music, confirming a general practice which still had its adherents in the reign of James I.[1] Tomkins was not one of those adherents: he embraced the new art of fantasia with its indomitably instrumental personality, its rhythmical freedom apt for the subtleties of the bow, and its wide variety of melodic leaps, safe and sure upon

so many equal and truly-sized viols; and so exactly strung, tuned, and played upon, as no one part was any impediment to the other.[2]

Dance-forms held an almost equal fascination for him, and it is not without significance that his most famous work is a Pavan, printed in 1610 by Thomas Simpson, and still available in six manuscript sources, four for viols and two for keyboard instruments.

Tomkins's strong preference for genuine viol music can hardly be doubted, for a mere three of his sixty or more verse anthems were provided with an alternative accompaniment for viols. Where vocal music was concerned, his chosen instrument was the organ, and he may even have felt that stringed instruments were out of place in service time. At home, however, the chest of viols was distinctly welcome. His brother Robert was a professional player in the King's service, and his neighbours Humphrey and John Withy (whose names are inscribed in an unfortunately incomplete set of part-books at Oxford [3] were assiduous collectors and players of consort music. Their part-books are dated 1642,

[1] For a discussion and inventory of one of the earliest and largest of these anthologies (British Museum, Add. MS 31390) see the article by Jeremy Noble, *Le Répertoire instrumental anglais (1550–85)*.

[2] Mace, *Music's Monument*, p. 234.

[3] Bodley MS [Mus. Sch.] E 415-8. At the end of 417 is written 'Mr. Tho: Tomkins / Mr. Humphrey Withy 1642'; 418 (ff. 17 and 25v) mentions J. Withy.

when trouble was already brewing in and about the city
of Worcester, thanks to the attentions of Essex's unruly
troops. Then, perhaps more than ever, North's *bon mot*
on the subject of violence versus viols held good:

> And amongst other arts, music flourished, and exceedingly
> improved, for the King being a virtuous prince loved an entertain-
> ment so commendable as that was; and the fantasia manner held
> through his reign and during the troubles and when most other good
> arts languished music held up her head, not at court nor (in the
> cant of those times) profane theatres, but in private society, for
> many chose rather to fiddle at home, than to go out and be knocked
> on the head abroad; and the entertainment was very much courted
> and made use of not only in country but in city families, in which
> many of the ladies were good consortiers, and in this state was
> music daily improving more or less till the time of (in all other
> respects but music) the happy restoration.[1]

The viol-players may sometimes have been joined in
consort by the chamber organ of Nathaniel Tomkins,
this manner of performance being then current and very
much in fashion, as Mace and North affirmed many
years later.[2] But the rôle of the organ, when its part
was not expressly composed, remained a minor one,
strongly under the influence of the *basso seguente* tradition
and yet not strong enough to assert itself beyond that
rôle.

Tomkins certainly learnt much from the consort
music of his contemporaries, who had been busily
occupied with the exploitation of genuine instrumental
texture evolving, paradoxically enough, from the cantus-
firmus type of consort rather than copies of vocal models,
however sprightly and decorative the latter might be.
He can hold his own in the exacting and translucent

---

[1] North, *The Musical Grammarian*, pp. 18-19.

[2] Mace, *Music's Monument*, p. 234; North, *The Musical Grammarian*,
p. 28, and *Memoirs of Music*, p. 105.

style of the three-part fantasia, matching the best of Lupo, Mico, Ward, and Coperario, and even surpassing on occasion the music of his friend and colleague Orlando Gibbons. Similarly his two *In nomine* pieces display a keen sense of instrumental aptitude and technical skill, although they are of slighter stature than the keyboard settings of this particular melody. In the dances for five and six viols, Tomkins is often more sedate and serious than his fellows, rarely indulging in the flights of brilliant virtuosity that can be found in dances by Ferrabosco, Weelkes, Dering, and Phillips. His four six-part fantasias are worthy to stand by the finest of the consorts of his friends Coperario, Ward, and White, with whom he probably exchanged music whenever the opportunity presented itself. It is pleasant to think of a friendly rivalry between composers of similar stature and interests, and even if Tomkins surpassed them in age and ability he would (from what we know of his character and personality) have refrained from being either patronizing or aloof.

His consorts consist of a group of three-part fantasias, a single five-part fantasia which survives only in a keyboard version,[1] four six-part fantasias, two settings of *In nomine a* 3 and one *Ut re mi a* 4. The fourteen three-part fantasias are far from being stereotyped; indeed some of them go out of their way to appear downright unusual. A favourite example of the fantastic element is his modulating fantasia, no. 10,[2] which is a canon three in one at the fifth below.

Each repetition of the theme in each voice occurs one

[1] See p. 142.

[2] This numeration corresponds to the catalogue on p. 194. Of the consorts *a* 3, no. 7 is in *The Consort Player* (Stainer & Bell); no. 14 is in *Musica Britannica* ix, no. 13. The two *In nomine* pieces are to be found in *The Consort Player* and in Davison and Apel's *Historical Anthology of Music*, i, 202.

tone lower, so that the sixth statement leads back to the original key of C sharp minor. There are no jolts in this smooth descent by whole tones, since each part retains something of its own key-colour whilst contributing in a thoroughly convincing manner to the whole.

Ex.1

Kaleidoscopic but logical, the scheme must have appealed to Tomkins, for he allows the canon to perpetuate itself as far as three further statements, when a free codetta leads towards A minor, a new point, and a perfectly normal second half. Thus Tomkins achieves a nice artistic balance between a mechanical and modulatory introduction, and a freely composed continuation and ending. From a formal point of view, this is rare enough both in the music of Tomkins's contemporaries and in wider historical vistas. There is nevertheless a certain parallel to be drawn between Tomkins's three-part canon and Bach's two-part canon (with an independent but also repetitive part) in *Das musikalische Opfer*.[1] Both Tom-

---

[1] Canon *a* 2 per tonos (no. VI in Hans T. David's edition, published by G. Schirmer).

kins and Bach separate their thematic statements by whole-tone steps, Tomkins choosing the downward path and Bach the upward. But whereas Bach, by using canon at the octave, confirms and consolidates his temporary tonality, Tomkins seeks the other extreme by having the successive voice-parts enter a fifth below the previous statement of the theme, thus destroying on purpose any feeling of rigid tonality and building in its place a powerful and intriguing chromatic edifice.

There are, too, other remarkable fantasias among this group. Both 3 and 4 are to be noted for the broad sweep of their opening points, the former being maintained almost until the tripla section, and the latter encompassing a wide range in the first treble part, spanning well over two octaves. An unusual feature about 12 is the way in which it begins: quite atypical of the accepted fantasia style, the second bass states the theme, but remains silent while the theme is re-stated by the first bass beneath a counter-subject played by the treble viol.

Some of the passage-work is outstanding by reason of its brilliance and complexity: 1 and 2 contain extended passages in broken fourths, while 1 and 8 share a penchant for smoothly flowing broken thirds. Often one finds cascades of scales, crossing and intertwining in their headlong progress, and reaching a high pitch of excitement in 5, 11, 12, and 13. Academic devices, on the other hand, are rarely used, although diminution of the first point occurs in 5, and both 3 and 7 are enlivened by a short tripla section. The actual themes themselves may be lyrical or epigrammatic in quality, flowing or concise, yet invariably well balanced and adaptable. An opening paragraph of exceptional length and strength is found in 8 :

Ex.2

A completely different outlook is apparent from the very first notes of 11, where short and succinct phrases abound, with much variety of rhythm and movement:

Ex.3

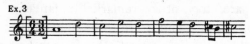

Fantasias 6 and 9 also exude radiant lyricism; 7 and 10, on the other hand, agree more with the temper of 11. In general, the structural scheme seems to be one of gradually increasing busyness, the longer note-values appearing near the beginning of the piece, and the shorter ones at the end. The middle section, often replete with a point of its own, acts as a transition from stately polyphony to scintillating peroration, though very occasionally (as in 14) there is a quieter atmosphere and a sense of elegant repose.

The two *In nomine* settings were certainly written as a pair, for they are contrasting and to a large extent complementary. The first has the cantus firmus in the middle voice, and the time is duple apart from a short passage in sextupla proportion about two-thirds of the way through the piece. First treble and bass are kept fairly well apart by the cantus firmus (in alto range), although they both touch extremes of compass from time to time and range widely over their respective tessituras. The left hand of the organist sometimes looms large in

the bass viol part, more especially perhaps at the very
end:

Ex.4

The second *In nomine* has its theme in the bass, in a
solemn trochaic rhythm. Above this quasi-ostinato,
only twice broken into figural patterns, the two trebles
display variety and agility in their neatly contrasted
sections, now thematic, now decorative. With a keyboard continuo, the texture would be not unlike that of
a trio-sonata, admittedly of a very special kind. The main
feature, however, is the ease with which Tomkins invents
new melodic and rhythmical ideas, gently persuading
the two parts to interchange their rôles, following one
another in lively imitation, then combining in chains of
thirds until the next theme is reached. Even North,
who had little enthusiasm for the *In nomine* in spite of
his sociological explanation of its vogue, may have
approved of this one:

But in the In nomines I never could see a cadence complete,
but proffers and baulks innumerable. That which was properly
termed Air was an entire stranger to this sort of harmony, and the
audience might sit with all the tranquillity in the world, and hear
continual shiftings of tones, with numberless syncopes and varieties,
such as they were, and not be in the least moved, if pleased it was
enough. And on the other side, if we consider that times were
peaceable, and men were not so much drawn from home to follow
the court, or city, or to travel as hath been since, but enjoyed
their fortunes plentifully at home, where anything to entertain the
time was welcome; and then such music, being loud and varie-
gated, pleased and never offended.[1]

No settings of *In nomine* for larger consorts of four,
five, or six viols by Thomas Tomkins are known to exist.

[1] North, *The Musical Grammarian*, p. 9.

For these more sonorous consorts he chose the fantasia.

The *Ut re mi* fantasia for four viols has, of course, certain affinities with the *In nomine*, as North noticed in his discussion of descant upon a plain-song:

> The plain-song was an order of plain notes of considerable length, perhaps a large or two breves; [1] very often the gamut notes ascending or descending, which were sung to the syllables of In nomine domini [*sic*].[2]

It is not as extensive or as elaborate as the keyboard version preserved in Paris and Oxford,[3] and in method and structure it is far more straightforward than the *Ut re mi* pavan. The hexachord, ascending and descending, is presented by the various instruments in turn, amid surrounding counterpoint of a somewhat solid though amiable nature. The keyboard version, in spite of its length, is nevertheless the more successful of the two, for there is more opportunity for decoration and disguise of the theme than in the consort, with its more limited technical resources.

With the five-part fantasia, exactly the opposite is true. But unfortunately its original form, as a consort, has not come down to us; all that remains is a reduction of the five parts for keyboard, and consequently (as so often happens in these cases) a good deal is left to the imagination. The keyboard version is nevertheless useful enough to demonstrate the lost excellences of this unique five-part consort.[4]

The four great six-part fantasias represent a noble achievement among Tomkins's consort music; indeed they rank along with the best of the five-part pavans as music of outstanding dignity and character. In spite of

---

[1] Here he writes a *longa*.   [2] North, *The Musical Grammarian*, p. 7.
[3] See p. 144.   [4] See p. 142.

the fact that the first three are firmly anchored to a G tonality (the fourth is in F) there is more than enough contrast of melody and style to set each work apart as a highly individual contribution to consort literature. Tomkins's near-symphonic outlook upon the development and integration of his themes can be seen at its clearest in the first of the group. The main subject:

has an invertible (and adjustable) counter-subject built on a *cambiata* figure:

and these are grafted on to an independent bicinium played by the two middle parts. Fragments of all these are used in close imitation to lead up to the first important cadence on a chord of G major. The E flat chord which follows introduced, together with its new colour, an ostensibly new point. But this has in fact evolved, by a process of augmentation and centonization, from the opening point and its counterpoint, in reverse order:

The tail of Ex. 7 is then used as a point in its own right, over a long pedal D; but after the next cadence on G there is a short section in free style, in the nature of transition. The first treble rises, then falls, with a touch of chromaticism, and a new point appears, some four bars in length, and remains active for some time with the aid of judiciously spaced rests, which lighten the texture to three or four voices for the most part. A common cadential suspension provides the idea and impetus for the next point, which is doubled either in sixths or thirds and has a distinctive counterpoint. From these three parts there is a gradual building up until the full consort is heard, with the unerringly logical suspension motive serving once again, and for the last time, as a fortification of the cadence. Throughout the fantasia Tomkins shows an instinctive feeling for musical equilibrium, the balance between texture and structure, and the appeal of melody and polyphony. Rarely at a loss for melodic ideas, he is not simply inventive and fertile because these things come naturally to him; he creates new material out of the old, binding together disparate elements and contrasting those that seem at first to be most alike.

The three other fantasias for six-part consort have similar though by no means identical virtues. A chromatic, curling descent characterizes the second fantasia, perhaps the best known of the four because of its availability in print.[1] The middle section abounds in lively dotted rhythms and syncopation, and at the end all is aglow with scale-motives which pile up on each other until a fine climax is reached.

The third fantasia has an initial point that pervades all six parts. The succeeding point, with its surge through an ascending fourth, tends towards key-transition, but shorter motives soon follow and their progress is mainly diatonic. Further points lean towards the harmonic and virtuosic elements respectively, and scales both ascending and descending cross and convolute until the final cadence.

[1] Edited by E. H. Fellowes (Stainer & Bell).

Like its fellows, the fourth fantasia is firmly con-
structed with motives strong in themselves yet lyrical
enough (as in the opening theme especially) to command
attention and remembrance. The individual parts are
of wide range and there is considerable and effective
crossing of parts, making for a smooth and even texture.
Much use is made of sequential motives within a theme,
especially in the middle section, which is more animated
in style. Contrary to custom, there is no display in the
coda, although syncopations and off-beat patterns play
a large part in the last few measures. In general, however,
the fantasias of Tomkins are not far removed from the
classical type described by North:

The method of the old fancies was to begin with a solemn
fugue, and all the parts entered with it one after another, and often
in different keys, which is the best garniture of fugues, and then
followed divers repeats, retorts, and reverts, of which art the
audience was little sensible, and being but labour in vain must be
passed upon account of industry and striving to do well; but with
all that, if the music was not so airy, it was sound and good, and after
the fugue spent nothing could be more full than the harmony was.
And then entered another fugue, intended to be more airy, and
performed much quicker, not unlike our Allegros, and when that
was spent, a tripla perhaps, or some yet freer air, but the tripla for
the most part is of the graver sort, and concluded after with a
l'envoye as they called it, and not with a jig as now the mode is,
but rather an adagio with this stately semiclose.[1] And of these
fancies whole volumes are left, scarce ever to be made use of but
either in the air for kites or in the fire for singeing pullets.[2]

Many of the dances must, alas, have gone the same
way. There are but two extant four-part dances by
Tomkins, and of nine pavans *a 5* three are so fragmentary
that reconstruction is an impossibility. A fine pavan

---

[1] Here North makes a fair guess at a decorated $^6_4$ $^5_3$ close *a* 4.
[2] North, *The Musical Grammarian*, pp. 12, 13.

and galliard *a* 6 has survived, however, and although they are not thematically related, and thus agree with the usual English custom in this respect, they are paired in the manuscript part-books at Oxford and Dublin. It may well be that none of these was intended for dancing, for they have a more learned air than the instrumental dances of Holborne, Phillips, Tregian, and Brade. In spite of the popularity of dancing at court, and the constant call for a lighter kind of music for masques and pageants, it seems that Tomkins was never called upon to provide music of this type. The Reformation had brought with it a strange new kind of decorum, banishing the choirboy plays and relieving the master of the choristers of his former versatility, whereby he not only provided plays and lyrics but also songs and dances. By the time Tomkins began to compose his dances for viols, many of the forms had been sublimated to the extent that their rhythmical interest was a secondary consideration.

The *Alman a* 4 [1] is sufficiently regular in the extent of its three strains to qualify for genuine dance-music, but even so the texture is eminently polyphonic and much use is made of short motives apt for development. It probably belongs to the same period as the later five-part pavans which date from 1640 onwards. These too make some use of imitation, together with occasional harmonic sequences, and they consist of the usual three strains, the middle one ending normally on the dominant or subdominant. The fourth pavan of the Bodleian set is based on the hexachord, but there is no attempt at chromatic treatment in the manner of the two versions of Ferrabosco's hexachord fantasia.[2] Tomkins uses prin-

[1] *Musica Britannica,* ix, no. 33.   [2] *Ibid.* nos. 23 and 29.

cipally the notes G to E in ascending and descending forms, although the third strain has C to A as a cantus firmus in two of the parts, now rhythmicized, now in regular and even notes. John Withy is the dedicatee of this musical merger of dance and cantus firmus, as the inscription on f. 25v of the bassus part-book proves.

The fifth pavan is of especial interest in view of the date, October 9, 1641, in three of the part-books. This date, together with the signatures of Thomas Tomkins and Humphrey Withy (1642) on the end-paper of the tenor book, helps to place the majority of these compositions in the later period of Tomkins's life. The length of the pavan, and the economy with which the thematic material is deployed, affords ample evidence of the composer's lively mind, and of his desire to remain active in spite of his wife's illness and the impending threat of the siege. He even found time to revise his early pavan, which had appeared in Thomas Simpson's *Opusculum neuer Pavanen, Galliarden, Couranten und Volten*, published in Frankfurt in 1610. In this revision, there is considerable alteration of the individual parts as well as a transposition up a minor third, which makes for greater brilliance within the emotional framework of the minor key. This same work had served as the basis of a keyboard pavan, where, of course, the opportunity to decorate and ornament the repeats of each strain had been grasped and exploited to the full.[1]

Although the six-part pavan[2] shows us Tomkins at his most dignified, the hint of a dactyl, reminiscent of countless chansons, lends a certain air of lightness to the opening point, whose rhythm is echoed at the beginning of the second strain. Its melodic shape, now in a new

[1] See p. 149.   [2] *Musica Britannica*, ix, nos. 92 and 93.

rhythmic pattern, is called to mind in the third strain, where (as in the previous two) the texture becomes progressively more dense as the cadence is approached. In the galliard, there is gracious exchange of phrases at the same pitch between the two treble parts, and similarly between the two bass parts, so that what Tomkins achieves is an elegant conversation between two quartets — the interchange of personalities rather than timbres — within the essentially six-part texture.

The prospect of a venerable church musician providing dances for a consort of viols was not unusual in Jacobean and Caroline society. Gibbons, Dering, Phillips, and Weelkes had all contributed noteworthy pieces for the fast-growing repertory, and there is no sign whatever that they were in any way ashamed of their contribution. If anything, the fault is an excess of learning rather than an excess of frivolity, for this dance music with a difference had, as we have seen, passed from the realm of the court masque and the ballroom to the quiet and intimacy of the home, and there it served as a leavening for the more serious fantasias and *In nomine* settings. English consort music had reached a high pitch of variety and excellence by the middle of the seventeenth century, and the situation is boldly summed up by Matthew Locke, in the very year of Tomkins's death, in the preface to his *Little Consort of Three Parts*:

> And for those mountebanks of wit, who think it necessary to disparage all they meet with of their own countrymen's, because there have been and are some excellent things done by strangers, I shall make bold to tell them (and I hope my known experience in this science will enforce them to confess me a competent judge) that I never yet saw any foreign instrumental composition (a few French corants excepted) worthy an Englishman's transcribing.

LIST OF WORKS
AND THEIR SOURCES

A LIST OF MANUSCRIPTS CONTAINING
MUSIC BY THOMAS TOMKINS

1	MS 1, Ely Cathedral Library	Ely
5	MS 5, Ely Cathedral Library	Ely
6	Mus. MS 6, Christ Church Library	Oxford
23	MS 23 H 13, Fitzwilliam Museum	Cambridge
24	RM 24 d 3, British Museum	London
28	MS 28, Ely Cathedral Library	Ely
30	MS 30 G 10, Fitzwilliam Museum	Cambridge
32	MS 32 G 29, Fitzwilliam Museum	Cambridge
61	Mus. MS 61, Christ Church Library	Oxford
62	Mus. MS 62, Christ Church Library	Oxford
64	MS [Mus. Sch.] C 64–9, Bodleian Library	Oxford
88	Mus. MS 88, Christ Church Library	Oxford
93	MS [Mus. Sch.] C 93, Bodleian Library	Oxford
180	MS 180, St John's College Library	Oxford
181	MS 181, St John's College Library	Oxford
212	MS [Mus. Sch.] D 212–6, Bodleian Library	Oxford
245	MS [Mus. Sch.] D 245–7, Bodleian Library	Oxford
341	MS Z.3.4. (1-6), Marsh's Library	Dublin
415	MS [Mus. Sch.] E 415–8, Bodleian Library	Oxford
437	Mus. MS 437, Christ Church Library	Oxford
530	G.5.30, Peterhouse Library	Cambridge
616	RCM MS 616, British Museum	London
645	M2 C 645 Case B, The General Library, University of California	Berkeley
698	Mus. MSS 698, 700, 702, 704, 706, Christ Church Library	Oxford
791	MS 791, St. Michael's College Library	Tenbury

1001	Mus. MS 1001, Christ Church Library	Oxford
1002	Mus. MS 1002, Christ Church Library	Oxford
1004	MS 1004, St. Michael's College Library	Tenbury
1018	Mus. MS 1018–20, Christ Church Library	Oxford
1021	MS 1021, St. Michael's College Library	Tenbury
1045	RCM MSS 1045–51, British Museum	London
1113	Mus. MS 1113, Christ Church Library	Oxford
1122	Rés. 1122, Conservatoire de Musique	Paris
1176	MS 1176, St. Michael's College Library	Tenbury
1186	Rés. 1186, Conservatoire de Musique	Paris
1220	Mus. MS 1220–4, Christ Church Library	Oxford
1227	Mus. MS 1227, Christ Church Library	Oxford
1303	MS 1303, St. Michael's College Library	Tenbury
1382	MS 1382, St. Michael's College Library	Tenbury
3665	Egerton MS 3665, British Museum	London
4076	RCM MS 4076, British Museum	London
4078	RCM MS 4078, British Museum	London
4080	RCM MS 4080, British Museum	London
4081	RCM MS 4081, British Museum	London
4087	RCM MS 4087, British Museum	London
4142	Harley MS 4142, British Museum	London
5611	Drexel MS 5611, Public Library	New York
5612	Drexel MS 5612, Public Library	New York
6346	Harley MS 6346, British Museum	London
7337	Harley MS 7337, British Museum	London
7339	Harley MS 7339, British Museum	London
11587	Add. MS 11587, British Museum	London
17784	Add. MS 17784, British Museum	London
17786	Add. MS 17786–91, British Museum	London
17792	Add. MS 17792; 17796, British Museum	London
17793	Add. MS 17793–5, British Museum	London
29289	Add. MS 29289, British Museum	London
29366	Add. MS 29366, British Museum	London
29372	Add. MS 29372–7, British Museum	London
29427	Add. MS 29427, British Museum	London
29996	Add. MS 29996, British Museum	London
30478	Add. MS 30478–9, British Museum	London
30826	Add. MS 30826–8, British Museum	London
31443	Add. MS 31443, British Museum	London

SEVENTEENTH-CENTURY part-books or scores in college or cathedral libraries are shown by the following sigla:

d   Durham Cathedral.

h   Hereford Cathedral.

l   Lichfield Cathedral.

p   Peterhouse, Cambridge.

w   Worcester Cathedral.

y   York Minster.

Unpublished modern transcriptions are shown as follows:

c   Cavanaugh, R. W. *The Anthems in Musica Deo Sacra by Thomas Tomkins.* University Microfilms, Doctoral Dissertation Series, No. 5649. (Ann Arbor, Michigan.)

r   Ramsbotham, A. *Musica Deo Sacra*, scored for the projected second series of *Tudor Church Music.* (London University Music Library.)

A LIST OF EARLY PRINTED BOOKS
CONTAINING MUSIC BY
THOMAS TOMKINS

1601   *The Triumphs of Oriana* (Thomas Morley, editor), London.
        Cambridge, University Library.
        London, British Museum.
        London, Royal College of Music.
        Oxford, Bodleian Library (3 copies).
        Oxford, Christ Church Library.

1610   *Opusculum neuer Pavanen, Galliarden, Couranten und Volten.*
        Auf allerhand musikalischen Instrumenten sonderlich auf Violen
        zu gebrauchen (Thomas Simpson, editor), Frankfurt.
        Berlin, Öffentliche Wissenschaftliche Bibliothek.
        Hamburg, Staats- und Universitäts-Bibliothek.
        Nuremberg, Bibliothek des germanischen Museums.

1622   *Songs of 3.4.5. and 6. parts*, London.
        London, British Museum.
        London, Royal College of Music.
        Oxford, Bodleian Library (2 copies).
        Oxford, Christ Church Library.
        San Marino, California, Huntington Library.

1668   *Musica Deo Sacra et Ecclesiae Anglicanae: or, Music dedicated to*
        the Honour and Service of God, and to the Use of Cathedral and
        other Churches of England, especially of the Chapel Royal of King
        Charles the First, London.
        London, British Museum.
        London, Royal College of Music.
        Oxford, Christ Church Library (2 copies).
        San Marino, California, Huntington Library.
        St. David's Cathedral.
        Tenbury, St. Michael's College.
        Worcester Cathedral.

A SHORT-TITLE LIST OF PUBLICATIONS
CONTAINING MUSIC BY
THOMAS TOMKINS

(1) CHURCH MUSIC

A Atkins, Sir Ivor (Novello; Oxford University Press).

B Boyce, William, *Cathedral Music*, revised and augmented by Joseph Warren (1849).

D *The CL Psalms of David* (1615).

E *The English Madrigal School*, vol. xviii (1922).

H *Historical Anthology of Music*, ed. Davison and Apel. Vol. 1 (1947).

J Jebb, J., *Choral Responses* (1847).

M *Musica Deo Sacra* (1668).

O Ouseley, F. A. G., *Cathedral Services* (1873).

P Parish Choir Book (Novello).

R Ravenscroft, T., *The Whole Book of Psalms* (1621).

Ro Rose, B. W. G., Anthems from *Musica Deo Sacra* (Stainer & Bell; Schott).

S *Songs of 3.4.5. and 6. parts* (1622).

St Stevens, D. W., Anthems from *Musica Deo Sacra* (Hinrichsen; Concordia Publishing House).

T *Tudor Church Music*, vol. viii (1928).

T⁸ *Tudor Church Music*, Octavo edition (Oxford University Press).

(2) SECULAR VOCAL MUSIC

E *The English Madrigal School*, vol. xviii (1922).

EU Euterpe Series (Oxford University Press).

GW Gwynn Williams, W.S. (Gwynn Publishing Company).

MT *The Musical Times*.

OR Oriana Series (Novello).

S *Songs of 3.4.5. and 6. parts* (1622).

TO *The Triumphs of Oriana* (1601).

SWB W. Barclay Squire, *Ausgewählte Madrigale* (Breitkopf).

(3) KEYBOARD MUSIC

AP   André Pirro, *L'Art des organistes*, in Lavignac's *Encyclopédie de la musique*, ii, 2.

FB   *Fitzwilliam Virginal Book*, ed. Maitland and Squire (Breitkopf).

FD   Frank Dawes, *Two Elizabethan Keyboard Duets*; Early Keyboard Music, Book 4 (Schott).

HM   Hugh M. Miller, *The Earliest Keyboard Duets*, in *The Musical Quarterly*, xxix (1943), 439.

M5   *Musica Britannica*, v, ed. Stephen D. Tuttle.

MG   Margaret Glyn, *Thirty Virginal Pieces* (Stainer & Bell).

(4) CONSORT MUSIC

CPS   Consort Player Series (Stainer & Bell).

EHF   E. H. Fellowes (Stainer & Bell).

H   *Historical Anthology of Music*, ed. Davison and Apel. Vol. 1 (1947).

M9   *Musica Britannica*, ix, ed. Thurston Dart and William Coates.

TS   Thomas Simpson, *Opusculum neuer Pavanen* . . . (1610)

VGS   Viola da Gamba Society Publications (Schott).

SERVICES

Title (*Verse Services italicized*)	MS Sources	Printed Editions	Remarks
First (Venite, Te Deum, Benedictus, Kyrie, Creed, Magnificat, Nunc Dimittis)	d p y 28 88 180 437 1220 29289	B M O P T	p has an extra copy of *Kyrie*
Second (Venite, Te Deum, Jubilate, Kyrie, Creed, Magnificat, Nunc Dimittis)	y 181 1002 1227	A M T	A contains only (T J M N); y lacks *Venite*
Third (T J M N)	791	M T T⁸	Called 'Mr. Tomkins's Great Service' in 791
Fourth (T M N)	791	M T	
Fifth (T J M N)		M T	
[*Sixth*] (M N)	d 791		incomplete
[*Seventh*] (M N)	791		incomplete

PRECES AND PSALMODY

Preces	p 180	J M T	
Responses	p	J	
First Litany	p	J	
Second Litany ('Common Litany')	p	J	
Ps. xlvii: O clap your hands	180	M T	Whitsunday
Ps. xv: Lord who shall dwell	180	M T	Ascension

Title	MS Sources	Printed Editions	Remarks
Psalm tunes:			
Dunfermline	31421	D R	
Martyrs	r	M	
Old 113th	r	M	
St. David's	r	M	
Windsor	r	M	
Worcester	31421	D R	
York	r	M	

ANTHEMS

Title (*Verse Anthems italicized*)	MS Sources	Printed Editions	Remarks
Above the stars my saviour dwells	d r 180 212 791 1220 4142 6346 17784 30478	M	212 includes string parts
Almighty and everlasting God we humbly beseech Thy majesty	d r 180 791 6346 30478	M	Purification; Listed as a full anthem in 6346 *
Almighty and everlasting God which hatest nothing that Thou hast made	c r 181 1045 1642 6346	B M St	Ash Wednesday
Almighty God the fountain of all wisdom	r d y 181 645 1004 1382 4142 6346 7337 17792 30478 31443	M	'A collect after the Offertory' (6346)
Almighty God which hast instructed	r 181 791 6346 30478	M	St. Mark

* 6346 gives different texts for full and verse anthems, thus postulating a lost full anthem for this feast.

Title (*Verse Anthems italicized*)	MS Sources	Printed Editions	Remarks
Almighty God which hast knit together	d p r 181 30478	M	All Saints
Almighty God who hast given	r 180	M	Christmas
Almighty God whose praise	r 181	M	Holy Innocents
Arise O Lord and have mercy	r 6346	M	
Arise O Lord God lift up thy hand	c r	M	
Arise O Lord into thy resting place	r 6346	M	
Awake up my glory	r	M	
Be strong and of good courage	r	M	Coronation of James I
Behold I bring you glad tidings; Glory be to God in the highest	c r 5 791 1382	M	Christmas; 5 contains second part only
Behold it is Christ	r	M	
Behold the hour cometh	p r	M Ro	
Blessed be the Lord God of Israel	d p r 180 791 1220 4142 6346 30478	M	Listed as a full anthem in 6346
Blessed is he that considereth [O Lord graciously accept]	r	M	
Blessed is he whose unrighteousness	c r	M	Penitential Psalm 2
Christ rising again from the dead	r 181 791	M	Easter
Come let us go up	r	M	
Deal with me O Lord	r	M	
Dear Lord of Life	r 61		r gives parts only, no score
Death is swallowed up	1382		

Title (*Verse Anthems italicized*)	MS Sources	Printed Editions	Remarks
Deliver me from mine enemies	r 30478	M	
From deepest horror of sad penitence	29372		
Give ear unto my words; My voice shalt thou hear	r	M	for men's voices
Give sentence with me O God	d p r 180 791 6346 30478	M	
Glory be to God on high	c r 791 1382	M	*Gloria in excelsis Deo*
Glory be to the Father	r	M	
God who as at this time	p r 181 791	M St	Whitsunday
Grant us, gracious Lord, so to eat	6346		' For the Communion '
Great and marvellous	r	M P T⁸	
Have mercy	r 1382	M	
Have mercy upon me O God	c r	M	Penitential Psalm 4
He that hath pity on the poor	r	M P	
Hear me when I call	r	M	
Hear my prayer O good Lord	r 791	M	Verses for 2 countertenors
Hear my prayer, O Lord	r 791 6346	M	Verses for medius and bass
Hear my prayer O Lord	c r	M	Penitential Psalm 5
Hear my prayer O Lord	c r	M	Penitential Psalm 7
Holy holy holy Lord God	r 1382	M	*Sanctus*, with *Alleluias*
I am the resurrection; I heard a voice from heaven	r	A M	For the Burial Service
I have gone astray	r	M	

Title (*Verse Anthems italicized*)	MS Sources	Printed Editions	Remarks
I will lift up mine eyes	r 791 6346 30478	M	(= *My help cometh*)
It is my well-beloved's voice	62 616 4080 29372 29427	E S	Dedicated to Theophilus Aylmer
Jesus came when the doors were shut	p r 181 6346 30478		r gives parts only, no score
Know you not	r 61 698 1382		r gives cantus only, from 61. Funeral anthem for Prince Henry
Leave O my soul	r 791	M	
Lord enter not into judgment	r 1382 17792	M	
Merciful Lord we beseech thee	r 181	M	St. John
My beloved spake	p r y 791 6346	M Ro	
My dwelling is above	791 6346		
My shepherd is the living Lord	r 4142 17784 30478	M Ro	' Psalm 23 of the ordinary metre ' (M)
Not in the merits	r 791	M	(791 has *Stripped of my merits*)
O be favourable unto Sion	r	M	
O give thanks unto the Lord	r	M T⁸	for men's voices
O God the proud are risen up	c r 5 181	M	645 contains two different settings

Title (*Verse Anthems italicized*)	MS Sources	Printed Editions	Remarks
	645		
	1382		
	6346		
	7339		
O God wonderful art thou	c r	M T[8]	
O how amiable are thy dwellings	r	M	for men's voices
O Israel if thou return	r	M	
O Lord do away as the night	r	M	
O Lord God of hosts	r	M	
O Lord God of hosts	r	M	
O Lord grant the King a long life	r	M	Coronation of Charles I
	791		
O Lord how glorious	r	M	
O Lord how manifold	c r	M	
O Lord I have loved	p r y	M P	
	1		
	23		
	30		
	180		
	6346		
O Lord let me know mine end	r d y	M	
	180		
	791		
	1045		
	1220		
	1382		
	6346		
	29366		
	29427		
	30478		
O Lord open thou our lips	r	M	
O Lord rebuke me not	c r	M	
O Lord thou hast dealt	r	M	
	791		
O Lord wipe away my sins	1382		
O praise the Lord all ye heathen	r	M	*a* 5
O praise the Lord all ye heathen	c r	M T[8]	*a* 12
	5		
	7339		

Title (*Verse Anthems italicized*)	MS Sources	Printed Editions	Remarks
O pray for the peace of Jerusalem	d p r 1 28 180 791 1045 1220 6346 30478	M	
O pray for the peace of Jerusalem	r 181 4142	B M T⁸	
O sing unto the Lord a new song	d r 180 1382 6346 17786 29366 30478	M Ro	
O that the salvation	r	M	
O think upon thy servant	791 6346		
Out of the deep	d r 181 791 30478	M	
Out of the deep have I called	c r	M	Penitential Psalm 6
Praise the Lord O my soul	r 791 1045 6346	M	
Praise the Lord O my soul	r 181	M T⁸	
Praise the Lord O ye servants	r	M	
Put me not to rebuke	c r	M	Penitential Psalm 3
Rejoice, rejoice	17792		
Remember me O Lord	r	M	for men's voices
Sadock the priest	6346		Coronation of Charles I
Set up thyself O God	w		incomplete

Title (*Verse Anthems italicized*)	MS Sources	Printed Editions	Remarks
Sing unto God	p r 791 29372	M	
Stephen being full of the Holy Ghost	d r 6346 30478	M	St. Stephen
Sweet Saviour	791		
The heavens declare the glory	r	M	for men's voices
The hills stand about Jerusalem	r	M	
The Lord bless us	791 1382		
The Lord even the most mighty	r 791 1382	M	
Then David mourned	r	M Ro	
Thou art my King, O God	c d h l p r y 1 6 28 180 791 1001 1045 1176 1220 1382 4142 6346 17784 29372 30478	M Ro	29372 includes string parts. Arranged by Edmund Hooper for 2 bass soloists rather than one: thus in 791, 1045, and part-books at Durham and Windsor
Thou healest the broken	r	M	
Turn thou us	c r 7339	M	canon four in one
Turn thou us O good Lord	r 5 791 1382 30478	M	

Title (*Verse Anthems italicized*)	MS Sources	Printed Editions	Remarks
Turn unto the Lord	p r 4078 17792	E S	Dedicated to Nathaniel Tomkins
When David heard	r 29372	E H M S	Dedicated to Thomas Myriell
Who can tell how oft he offendeth	r	M	
Who is this that cometh	r 181 6346	M	St. George
Who shall ascend the hill of God	c r	M	
Whom have I in heaven	r	M	
Why art thou so full of heaviness	c r	M	
Withdraw not thou thy mercy	r 1021 6346	M	Listed among verse anthems in 6346
Woe is me	17792	E S	Dedicated to John Tomkins
Ye people all	1045		

SECULAR VOCAL MUSIC

Title	MS Source	Printed Edition	Dedicatee
Adieu, ye city-prisoning towers	616 4087	E S	William White
Cloris, whenas I woo		E S	Orlando Gibbons
Come, shepherds, sing with me		E S	Nathaniel Giles
Fauns and satyrs tripping, The		E EU OR TO	Queen Elizabeth I
Fond men that do so highly prize	616	E S	Nicholas Tomkins
Fusca, in thy starry eyes	616	E S WBS	Phineas Fletcher
How great delight	616	E S	William Cross
Love, cease tormenting	616	E S	Thomas Day
Music Divine	616 4076	E S	Dr. Heather
No more will I thy love	616	E S	William Walker
O let me die for true love	616	E S	John Daniel
O let me live for true love	616	E S	John Dowland
Oft did I marle	29372	E S	John Ward
Our hasty life away doth post	616 11587	E S	Thomas Tomkins senr.
Oyez! has any found a lad?	616	E MT S WBS	John Coperario
Phyllis, now cease to move me	616	E O S	Henry Molle
Phyllis, yet see him dying	616	E S	Nicholas Carlton
See, see, the shepherd's queen	616	E O S WBS	John Stevens
Sure there is no god of love	616	E GW S	Humphrey Withy
To the shady woods	616 4081	E S	Robert Chetwode
Too much I once lamented	616	E S	William Byrd
Was ever wretch tormented	616	E S	Giles Tomkins
Weep no more thou sorry boy	616	E MT S	Peregrine Tomkins

Title	MS Source	Printed Edition	Dedicatee
When I observe	616	E S	Thomas Warwick
Yet again, as soon revived	616	E S	Robert Tomkins

KEYBOARD MUSIC

Title	MS Source	Printed Edition	Remarks
Barafostus' Dream	32	FB M5^{62}	
Bitts or morcells	1122	M5^{73}	fragments
Clarifica me pater	1122	M5^{4}	September, 1650
Fancy	1122	M5^{22}	September 9, 1646
Fancy	1122	M5^{23}	July 8, 1647
Fancy	1122	M5^{25}	October 24, 1648
Fancy	1113	M5^{29}	
Fancy: for two to play	29996	M5^{32} FD HM	
Fancy: for viols	1122	M5^{33}	
Fortune my foe	1122	M5^{61}	July 4, 1654
Galliard	5612	M5^{60}	
Galliard, The hunting	32	FB M5^{58}	
Galliard, The Lady Folliot's	5612	M5^{59}	
Go from my window	1122	M5^{72}	fragment
Ground	32	FB M5^{39}	
Ground	29996	M5^{40}	
In nomine (version 1)	1122	AP M5^{5}	January 20–28, 1647
In nomine (version 2)	1122	M5^{6}	January 20, 1647 — August 2, 1650
In nomine	1122	M5^{7}	May, 1648
In nomine	1122	M5^{8}	June 16, 1648
In nomine	1122	M5^{9}	October 27, 1648
In nomine (version 1)	1122	M5^{10}	February, 1650
In nomine (version 2)	1122	M5^{11}	February 14, 1650

Title	MS Source	Printed Edition	Remarks
In nomine	1122	M5^{12}	June 28, 1652
Miserere	1122	M5^{13}	September 15, 1648
Miserere	1122	M5^{14}	October 7, 1648
Miserere	1122	M5^{15}	May 26, 1651
Miserere	1122	M5^{16}	February 3–4, 1652
Miserere	1122	M5^{17}	
Miserere	1122	M5^{18}	
Miserere	1122	M5^{19}	
Miserere	1122	M5^{20}	
Offertory	93	M5^{21}	1637
Pavan	1122	M5^{51}	September 10, 1647
Pavan	1122	M5^{52}	September 14, 1647
Pavan, A sad; for these distracted times	1122	M5^{53}	February 14, 1649
Pavan	1122	M5^{54}	August 20, 1650
Pavan, Short	1122	M5^{55}	July 19, 1654
Pavan	32 1113	FB M5^{56}	String version in M9^{73}
Pavan, Lord Canterbury	29996	FD M5^{57}	1647
Pavan & Galliard, Earl Strafford	1122	M5$^{41-2}$	September 29, 1647 (short version)
Pavan & Galliard, Earl Strafford	1122	M5$^{43-4}$	October 2, 1647 (long version)
Pavan & Galliard	1122	M5$^{45-6}$	April, 1650 October 1, 1650
Pavan & Galliard	1122	M5$^{47-8}$	September 4, 1654 September 7, 1654
Pavan & Galliard, of three parts	1122	M5$^{49-50}$	
Plainsong, On a	1113	M5^{68}	
Prelude	1122	M5^{1}	
Prelude, Piece of a	1122	M5^{2}	July 9, 1647
Prelude	1122	M5^{3}	
Robin Hood	24	M5^{63}	
Round, The perpetual	1122	M5^{66}	September 7–8, 1654

Title	MS Source	Printed Edition	Remarks
Toy: made at Poole Court	1122	MG M5[67]	
Toy: Mr. Curch	32	FB M5[69]	Entitled *Almain*
	1113		in 1113.
	5612		Attr. to
			Farnaby in 32
Ut mi re	93	M5[38]	
Ut re mi fa sol la; for a beginner	1122	M5[34]	
Ut re mi fa sol la	93	M5[35]	For string
	1122		versions see
			p. 196
Ut re mi fa sol la	1122	M5[36]	
Ut re mi fa sol la	1122	M5[37]	
Ut re mi fa sol la	1122	M5[70]	fragment
Ut re mi fa sol la	1122	M5[71]	June 30, 1654
			fragment
Verse, of three parts	1122	M5[26]	August 12, 1650
Verse, A short	29996	FD M5[27]	
Verse, A substantial; maintaining the point	1122	M5[31]	
[Verse] (i)	93		Dedicated to
			Archdeacon
			Thornborough
[Verse] (ii)	93		Dedicated to
			Archdeacon
			Thornborough
[Verse] (iii)	93		Dedicated to
			Archdeacon
			Thornborough
Voluntary	1122	M5[24]	August 10 —
			September 10
			1647
Voluntary	5611	M5[28]	
Voluntary	5611	M5[30]	
What if a day	5612	MG M5[64]	
Worcester Brawls	32	FB MG M5[65]	

CONSORT MUSIC

Title	MS Sources	Printed Editions	Remarks
Alman *a* 4	341	M9[33]	
Fantasia *a* 3 (1)	245		Numerical
	347		order as in
	17792		245
Fantasia *a* 3 (2)	245		
	347		
	1018		
	17792		
Fantasia *a* 3 (3)	245		
	347		
	1018		
	17792		
Fantasia *a* 3 (4)	245		
	347		
	1018		
	17792		
Fantasia *a* 3 (5)	245		
	347		
	1018		
	17792		
Fantasia *a* 3 (6)	245		
	1018		
	17792		
Fantasia *a* 3 (7)	245	CPS	
	347		
	1018		
	17792		
Fantasia *a* 3 (8)	245		
	347		
	1018		
	17792		
Fantasia *a* 3 (9)	245		
	347		
	1018		
	17792		

Title	MS Sources	Printed Editions	Remarks
Fantasia *a* 3 (10)	245 347 1018 17792		
Fantasia *a* 3 (11)	245 17792		
Fantasia *a* 3 (12)	245 347 17792		
Fantasia *a* 3 (13)	245 347 17792		
Fantasia *a* 3 (14)	245 347 17793	M9[13] VGS	
Fantasia *a* 5	1122	M5[33]	Keyboard version: original not extant
Fantasia *a* 6 (1)	64 341		Numerical order as in 64
Fantasia *a* 6 (2)	64 341	EHF	
Fantasia *a* 6 (3)	64 341		
Fantasia *a* 6 (4)	64 341		
In nomine *a* 3 (1)	245 1018 17792	CPS	Numerical order as in 245
In nomine *a* 3 (2)	245 347 1018 17792	H	
Pavan *a* 5 (1)	415 17792		Numerical order as in 415, which lacks one part-book
Pavan *a* 5 (2)	415		
Pavan *a* 5 (3)	415		
Pavan *a* 5 (4)	415		
Pavan *a* 5 (5)	415		

Title	MS Sources	Printed Editions	Remarks
Pavan *a* 5 (6)	415 3665 17792 30826	TS M9[73]	For keyboard versions see p. 192
Pavan *a* 5 [7]	17792		
Pavan *a* 5 [8]	17792		
Pavan *a* 5 [9]	30826		3 parts only
Pavan & Galliard *a* 6	64 341	M9[91-2]	
Ut re mi *a* 4	64 341		For keyboard versions see p. 193

BIBLIOGRAPHY

Abingdon, T., *The Antiquities of Worcester Cathedral.* (1717.)

Amphlett, John, ed. *A Survey of Worcester by Thomas Habington.* (Worcestershire Historical Society, 1895.)

Arkwright, G. E. P., *Catalogue of Music in the Library of Christ Church, Oxford.* (1915.)

Armitt, M. L., *Old English Viol Music* in *The Quarterly Musical Review,* iv (1888), 175, 243.

Atkins, Sir Ivor, *The Early Occupants of the Office of Organist and Master of the Choristers of the Cathedral Church of Christ and the Blessed Virgin Mary, Worcester.* (Worcestershire Historical Society, 1918.)

Aubrey, John, *Brief Lives,* ed. Oliver Lawson Dick. (1950.)

Birch, Thomas, *The Life of Henry, Prince of Wales, eldest son of King James I.* (1760.)

Bloxam, J. R., *A Register of the Presidents, Fellows, Demies, Instructors in Grammar and in Music, Chaplains, Clerks, Choristers and other members of Saint Mary Magdalen College in the University of Oxford.* (1853–5.)

Bontoux, Germaine, *La Chanson en Angleterre au temps d'Élisabeth.* (1936.)

Boorman, P., *Thomas Tomkins: A Great Composer.* (Report of the Friends of St. David's Cathedral, 1956.)

Boyd, M. C., *Elizabethan Music and Music Criticism.* (1940.)

Bukofzer, M. F., ed. *John Dunstable, Complete Works* (*Musica Britannica,* viii). (1955.)

Music in the Baroque Era. (1947.)

Bund, J. W. Willis, ed. *Diary of Henry Townshend of Elmley Lovett, 1640–1663.* (Worcestershire Historical Society, 1920.)

Burney, C., *General History of Music* (1776–89). New edition by Frank Mercer (1935).

Butler, Charles, *The Principles of Musick.* (1636.)

Cavanaugh, R. W., *The Anthems in Musica Deo Sacra by Thomas Tomkins.* University Microfilms, Doctoral Dissertation Series, No. 5649. (1953.)

Clifford, James, *The Divine Services and Anthems usually sung in the Cathedrals and Collegiate Choirs in the Church of England.* (1663.)

Dart, R. T., *Jacobean Consort Music* in *Proceedings of The Royal Musical Association,* 81 (1954–5), 63.

Dart, R. T., and Coates, W., *Jacobean Consort Music (Musica Britannica,* ix). (1955.)

Davey, H., *Die ältesten Musik-Handschriften auf englischen Bibliotheken* in *Monatshefte für Musikgeschichte,* xxxiv (1902), 33.

Dawes, F., *Nicholas Carlton and the Earliest Keyboard Duet* in *The Musical Times,* xcii (1951), 542.

Dickson, W. E., *A Catalogue of Ancient Choral Services and Anthems Preserved among the Manuscript Scores and Part-Books in the Cathedral Church of Ely.* (1861.)

Dugdale, William, *A short view of the late troubles in England.* (1681.)

Ede, W. M., *The Cathedral Church of Christ and the Blessed Virgin Mary of Worcester.* (1925.)

Eitner, R., *Biographisch-bibliographisches Quellenlexikon.* (1899–1904.)

Emden, C. S., *Lives of Elizabethan Song Composers: Some New Facts* in *Review of English Studies,* ii (1926), 416.

Fellowes, E. H., *Orlando Gibbons.* (1951.)

English Cathedral Music from Edward VI to Edward VII. (1941.)

The Catalogue of Manuscripts in the Library of St. Michael's College, Tenbury. (1934.)

English Madrigal Composers. (1921.)

The English Madrigal. (1925.)

ed. *The English Madrigal School,* Vol. xviii: *Thomas Tomkins, Songs of 3. 4. 5. and 6. parts.* (1922.)

Fétis, F. J., *Biographie universelle des musiciens.* (1860–5.)

Fletcher, P., *The Poems of Phineas Fletcher, B.D.* (ed. A. B. Grosart). (1869.)

Fosbroke, T. D., *An Original History of the City of Gloucester.* (1819.)

Foster, M. B., *Anthems and Anthem Composers.* (1901.)

Frere, W. H., ed. *Antiphonale Sarisburiense.* (*Plainsong and Medieval Music Society,* 1901–25.)

Frost, M., *English and Scottish Psalm and Hymn Tunes.* (1953.)

Glyn, M. H., *About Elizabethan Virginal Music and its Composers.* (1924; revised ed. 1934.)

Green, M. A. E., *Calendar of the Proceedings of the Committee for Compounding (1643–1660).* (1890.)

Green, V., *A History of Worcester.* (1796.)

Grove, Sir George, *Dictionary of Music and Musicians.* 5th edition, edited by Eric Blom. (1954.)

Guarini, G. B., *Delle opere del Cavalier Battista Guarini.* (1737.)

Hawkins, J., *A General History of the Science and Practice of Music.* (1776.)

Hayes, W., *Remarks on Mr. Avison's Essay on Musical Expression.* (1753.)

Hitchins, F., *History of Cornwall.* (1824.)

Hughes, Dom A., *Catalogue of the Musical Manuscripts at Peterhouse, Cambridge.* (1953.)

Hughes-Hughes, A., *Catalogue of Manuscript Music in the British Museum.* (1906.)

Jebb, J., ed. *The Choral Responses and Litanies of the United Church of England and Ireland.* (1847.)

Lafontaine, H. C. de, *The King's Musick.* (1909.)

Lawes, Henry, *The Treasury of Musick; containing Ayres and Dialogues to sing to the Theorbo Lute or Basse Viol.* (1669.)

Le Neve, J., *Fasti Ecclesiae Anglicanae,* ed. T. Duffus Hardy. (1854.)

Leach, A. F., *Documents illustrating Early Education in Worcester, 1685–1700.* (Worcestershire Historical Society, 1913.)

Legg, J. W., *English Orders for Consecrating Churches.* (*Henry Bradshaw Society,* xli) (1911).

The Coronation Order of King James I. (1902.)

Mace, Thomas, *Musick's Monument.* (1676.)

Maitland, J. A. F., and Squire, B., ed. *The Fitzwilliam Virginal Book.* (1894–9.)

Meyer, E. H., *Die mehrstimmige Spielmusik des 17. Jahrhunderts in Nord- und Mitteleuropa.* (1934.)

English Chamber Music. (1946.)

Miller, H. M., *Pretty Wayes: For Young Beginners to Looke on* in *The Musical Quarterly,* xxxiii (1947), 543.

The Earliest Keyboard Duets in *The Musical Quarterly,* xxix (1943), 439.

Morley, T., *A Plain and Easy Introduction to Practical Music,* ed. Alec Harman. (1952.)

Nagel, W., *Annalen der englischen Hofmusik* in *Monatshefte für Musik-geschichte [Beilage]*, *xxvi*. (1894.)

Geschichte der Musik in England. (1894–7.)

Nash, T., *Quaternio, or a Fourfold Way to a Happy Life.* (1633.)

Naylor, E. J. W., *An Elizabethan Virginal Book.* (1905.)

Noake, J., *The Monastery and Cathedral of Worcester.* (1866.)

Noble, J., *Le Répertoire instrumental anglais (1550–1585)* in *La Musique instrumentale de la Renaissance.* (1955.)

North, R., *Memoirs of Music,* ed. E. F. Rimbault. (1846.)

The Musical Grammarian, ed. H. Andrews. (1925.)

Ouseley, F. A. G., *Cathedral Services.* (1853.)

Pfeilschifter, O., *Die englische Kirchenmusik der Tudorepoche.* (Dissertation, Munich, 1949.)

Pulver, J., *A Biographical Dictionary of Old English Music.* (1927.)

Ramsbotham, A., ed. *Thomas Tomkins: Services in Tudor Church Music,* viii. (1928.)

Reese, G., *The Origin of the English In Nomine* in *Journal of the American Musicological Society,* ii (1949), 7.

Music in the Renaissance. (1954.)

Rimbault, E. F., *Bibliotheca Madrigaliana.* (1847.)

The Old Cheque Book, or Book of Remembrance, of the Chapel Royal, from 1561 to 1744. (1872.)

Robertson, D., *Sarum Close.* (1938.)

Rose, B. W. G., *Thomas Tomkins* in *Proceedings of the Royal Musical Association,* 82 (1955–6), 89.

Sartori, Claudio, *Une Pratique des musiciens lombards (1582–1639)* in *La Musique instrumentale de la Renaissance.* (1955.)

Simpson, Christopher, *A Compendium of Practical Musick.* (1667.)

Smith and Onslow, *Diocesan History of Worcester.* (1883.)

Squire, W. B., ed. *Ausgewählte Madrigale.* (1903–13.)

Stevens, D. W., ed. *Altenglische Orgelmusik.* (1954.)

La Vie et l'œuvre de Thomas Tomkins, in *Revue de Musicologie,* 115 (1957), *s.v.* Séances de la Société.

ed. *The Mulliner Book (Musica Britannica,* i). (1951.)

The Mulliner Book: A Commentary. (1952.)

Thomas Tomkins — Keyboard Music (review of *Musica Britannica,* v), in *The Musical Quarterly,* xlii (1956), 402.

Thomas Tomkins, Last of the Elizabethan Virginalists, in *Étude* (July–August 1956), 16.

Thomas Tomkins : 1572–1656, in *The Listener* (June 7, 1956).

Tudor Church Music. (1955.)

Taylor, S. de B., *Thomas Tomkins: A Short Account of his Life and Works.* (n.d.)

Toy, John, *A Sermon, preached in the Cathedral Church of Worcester . . . at the funeral of Mrs. Alice Tomkins.* (1642.)

Worcester Elegy and Eulogy. (1638.)

Tuttle, S. D., ed. *Thomas Tomkins: Keyboard Music (Musica Britannica, v).* (1955.)

Van den Borren, C., *The Sources of Keyboard Music in England.* (1914.)

Willis, B., *A Survey of the Cathedrals.* (1727–30.)

Wither, George, *The Hymns and Songs of the Church.* (1623.)

Wood, A., *Athenae Oxonienses; Fasti Oxonienses*, ed. Bliss. (1813–17.)

Woodfill, W., *Musicians in English Society.* (1953.)

DISCOGRAPHY

This is not an exhaustive list, but the four discs considered as a group offer a fair cross-section of Tomkins's music, sacred and secular.

Magdalen College Choir, dir. Bernard Rose:
Responses; Psalm 15; Te Deum and Benedictus (First Service); Above the stars; Almighty God, the fountain of all wisdom; Holy, holy, holy; My shepherd is the living Lord; Turn unto the Lord; When David heard. Voluntary and Fancy (organ).

Argo RG 249 (stereo, ZRG 5249)

Ambrosian Singers and Players, dir. Denis Stevens:
Thou art my king, O God; O clap your hands; Then David mourned; God who as at this time; Above the stars; The heavens declare; Jubilate (Fifth Service). Three Voluntaries (organ).

Expériences Anonymes EA 27 (stereo, MHS 687)

SONGS AND CONSORT MUSIC

Ambrosian Consort, dir. Denis Stevens
In Nomine Players
Music Divine; How great delight; O let me live; O let me die; Sure there is no god of love; When I observe; Oft did I marle; Our hasty life; Too much I once lamented; Was ever wretch tormented; Adieu, ye city-prisoning towers. Pavan in A minor; Fantasia *a* 3; Alman *a* 4; Pavan in F.

Expériences Anonymes EA 28 (stereo, MHS 688)

Thurston Dart (harpsichord)
Clarifica me pater; Pavan and Galliard in G; Pavan and Galliard (Earl of Strafford); Pavan and Galliard in A minor; Toy made at Poole Court; Voluntary; What if a day; Worster Braules.

Oiseau Lyre OL 50076

THE TOMKINS FAMILY (1495–1840)

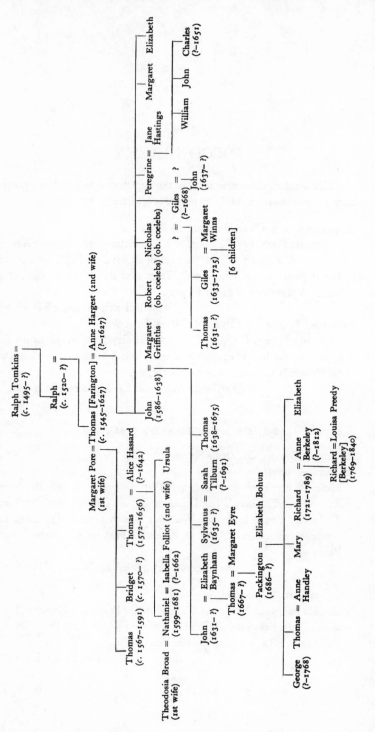

INDEX

Titles of musical works are shown in *italics*: they are by Thomas Tomkins if no other composer's name is specified. To distinguish between similar titles in references to instrumental music, the keyboard works have been given their *Musica Britannica* numbers (e.g. M5²²), while string music is numbered in accordance with the catalogue on p. 194.

CATALOGUE OF DOVER BOOKS

Books Explaining Science and Mathematics

WHAT IS SCIENCE?, N. Campbell. The role of experiment and measurement, the function of mathematics, the nature of scientific laws, the difference between laws and theories, the limitations of science, and many similarly provocative topics are treated clearly and without technicalities by an eminent scientist. "Still an excellent introduction to scientific philosophy," H. Margenau in PHYSICS TODAY. "A first-rate primer . . . deserves a wide audience," SCIENTIFIC AMERICAN. 192pp. 5⅜ x 8.   S43 Paperbound **$1.25**

THE NATURE OF PHYSICAL THEORY, P. W. Bridgman. A Nobel Laureate's clear, non-technical lectures on difficulties and paradoxes connected with frontier research on the physical sciences. Concerned with such central concepts as thought, logic, mathematics, relativity, probability, wave mechanics, etc. he analyzes the contributions of such men as Newton, Einstein, Bohr, Heisenberg, and many others. "Lucid and entertaining . . . recommended to anyone who wants to get some insight into current philosophies of science," THE NEW PHILOSOPHY. Index. xi + 138pp. 5⅜ x 8.   S33 Paperbound **$1.25**

EXPERIMENT AND THEORY IN PHYSICS, Max Born. A Nobel Laureate examines the nature of experiment and theory in theoretical physics and analyzes the advances made by the great physicists of our day: Heisenberg, Einstein, Bohr, Planck, Dirac, and others. The actual process of creation is detailed step-by-step by one who participated. A fine examination of the scientific method at work. 44pp. 5⅜ x 8.   S308 Paperbound **75¢**

THE PSYCHOLOGY OF INVENTION IN THE MATHEMATICAL FIELD, J. Hadamard. The reports of such men as Descartes, Pascal, Einstein, Poincaré, and others are considered in this investigation of the method of idea-creation in mathematics and other sciences and the thinking process in general. How do ideas originate? What is the role of the unconscious? What is Poincaré's forgetting hypothesis? are some of the fascinating questions treated. A penetrating analysis of Einstein's thought processes concludes the book. xiii + 145pp. 5⅜ x 8.   T107 Paperbound **$1.25**

THE NATURE OF LIGHT AND COLOUR IN THE OPEN AIR, M. Minnaert. Why are shadows sometimes blue, sometimes green, or other colors depending on the light and surroundings? What causes mirages? Why do multiple suns and moons appear in the sky? Professor Minnaert explains these unusual phenomena and hundreds of others in simple, easy-to-understand terms based on optical laws and the properties of light and color. No mathematics is required but artists, scientists, students, and everyone fascinated by these "tricks" of nature will find thousands of useful and amazing pieces of information. Hundreds of observational experiments are suggested which require no special equipment. 200 illustrations; 42 photos. xvi + 362pp. 5⅜ x 8.   T196 Paperbound **$2.00**

THE UNIVERSE OF LIGHT, W. Bragg. Sir William Bragg, Nobel Laureate and great modern physicist, is also well known for his powers of clear exposition. Here he analyzes all aspects of light for the layman: lenses, reflection, refraction, the optics of vision, x-rays, the photoelectric effect, etc. He tells you what causes the color of spectra, rainbows, and soap bubbles, how magic mirrors work, and much more. Dozens of simple experiments are described. Preface. Index. 199 line drawings and photographs, including 2 full-page color plates. x + 283pp. 5⅜ x 8.   T538 Paperbound **$1.85**

SOAP-BUBBLES: THEIR COLOURS AND THE FORCES THAT MOULD THEM, C. V. Boys. For continuing popularity and validity as scientific primer, few books can match this volume of easily-followed experiments, explanations. Lucid exposition of complexities of liquid films, surface tension and related phenomena, bubbles' reaction to heat, motion, music, magnetic fields. Experiments with capillary attraction, soap bubbles on frames, composite bubbles, liquid cylinders and jets, bubbles other than soap, etc. Wonderful introduction to scientific method, natural laws that have many ramifications in areas of modern physics. Only complete edition in print. New Introduction by S. Z. Lewin, New York University. 83 illustrations; 1 full-page color plate. xii + 190pp. 5⅜ x 8½.   T542 Paperbound **95¢**

THE STORY OF X-RAYS FROM RONTGEN TO ISOTOPES, A. R. Bleich, M.D. This book, by a member of the American College of Radiology, gives the scientific explanation of x-rays, their applications in medicine, industry and art, and their danger (and that of atmospheric radiation) to the individual and the species. You learn how radiation therapy is applied against cancer, how x-rays diagnose heart disease and other ailments, how they are used to examine mummies for information on diseases of early societies, and industrial materials for hidden weaknesses. 54 illustrations show x-rays of flowers, bones, stomach, gears with flaws, etc. 1st publication. Index. xix + 186pp. 5⅜ x 8.   T622 Paperbound **$1.50**

SPINNING TOPS AND GYROSCOPIC MOTION, John Perry. A classic elementary text of the dynamics of rotation — the behavior and use of rotating bodies such as gyroscopes and tops. In simple, everyday English you are shown how quasi-rigidity is induced in discs of paper, smoke rings, chains, etc., by rapid motions; why a gyrostat falls and why a top rises; precession; how the earth's motion affects climate; and many other phenomena. Appendix on practical use of gyroscopes. 62 figures. 128pp. 5⅜ x 8.   T416 Paperbound **$1.25**

SNOW CRYSTALS, W. A. Bentley, M. J. Humphreys. For almost 50 years W. A. Bentley photographed snow flakes in his laboratory in Jericho, Vermont; in 1931 the American Meteorological Society gathered together the best of his work, some 2400 photographs of snow flakes, plus a few ice flowers, windowpane frosts, dew, frozen rain, and other ice formations. Pictures were selected for beauty and scientific value. A very valuable work to anyone in meteorology, cryology; most interesting to layman; extremely useful for artist who wants beautiful, crystalline designs. All copyright free. Unabridged reprint of 1931 edition. 2453 illustrations. 227pp. 8 x 10½.   T287 Paperbound **$3.00**

A DOVER SCIENCE SAMPLER, edited by George Barkin. A collection of brief, non-technical passages from 44 Dover Books Explaining Science for the enjoyment of the science-minded browser. Includes work of Bertrand Russell, Poincaré, Laplace, Max Born, Galileo, Newton; material on physics, mathematics, metallurgy, anatomy, astronomy, chemistry, etc. You will be fascinated by Martin Gardner's analysis of the sincere pseudo-scientist, Moritz's account of Newton's absentmindedness, Bernard's examples of human vivisection, etc. Illustrations from the Diderot Pictorial Encyclopedia and De Re Metallica. 64 pages.   **FREE**

THE STORY OF ATOMIC THEORY AND ATOMIC ENERGY, J. G. Feinberg. A broader approach to subject of nuclear energy and its cultural implications than any other similar source. Very readable, informal, completely non-technical text. Begins with first atomic theory, 600 B.C. and carries you through the work of Mendelejeff, Röntgen, Madame Curie, to Einstein's equation and the A-bomb. New chapter goes through thermonuclear fission, binding energy, other events up to 1959. Radioactive decay and radiation hazards, future benefits, work of Bohr, moderns, hundreds more topics. "Deserves special mention . . . not only authoritative but thoroughly popular in the best sense of the word," Saturday Review. Formerly, "The Atom Story." Expanded with new chapter. Three appendixes. Index. 34 illustrations. vii + 243pp. 5⅜ x 8.   T625 Paperbound **$1.60**

THE STRANGE STORY OF THE QUANTUM, AN ACCOUNT FOR THE GENERAL READER OF THE GROWTH OF IDEAS UNDERLYING OUR PRESENT ATOMIC KNOWLEDGE, B. Hoffmann. Presents lucidly and expertly, with barest amount of mathematics, the problems and theories which led to modern quantum physics. Dr. Hoffmann begins with the closing years of the 19th century, when certain trifling discrepancies were noticed, and with illuminating analogies and examples takes you through the brilliant concepts of Planck, Einstein, Pauli, Broglie, Bohr, Schroedinger, Heisenberg, Dirac, Sommerfeld, Feynman, etc. This edition includes a new, long postscript carrying the story through 1958. "Of the books attempting an account of the history and contents of our modern atomic physics which have come to my attention, this is the best," H. Margenau, Yale University, in "American Journal of Physics." 32 tables and line illustrations. Index. 275pp. 5⅜ x 8.   T518 Paperbound **$1.50**

SPACE AND TIME, E. Borel. Written by a versatile mathematician of world renown with his customary lucidity and precision, this introduction to relativity for the layman presents scores of examples, analogies, and illustrations that open up new ways of thinking about space and time. It covers abstract geometry and geographical maps, continuity and topology, the propagation of light, the special theory of relativity, the general theory of relativity, theoretical researches, and much more. Mathematical notes. 2 Indexes. 4 Appendices. 15 figures. xvi + 243pp. 5⅜ x 8.   T592 Paperbound **$1.75**

FROM EUCLID TO EDDINGTON: A STUDY OF THE CONCEPTIONS OF THE EXTERNAL WORLD, Sir Edmund Whittaker. A foremost British scientist traces the development of theories of natural philosophy from the western rediscovery of Euclid to Eddington, Einstein, Dirac, etc. The inadequacy of classical physics is contrasted with present day attempts to understand the physical world through relativity, non-Euclidean geometry, space curvature, wave mechanics, etc. 5 major divisions of examination: Space; Time and Movement; the Concepts of Classical Physics; the Concepts of Quantum Mechanics; the Eddington Universe 212pp. 5⅜ x 8.
T491 Paperbound **$1.35**

Nature, Biology,

NATURE RECREATION: Group Guidance for the Out-of-doors, William Gould Vinal. Intended for both the uninitiated nature instructor and the education student on the college level, this complete "how-to" program surveys the entire area of nature education for the young. Philosophy of nature recreation; requirements, responsibilities, important information for group leaders; nature games; suggested group projects; conducting meetings and getting discussions started; etc. Scores of immediately applicable teaching aids, plus completely updated sources of information, pamphlets, field guides, recordings, etc. Bibliography. 74 photographs. + 310pp. 5⅜ x 8½. T1015 Paperbound **$1.75**

HOW TO KNOW THE WILD FLOWERS, Mrs. William Starr Dana. Classic nature book that has introduced thousands to wonders of American wild flowers. Color-season principle of organization is easy to use, even by those with no botanical training, and the genial, refreshing discussions of history, folklore, uses of over 1,000 native and escape flowers, foliage plants are informative as well as fun to read. Over 170 full-page plates, collected from several editions, may be colored in to make permanent records of finds. Revised to conform with 1950 edition of Gray's Manual of Botany. xlii + 438pp. 5⅜ x 8½. T332 Paperbound **$2.00**

HOW TO KNOW THE FERNS, F. T. Parsons. Ferns, among our most lovely native plants, are all too little known. This classic of nature lore will enable the layman to identify almost any American fern he may come across. After an introduction on the structure and life of ferns, the 57 most important ferns are fully pictured and described (arranged upon a simple identification key). Index of Latin and English names. 61 illustrations and 42 full-page plates. xiv + 215pp. 5⅜ x 8. T740 Paperbound **$1.35**

MANUAL OF THE TREES OF NORTH AMERICA, Charles Sprague Sargent. Still unsurpassed as most comprehensive, reliable study of North American tree characteristics, precise locations and distribution. By dean of American dendrologists. Every tree native to U.S., Canada, Alaska, 185 genera, 717 species, described in detail—leaves, flowers, fruit, winterbuds, bark, wood, growth habits etc. plus discussion of varieties and local variants, immaturity variations. Over 100 keys, including unusual 11-page analytical key to genera, aid in identification. 783 clear illustrations of flowers, fruit, leaves. An unmatched permanent reference work for all nature lovers. Second enlarged (1926) edition. Synopsis of families. Analytical key to genera. Glossary of technical terms. Index. 783 illustrations, 1 map. Two volumes. Total of 982pp. 5⅜ x 8. T277 Vol. I Paperbound **$2.25**
T278 Vol. II Paperbound **$2.25**
The set **$4.50**

TREES OF THE EASTERN AND CENTRAL UNITED STATES AND CANADA, W. M. Harlow. A revised edition of a standard middle-level guide to native trees and important escapes. More than 140 trees are described in detail, and illustrated with more than 600 drawings and photographs. Supplementary keys will enable the careful reader to identify almost any tree he might encounter. xiii + 288pp. 5⅜ x 8. T395 Paperbound **$1.35**

GUIDE TO SOUTHERN TREES, Ellwood S. Harrar and J. George Harrar. All the essential information about trees indigenous to the South, in an extremely handy format. Introductory essay on methods of tree classification and study, nomenclature, chief divisions of Southern trees, etc. Approximately 100 keys and synopses allow for swift, accurate identification of trees. Numerous excellent illustrations, non-technical text make this a useful book for teachers of biology or natural science, nature lovers, amateur naturalists. Revised 1962 edition. Index. Bibliography. Glossary of technical terms. 920 illustrations; 201 full-page plates. ix + 709pp. 4⅝ x 6⅜. T945 Paperbound **$2.35**

FRUIT KEY AND TWIG KEY TO TREES AND SHRUBS, W. M. Harlow. Bound together in one volume for the first time, these handy and accurate keys to fruit and twig identification are the only guides of their sort with photographs (up to 3 times natural size). "Fruit Key": Key to over 120 different deciduous and evergreen fruits. 139 photographs and 11 line drawings. Synoptic summary of fruit types. Bibliography. 2 Indexes (common and scientific names). "Twig Key": Key to over 160 different twigs and buds. 173 photographs. Glossary of technical terms. Bibliography. 2 Indexes (common and scientific names). Two volumes bound as one. Total of xvii + 126pp. 5⅝ x 8⅜. T511 Paperbound **$1.25**

INSECT LIFE AND INSECT NATURAL HISTORY, S. W. Frost. A work emphasizing habits, social life, and ecological relations of insects, rather than more academic aspects of classification and morphology. Prof. Frost's enthusiasm and knowledge are everywhere evident as he discusses insect associations and specialized habits like leaf-rolling, leaf-mining, and case-making, the gall insects, the boring insects, aquatic insects, etc. He examines all sorts of matters not usually covered in general works, such as: insects as human food, insect music and musicians, insect response to electric and radio waves, use of insects in art and literature. The admirably executed purpose of this book, which covers the middle ground between elementary treatment and scholarly monographs, is to excite the reader to observe for himself. Over 700 illustrations. Extensive bibliography. x + 524pp. 5⅜ x 8. T517 Paperbound **$2.50**

CATALOGUE OF DOVER BOOKS

COMMON SPIDERS OF THE UNITED STATES, J. H. Emerton. Here is a nature hobby you can pursue right in your own cellar! Only non-technical, but thorough, reliable guide to spiders for the layman. Over 200 spiders from all parts of the country, arranged by scientific classification, are identified by shape and color, number of eyes, habitat and range, habits, etc. Full text, 501 line drawings and photographs, and valuable introduction explain webs, poisons, threads, capturing and preserving spiders, etc. Index. New synoptic key by S. W. Frost. xxiv + 225pp. 5⅜ x 8.   T223 Paperbound **$1.45**

THE LIFE STORY OF THE FISH: HIS MANNERS AND MORALS, Brian Curtis. A comprehensive, non-technical survey of just about everything worth knowing about fish. Written for the aquarist, the angler, and the layman with an inquisitive mind, the text covers such topics as evolution, external covering and protective coloration, physics and physiology of vision, maintenance of equilibrium, function of the lateral line canal for auditory and temperature senses, nervous system, function of the air bladder, reproductive system and methods—courtship, mating, spawning, care of young—and many more. Also sections on game fish, the problems of conservation and a fascinating chapter on fish curiosities. "Clear, simple language . . . excellent judgment in choice of subjects . . . delightful sense of humor," New York Times. Revised (1949) edition. Index. Bibliography of 72 items. 6 full-page photographic plates. xii + 284pp. 5⅜ x 8.   T929 Paperbound **$1.65**

BATS, Glover Morrill Allen. The most comprehensive study of bats as a life-form by the world's foremost authority. A thorough summary of just about everything known about this fascinating and mysterious flying mammal, including its unique location sense, hibernation and cycles, its habitats and distribution, its wing structure and flying habits, and its relationship to man in the long history of folklore and superstition. Written on a middle-level, the book can be profitably studied by a trained zoologist and thoroughly enjoyed by the layman. "An absorbing text with excellent illustrations. Bats should have more friends and fewer thoughtless detractors as a result of the publication of this volume," William Beebe, Books. Extensive bibliography. 57 photographs and illustrations. x + 368pp. 5⅜ x 8½.
T984 Paperbound **$2.00**

BIRDS AND THEIR ATTRIBUTES, Glover Morrill Allen. A fine general introduction to birds as living organisms, especially valuable because of emphasis on structure, physiology, habits, behavior. Discusses relationship of bird to man, early attempts at scientific ornithology, feathers and coloration, skeletal structure including bills, legs and feet, wings. Also food habits, evolution and present distribution, feeding and nest-building, still unsolved questions of migrations and location sense, many more similar topics. Final chapter on classification, nomenclature. A good popular-level summary for the biologist; a first-rate introduction for the layman. Reprint of 1925 edition. References and index. 51 illustrations. viii + 338pp. 5⅜ x 8½.   T957 Paperbound **$1.85**

LIFE HISTORIES OF NORTH AMERICAN BIRDS, Arthur Cleveland Bent. Bent's monumental series of books on North American birds, prepared and published under auspices of Smithsonian Institute, is the definitive coverage of the subject, the most-used single source of information. Now the entire set is to be made available by Dover in inexpensive editions. This encyclopedic collection of detailed, specific observations utilizes reports of hundreds of contemporary observers, writings of such naturalists as Audubon, Burroughs, William Brewster, as well as author's own extensive investigations. Contains literally everything known about life history of each bird considered: nesting, eggs, plumage, distribution and migration, voice, enemies, courtship, etc. These not over-technical works are musts for ornithologists, conservationists, amateur naturalists, anyone seriously interested in American birds.

BIRDS OF PREY. More than 100 subspecies of hawks, falcons, eagles, buzzards, condors and owls, from the common barn owl to the extinct caracara of Guadaloupe Island. 400 photographs. Two volume set. Index for each volume. Bibliographies of 403, 520 items. 197 full-page plates. Total of 907pp. 5⅜ x 8½.   Vol. I T931 Paperbound **$2.50**
                                                         Vol. II T932 Paperbound **$2.50**

WILD FOWL. Ducks, geese, swans, and tree ducks—73 different subspecies. Two volume set. Index for each volume. Bibliographies of 124, 144 items. 106 full-page plates. Total of 685pp. 5⅜ x 8½.   Vol. I T285 Paperbound **$2.50**
                                                         Vol. II T286 Paperbound **$2.50**

SHORE BIRDS. 81 varieties (sandpipers, woodcocks, plovers, snipes, phalaropes, curlews, oyster catchers, etc.). More than 200 photographs of eggs, nesting sites, adult and young of important species. Two volume set. Index for each volume. Bibliographies of 261, 188 items. 121 full-page plates. Total of 860pp. 5⅜ x 8½.   Vol. I T933 Paperbound **$2.35**
                                                         Vol. II T934 Paperbound **$2.35**

THE LIFE OF PASTEUR, R. Vallery-Radot. 13th edition of this definitive biography, cited in Encyclopaedia Britannica. Authoritative, scholarly, well-documented with contemporary quotes, observations; gives complete picture of Pasteur's personal life; especially thorough presentation of scientific activities with silkworms, fermentation, hydrophobia, inoculation, etc. Introduction by Sir William Osler. Index. 505pp. 5⅜ x 8.   T632 Paperbound **$2.00**

Puzzles, Mathematical Recreations

SYMBOLIC LOGIC and THE GAME OF LOGIC, Lewis Carroll. "Symbolic Logic" is not concerned with modern symbolic logic, but is instead a collection of over 380 problems posed with charm and imagination, using the syllogism, and a fascinating diagrammatic method of drawing conclusions. In "The Game of Logic" Carroll's whimsical imagination devises a logical game played with 2 diagrams and counters (included) to manipulate hundreds of tricky syllogisms. The final section, "Hit or Miss" is a lagniappe of 101 additional puzzles in the delightful Carroll manner. Until this reprint edition, both of these books were rarities costing up to $15 each. Symbolic Logic: Index. xxxi + 199pp. The Game of Logic: 96pp. 2 vols. bound as one. 5⅜ x 8.　　　　　　　　　　　　　　　　T492 Paperbound **$1.75**

PILLOW PROBLEMS and A TANGLED TALE, Lewis Carroll. One of the rarest of all Carroll's works, "Pillow Problems" contains 72 original math puzzles, all typically ingenious. Particularly fascinating are Carroll's answers which remain exactly as he thought them out, reflecting his actual mental process. The problems in "A Tangled Tale" are in story form, originally appearing as a monthly magazine serial. Carroll not only gives the solutions, but uses answers sent in by ·readers to discuss wrong approaches and misleading paths, and grades them for insight. Both of these books were rarities until this edition, "Pillow Problems" costing up to $25, and "A Tangled Tale" $15. Pillow Problems: Preface and Introduction by Lewis Carroll. xx + 109pp. A Tangled Tale: 6 illustrations. 152pp. Two vols. bound as one. 5⅜ x 8.　　　　　　　　　　　　　　T493 Paperbound **$1.50**

AMUSEMENTS IN MATHEMATICS, Henry Ernest Dudeney. The foremost British originator of mathematical puzzles is always intriguing, witty, and paradoxical in this classic, one of the largest collections of mathematical amusements. More than 430 puzzles, problems, and paradoxes. Mazes and games, problems on number manipulation, unicursal and other route problems, puzzles on measuring, weighing, packing, age, kinship, chessboards, joiners', crossing river, plane figure dissection, and many others. Solutions. More than 450 illustrations. vii +. 258pp. 5⅜ x 8.　　　　　　　　　　　　　　　　T473 Paperbound **$1.25**

THE CANTERBURY PUZZLES, Henry Dudeney. Chaucer's pilgrims set one another problems in story form. Also Adventures of the Puzzle Club, the Strange Escape of the King's Jester, the Monks of Riddlewell, the Squire's Christmas Puzzle Party, and others. All puzzles are original, based on dissecting plane figures, arithmetic, algebra, elementary calculus and other branches of mathematics, and purely logical ingenuity. "The limit of ingenuity and intricacy," The Observer. Over 110 puzzles. Full Solutions. 150 illustrations. vii + 225pp. 5⅜ x 8.　　　　　　　　　　　　　　　　　　　　　　　　　　T474 Paperbound **$1.25**

MATHEMATICAL EXCURSIONS, H. A. Merrill. Even if you hardly remember your high school math, you'll enjoy the 90 stimulating problems contained in this book and you will come to understand a great many mathematical principles with surprisingly little effort. Many useful shortcuts and diversions not generally known are included: division by inspection, Russian peasant multiplication, memory systems for pi, building odd and even magic squares, square roots by geometry, dyadic systems, and many more. Solutions to difficult problems. 50 illustrations. 145pp. 5⅜ x 8.　　　　　　　　　　　　T350 Paperbound **$1.00**

MAGIC SQUARES AND CUBES, W. S. Andrews. Only book-length treatment in English, a thorough non-technical description and analysis. Here are nasik, overlapping, pandiagonal, serrated squares; magic circles, cubes, spheres, rhombuses. Try your hand at 4-dimensional magical figures! Much unusual folklore and tradition included. High school algebra is sufficient. 754 diagrams and illustrations. viii + 419pp. 5⅜ x 8.　　　　　　　T658 Paperbound **$1.85**

CALIBAN'S PROBLEM BOOK: MATHEMATICAL, INFERENTIAL AND CRYPTOGRAPHIC PUZZLES, H. Phillips (Caliban), S. T. Shovelton, G. S. Marshall. 105 ingenious problems by the greatest living creator of puzzles based on logic and inference. Rigorous, modern, piquant; reflecting their author's unusual personality, these intermediate and advanced puzzles all involve the ability to reason clearly through complex situations; some call for mathematical knowledge, ranging from algebra to number theory. Solutions. xi + 180pp. 5⅜ x 8.　　　　　　　　　　　　　　　　　　　　　　　　　　T736 Paperbound **$1.25**

MATHEMATICAL PUZZLES FOR BEGINNERS AND ENTHUSIASTS, G. Mott-Smith. 188 mathematical puzzles based on algebra, dissection of plane figures, permutations, and probability, that will test and improve your powers of inference and interpretation. The Odic Force, The Spider's Cousin, Ellipse Drawing, theory and strategy of card and board games like tit-tat-toe, go moku, salvo, and many others. 100 pages of detailed mathematical explanations. Appendix of primes, square roots, etc. 135 illustrations. 2nd revised edition. 248pp. 5⅜ x 8.　　　　　　　　　　　　　　　　　　　　　　　　　　T198 Paperbound **$1.00**

MATHEMAGIC, MAGIC PUZZLES, AND GAMES WITH NUMBERS, R. V. Heath. More than 60 new puzzles and stunts based on the properties of numbers. Easy techniques for multiplying large numbers mentally, revealing hidden numbers magically, finding the date of any day in any year, and dozens more. Over 30 pages devoted to magic squares, triangles, cubes, circles, etc. Edited by J. S. Meyer. 76 illustrations. 128pp. 5⅜ x 8.　　　　　T110 Paperbound **$1.00**

THE BOOK OF MODERN PUZZLES, G. L. Kaufman. A completely new series of puzzles as fascinating as crossword and deduction puzzles but based upon different principles and techniques. Simple 2-minute teasers, word labyrinths, design and pattern puzzles, logic and observation puzzles — over 150 braincrackers. Answers to all problems. 116 illustrations. 192pp. 5⅜ x 8.
T143 Paperbound **$1.00**

NEW WORD PUZZLES, G. L. Kaufman. 100 ENTIRELY NEW puzzles based on words and their combinations that will delight crossword puzzle, Scrabble and Jotto fans. Chess words, based on the moves of the chess king; design-onyms, symmetrical designs made of synonyms; rhymed double-crostics; syllable sentences; addle letter anagrams; alphagrams; linkograms; and many others all brand new. Full solutions. Space to work problems. 196 figures. vi + 122pp. 5⅜ x 8.
T344 Paperbound **$1.00**

MAZES AND LABYRINTHS: A BOOK OF PUZZLES, W. Shepherd. Mazes, formerly associated with mystery and ritual, are still among the most intriguing of intellectual puzzles. This is a novel and different collection of 50 amusements that embody the principle of the maze: mazes in the classical tradition; 3-dimensional, ribbon, and Möbius-strip mazes; hidden messages; spatial arrangements; etc.—almost all built on amusing story situations. 84 illustrations. Essay on maze psychology. Solutions. xv + 122pp. 5⅜ x 8.
T731 Paperbound **$1.00**

MAGIC TRICKS & CARD TRICKS, W. Jonson. Two books bound as one. 52 tricks with cards, 37 tricks with coins, bills, eggs, smoke, ribbons, slates, etc. Details on presentation, misdirection, and routining will help you master such famous tricks as the Changing Card, Card in the Pocket, Four Aces, Coin Through the Hand, Bill in the Egg, Afghan Bands, and over 75 others. If you follow the lucid exposition and key diagrams carefully, you will finish these two books with an astonishing mastery of magic. 106 figures. 224pp. 5⅜ x 8. T909 Paperbound **$1.00**

PANORAMA OF MAGIC, Milbourne Christopher. A profusely illustrated history of stage magic, a unique selection of prints and engravings from the author's private collection of magic memorabilia, the largest of its kind. Apparatus, stage settings and costumes; ingenious ads distributed by the performers and satiric broadsides passed around in the streets ridiculing pompous showmen; programs; decorative souvenirs. The lively text, by one of America's foremost professional magicians, is full of anecdotes about almost legendary wizards: Dede, the Egyptian; Philadelphia, the wonder-worker; Robert-Houdin, "the father of modern magic;" Harry Houdini; scores more. Altogether a pleasure package for anyone interested in magic, stage setting and design, ethnology, psychology, or simply in unusual people. A Dover original. 295 illustrations; 8 in full color. Index. viii + 216pp. 8⅜ x 11¼.
T774 Paperbound **$2.25**

HOUDINI ON MAGIC, Harry Houdini. One of the greatest magicians of modern times explains his most prized secrets. How locks are picked, with illustrated picks and skeleton keys; how a girl is sawed into twins; how to walk through a brick wall — Houdini's explanations of 44 stage tricks with many diagrams. Also included is a fascinating discussion of great magicians of the past and the story of his fight against fraudulent mediums and spiritualists. Edited by W.B. Gibson and M.N. Young. Bibliography. 155 figures, photos. xv + 280pp. 5⅜ x 8.
T384 Paperbound **$1.35**

MATHEMATICS, MAGIC AND MYSTERY, Martin Gardner. Why do card tricks work? How do magicians perform astonishing mathematical feats? How is stage mind-reading possible? This is the first book length study explaining the application of probability, set theory, theory of numbers, topology, etc., to achieve many startling tricks. Non-technical, accurate, detailed! 115 sections discuss tricks with cards, dice, coins, knots, geometrical vanishing illusions, how a Curry square "demonstrates" that the sum of the parts may be greater than the whole, and dozens of others. No sleight of hand necessary! 135 illustrations. xii + 174pp. 5⅜ x 8.
T335 Paperbound **$1.00**

EASY-TO-DO ENTERTAINMENTS AND DIVERSIONS WITH COINS, CARDS, STRING, PAPER AND MATCHES, R. M. Abraham. Over 300 tricks, games and puzzles will provide young readers with absorbing fun. Sections on card games; paper-folding; tricks with coins, matches and pieces of string; games for the agile; toy-making from common household objects; mathematical recreations; and 50 miscellaneous pastimes. Anyone in charge of groups of youngsters, including hard-pressed parents, and in need of suggestions on how to keep children sensibly amused and quietly content will find this book indispensable. Clear, simple text, copious number of delightful line drawings and illustrative diagrams. Originally titled "Winter Nights Entertainments." Introduction by Lord Baden Powell. 329 illustrations. v + 186pp. 5⅜ x 8½.
T921 Paperbound **$1.00**

STRING FIGURES AND HOW TO MAKE THEM, Caroline Furness Jayne. 107 string figures plus variations selected from the best primitive and modern examples developed by Navajo, Apache, pygmies of Africa, Eskimo, in Europe, Australia, China, etc. The most readily understandable, easy-to-follow book in English on perennially popular recreation. Crystal-clear exposition; step-by-step diagrams. Everyone from kindergarten children to adults looking for unusual diversion will be endlessly amused. Index. Bibliography. Introduction by A. C. Haddon. 17 full-page plates. 960 illustrations. xxiii + 401pp. 5⅜ x 8½.
T152 Paperbound **$2.00**

Entertainments, Humor

ODDITIES AND CURIOSITIES OF WORDS AND LITERATURE, C. Bombaugh, edited by M. Gardner. The largest collection of idiosyncratic prose and poetry techniques in English, a legendary work in the curious and amusing bypaths of literary recreations and the play technique in literature—so important in modern works. Contains alphabetic poetry, acrostics, palindromes, scissors verse, centos, emblematic poetry, famous literary puns, hoaxes, notorious slips of the press, hilarious mistranslations, and much more. Revised and enlarged with modern material by Martin Gardner. 368pp. 5⅜ x 8. T759 Paperbound **$1.75**

A NONSENSE ANTHOLOGY, collected by Carolyn Wells. 245 of the best nonsense verses ever written, including nonsense puns, absurd arguments, mock epics and sagas, nonsense ballads, odes, "sick" verses, dog-Latin verses, French nonsense verses, songs. By Edward Lear, Lewis Carroll, Gelett Burgess, W. S. Gilbert, Hilaire Belloc, Peter Newell, Oliver Herford, etc., 83 writers in all plus over four score anonymous nonsense verses. A special section of limericks, plus famous nonsense such as Carroll's "Jabberwocky" and Lear's "The Jumblies" and much excellent verse virtually impossible to locate elsewhere. For 50 years considered the best anthology available. Index of first lines specially prepared for this edition. Introduction by Carolyn Wells. 3 indexes: Title, Author, First lines. xxxiii + 279pp.
T499 Paperbound **$1.35**

THE BAD CHILD'S BOOK OF BEASTS, MORE BEASTS FOR WORSE CHILDREN, and A MORAL ALPHA-BET, H. Belloc. Hardly an anthology of humorous verse has appeared in the last 50 years without at least a couple of these famous nonsense verses. But one must see the entire volumes—with all the delightful original illustrations by Sir Basil Blackwood—to appreciate fully Belloc's charming and witty verses that play so subacidly on the platitudes of life and morals that beset his day—and ours. A great humor classic. Three books in one. Total of 157pp. 5⅜ x 8. T749 Paperbound **$1.00**

THE DEVIL'S DICTIONARY, Ambrose Bierce. Sardonic and irreverent barbs puncturing the pomposities and absurdities of American politics, business, religion, literature, and arts, by the country's greatest satirist in the classic tradition. Epigrammatic as Shaw, piercing as Swift, American as Mark Twain, Will Rogers, and Fred Allen, Bierce will always remain the favorite of a small coterie of enthusiasts, and of writers and speakers whom he supplies with "some of the most gorgeous witticisms of the English language" (H. L. Mencken). Over 1000 entries in alphabetical order. 144pp. 5⅜ x 8. T487 Paperbound **$1.00**

THE PURPLE COW AND OTHER NONSENSE, Gelett Burgess. The best of Burgess's early nonsense, selected from the first edition of the "Burgess Nonsense Book." Contains many of his most unusual and truly awe-inspiring pieces: 36 nonsense quatrains, the Poems of Patagonia, Alphabet of Famous Goops, and the other hilarious (and rare) adult nonsense that place him in the forefront of American humorists. All pieces are accompanied by the original Burgess illustrations. 123 illustrations. xiii + 113pp. 5⅜ x 8. T772 Paperbound **$1.00**

MY PIOUS FRIENDS AND DRUNKEN COMPANIONS and MORE PIOUS FRIENDS AND DRUNKEN COMPANIONS, Frank Shay. Folksingers, amateur and professional, and everyone who loves singing: here, available for the first time in 30 years, is this valued collection of 132 ballads, blues, vaudeville numbers, drinking songs, sea chanties, comedy songs. Songs of pre-Beatnik Bohemia; songs from all over America, England, France, Australia; the great songs of the Naughty Nineties and early twentieth-century America. Over a third with music. Woodcuts by John Held, Jr. convey perfectly the brash insouciance of an era of rollicking unabashed song. 12 illustrations by John Held, Jr. Two indexes (Titles and First lines and Choruses). Introductions by the author. Two volumes bound as one. Total of xvi + 235pp. 5⅜ x 8½.
T946 Paperbound **$1.25**

HOW TO TELL THE BIRDS FROM THE FLOWERS, R. W. Wood. How not to confuse a carrot with a parrot, a grape with an ape, a puffin with nuffin. Delightful drawings, clever puns, absurd little poems point out far-fetched resemblances in nature. The author was a leading physicist. Introduction by Margaret Wood White. 106 illus. 60pp. 5⅜ x 8.
T523 Paperbound **75¢**

PECK'S BAD BOY AND HIS PA, George W. Peck. The complete edition, containing both volumes, of one of the most widely read American humor books. The endless ingenious pranks played by bad boy "Hennery" on his pa and the grocery man, the outraged pomposity of Pa, the perpetual ridiculing of middle class institutions, are as entertaining today as they were in 1883. No pale sophistications or subtleties, but rather humor vigorous, raw, earthy, imaginative, and, as folk humor often is, sadistic. This peculiarly fascinating book is also valuable to historians and students of American culture as a portrait of an age. 100 original illustrations by True Williams. Introduction by E. F. Bleiler. 347pp. 5⅜ x 8.
T497 Paperbound **$1.50**

CATALOGUE OF DOVER BOOKS

THE HUMOROUS VERSE OF LEWIS CARROLL. Almost every poem Carroll ever wrote, the largest collection ever published, including much never published elsewhere: 150 parodies, burlesques, riddles, ballads, acrostics, etc., with 130 original illustrations by Tenniel, Carroll, and others. "Addicts will be grateful . . . there is nothing for the faithful to do but sit down and fall to the banquet," N. Y. Times. Index to first lines. xiv + 446pp. 5⅜ x 8.
T654 Paperbound **$2.00**

DIVERSIONS AND DIGRESSIONS OF LEWIS CARROLL. A major new treasure for Carroll fans! Rare privately published humor, fantasy, puzzles, and games by Carroll at his whimsical best, with a new vein of frank satire. Includes many new mathematical amusements and recreations, among them the fragmentary Part III of "Curiosa Mathematica." Contains "The Rectory Umbrella," "The New Belfry," "The Vision of the Three T's," and much more. New 32-page supplement of rare photographs taken by Carroll. x + 375pp. 5⅜ x 8.
T732 Paperbound **$2.00**

THE COMPLETE NONSENSE OF EDWARD LEAR. This is the only complete edition of this master of gentle madness available at a popular price. A BOOK OF NONSENSE, NONSENSE SONGS, MORE NONSENSE SONGS AND STORIES in their entirety with all the old favorites that have delighted children and adults for years. The Dong With A Luminous Nose, The Jumblies, The Owl and the Pussycat, and hundreds of other bits of wonderful nonsense. 214 limericks, 3 sets of Nonsense Botany, 5 Nonsense Alphabets, 546 drawings by Lear himself, and much more. 320pp. 5⅜ x 8.
T167 Paperbound **$1.00**

THE MELANCHOLY LUTE, The Humorous Verse of Franklin P. Adams ("FPA"). The author's own selection of light verse, drawn from thirty years of FPA's column, "The Conning Tower," syndicated all over the English-speaking world. Witty, perceptive, literate, these ninety-six poems range from parodies of other poets, Millay, Longfellow, Edgar Guest, Kipling, Masefield, etc., and free and hilarious translations of Horace and other Latin poets, to satiric comments on fabled American institutions—the New York Subways, preposterous ads, suburbanites, sensational journalism, etc. They reveal with vigor and clarity the humor, integrity and restraint of a wise and gentle American satirist. Introduction by Robert Hutchinson. vi + 122pp. 5⅜ x 8½.
T108 Paperbound **$1.00**

SINGULAR TRAVELS, CAMPAIGNS, AND ADVENTURES OF BARON MUNCHAUSEN, R. E. Raspe, with 90 illustrations by Gustave Doré. The first edition in over 150 years to reestablish the deeds of the Prince of Liars exactly as Raspe first recorded them in 1785—the genuine Baron Munchausen, one of the most popular personalities in English literature. Included also are the best of the many sequels, written by other hands. Introduction on Raspe by J. Carswell. Bibliography of early editions. xliv + 192pp. 5⅜ x 8.
T698 Paperbound **$1.00**

THE WIT AND HUMOR OF OSCAR WILDE, ed. by Alvin Redman. Wilde at his most brilliant, in 1000 epigrams exposing weaknesses and hypocrisies of "civilized" society. Divided into 49 categories—sin, wealth, women, America, etc.—to aid writers, speakers. Includes excerpts from his trials, books, plays, criticism. Formerly "The Epigrams of Oscar Wilde." Introduction by Vyvyan Holland, Wilde's only living son. Introductory essay by editor. 260pp. 5⅜ x 8.
T602 Paperbound **$1.00**

MAX AND MORITZ, Wilhelm Busch. Busch is one of the great humorists of all time, as well as the father of the modern comic strip. This volume, translated by H. A. Klein and other hands, contains the perennial favorite "Max and Moritz" (translated by C. T. Brooks), Plisch and Plum, Das Rabennest, Eispeter, and seven other whimsical, sardonic, jovial, diabolical cartoon and verse stories. Lively English translations parallel the original German. This work has delighted millions since it first appeared in the 19th century, and is guaranteed to please almost anyone. Edited by H. A. Klein, with an afterword. x + 205pp. 5⅝ x 8½.
T181 Paperbound **$1.15**

HYPOCRITICAL HELENA, Wilhelm Busch. A companion volume to "Max and Moritz," with the title piece (Die Fromme Helena) and 10 other highly amusing cartoon and verse stories, all newly translated by H. A. Klein and M. C. Klein: Adventure on New Year's Eve (Abenteuer in der Neujahrsnacht), Hangover on the Morning after New Year's Eve (Der Katzenjammer am Neujahrsmorgen), etc. English and German in parallel columns. Hours of pleasure, also a fine language aid. x + 205pp. 5⅝ x 8½.
T184 Paperbound **$1.00**

THE BEAR THAT WASN'T, Frank Tashlin. What does it mean? Is it simply delightful wry humor, or a charming story of a bear who wakes up in the midst of a factory, or a satire on Big Business, or an existential cartoon-story of the human condition, or a symbolization of the struggle between conformity and the individual? New York Herald Tribune said of the first edition: ". . . a fable for grownups that will be fun for children. Sit down with the book and get your own bearings." Long an underground favorite with readers of all ages and opinions. v + 51pp. Illustrated. 5⅜ x 8½.
T939 Paperbound **75¢**

RUTHLESS RHYMES FOR HEARTLESS HOMES and MORE RUTHLESS RHYMES FOR HEARTLESS HOMES, Harry Graham ("Col. D. Streamer"). Two volumes of Little Willy and 48 other poetic disasters. A bright, new reprint of oft-quoted, never forgotten, devastating humor by a precursor of today's "sick" joke school. For connoisseurs of wicked, wacky humor and all who delight in the comedy of manners. Original drawings are a perfect complement. 61 illustrations. Index. vi + 69pp. Two vols. bound as one. 5⅜ x 8½.
T930 Paperbound **75¢**

Say It language phrase books

These handy phrase books (128 to 196 pages each) make grammatical drills unnecessary for an elementary knowledge of a spoken foreign language. Covering most matters of travel and everyday life each volume contains:

> Over 1000 phrases and sentences in immediately useful forms — foreign language plus English.

> Modern usage designed for Americans. Specific phrases like, "Give me small change," and "Please call a taxi."

> Simplified phonetic transcription you will be able to read at sight.

> The only completely indexed phrase books on the market.

> Covers scores of important situations: — Greetings, restaurants, sightseeing, useful expressions, etc.

These books are prepared by native linguists who are professors at Columbia, N.Y.U., Fordham and other great universities. Use them independently or with any other book or record course. They provide a supplementary living element that most other courses lack. Individual volumes in:

Russian 75¢	Italian 75¢	Spanish 75¢	German 75¢
Hebrew 75¢	Danish 75¢	Japanese 75¢	Swedish 75¢
Dutch 75¢	Esperanto 75¢	Modern Greek 75¢	Portuguese 75¢
Norwegian 75¢	Polish 75¢	French 75¢	Yiddish 75¢
Turkish 75¢		English for German-speaking people 75¢	
English for Italian-speaking people 75¢		English for Spanish-speaking people 75¢	

Large clear type. 128-196 pages each. 3½ x 5¼. Sturdy paper binding.

Listen and Learn language records

LISTEN & LEARN is the only language record course designed especially to meet your travel and everyday needs. It is available in separate sets for FRENCH, SPANISH, GERMAN, JAPANESE, RUSSIAN, MODERN GREEK, PORTUGUESE, ITALIAN and HEBREW, and each set contains three 33⅓ rpm long-playing records—1½ hours of recorded speech by eminent native speakers who are professors at Columbia, New York University, Queens College.

Check the following special features found only in LISTEN & LEARN:

- **Dual-language recording. 812 selected phrases and sentences, over 3200 words,** spoken first in English, then in their foreign language equivalents. A suitable pause follows each foreign phrase, allowing you time to repeat the expression. You learn by unconscious assimilation.
- **128 to 206-page manual** contains everything on the records, plus a simple phonetic pronunciation guide.
- **Indexed for convenience. The only set on the market** that is completely indexed. No more puzzling over where to find the phrase you need. Just look in the rear of the manual.
- **Practical.** No time wasted on material you can find in any grammar. LISTEN & LEARN covers central core material with phrase approach. Ideal for the person with limited learning time.
- **Living, modern expressions,** not found in other courses. Hygienic products, modern equipment, shopping—expressions used every day, like "nylon" and "air-conditioned."
- **Limited objective.** Everything you learn, no matter where you stop, is immediately useful. You have to finish other courses, wade through grammar and vocabulary drill, before they help you.
- **High-fidelity recording.** LISTEN & LEARN records equal in clarity and surface-silence any record on the market costing up to $6.

"Excellent . . . the spoken records . . . impress me as being among the very best on the market," **Prof. Mario Pei,** Dept. of Romance Languages, Columbia University. "Inexpensive and well-done . . . it would make an ideal present," CHICAGO SUNDAY TRIBUNE. "More genuinely helpful than anything of its kind which I have previously encountered," **Sidney Clark,** well-known author of "ALL THE BEST" travel books.

UNCONDITIONAL GUARANTEE. Try LISTEN & LEARN, then return it within 10 days for full refund if you are not satisfied.

Each set contains three twelve-inch 33⅓ records, manual, and album.

SPANISH	the set $5.95	GERMAN	the set $5.95
FRENCH	the set $5.95	ITALIAN	the set $5.95
RUSSIAN	the set $5.95	JAPANESE	the set $6.95
PORTUGUESE	the set $5.95	MODERN GREEK	the set $5.95
MODERN HEBREW	the set $5.95		

Americana

THE EYES OF DISCOVERY, J. Bakeless. A vivid reconstruction of how unspoiled America appeared to the first white men. Authentic and enlightening accounts of Hudson's landing in New York, Coronado's trek through the Southwest; scores of explorers, settlers, trappers, soldiers. America's pristine flora, fauna, and Indians in every region and state in fresh and unusual new aspects. "A fascinating view of what the land was like before the first highway went through," Time. 68 contemporary illustrations, 39 newly added in this edition. Index. Bibliography. x + 500pp. 5⅜ x 8. T761 Paperbound **$2.25**

AUDUBON AND HIS JOURNALS, J. J. Audubon. A collection of fascinating accounts of Europe and America in the early 1800's through Audubon's own eyes. Includes the Missouri River Journals —an eventful trip through America's untouched heartland, the Labrador Journals, the European Journals, the famous "Episodes", and other rare Audubon material, including the descriptive chapters from the original letterpress edition of the "Ornithological Studies", omitted in all later editions. Indispensable for ornithologists, naturalists, and all lovers of Americana and adventure. 70-page biography by Audubon's granddaughter. 38 illustrations. Index. Total of 1106pp. 5⅜ x 8. T675 Vol I Paperbound **$2.25**
T676 Vol II Paperbound **$2.25**
The set **$4.50**

TRAVELS OF WILLIAM BARTRAM, edited by Mark Van Doren. The first inexpensive illustrated edition of one of the 18th century's most delightful books is an excellent source of first-hand material on American geography, anthropology, and natural history. Many descriptions of early Indian tribes are our only source of information on them prior to the infiltration of the white man. "The mind of a scientist with the soul of a poet," John Livingston Lowes. 13 original illustrations and maps. Edited with an introduction by Mark Van Doren. 448pp. 5⅜ x 8. T13 Paperbound **$2.00**

GARRETS AND PRETENDERS: A HISTORY OF BOHEMIANISM IN AMERICA, A. Parry. The colorful and fantastic history of American Bohemianism from Poe to Kerouac. This is the only complete record of hoboes, cranks, starving poets, and suicides. Here are Pfaff, Whitman, Crane, Bierce, Pound, and many others. New chapters by the author and by H. T. Moore bring this thorough and well-documented history down to the Beatniks. "An excellent account," N. Y. Times. Scores of cartoons, drawings, and caricatures. Bibliography. Index. xxviii + 421pp. 5⅝ x 8⅜. T708 Paperbound **$1.95**

THE EXPLORATION OF THE COLORADO RIVER AND ITS CANYONS, J. W. Powell. The thrilling first-hand account of the expedition that filled in the last white space on the map of the United States. Rapids, famine, hostile Indians, and mutiny are among the perils encountered as the unknown Colorado Valley reveals its secrets. This is the only uncut version of Major Powell's classic of exploration that has been printed in the last 60 years. Includes later reflections and subsequent expedition. 250 illustrations, new map. 400pp. 5⅝ x 8⅜. T94 Paperbound **$2.25**

THE JOURNAL OF HENRY D. THOREAU, Edited by Bradford Torrey and Francis H. Allen. Henry Thoreau is not only one of the most important figures in American literature and social thought; his voluminous journals (from which his books emerged as selections and crystallizations) constitute both the longest, most sensitive record of personal internal development and a most penetrating description of a historical moment in American culture. This present set, which was first issued in fourteen volumes, contains Thoreau's entire journals from 1837 to 1862, with the exception of the lost years which were found only recently. We are reissuing it, complete and unabridged, with a new introduction by Walter Harding, Secretary of the Thoreau Society. Fourteen volumes reissued in two volumes. Foreword by Henry Seidel Canby. Total of 1888pp. 8⅜ x 12¼. T312-3 Two volume set, Clothbound **$20.00**

GAMES AND SONGS OF AMERICAN CHILDREN, collected by William Wells Newell. A remarkable collection of 190 games with songs that accompany many of them; cross references to show similarities, differences among them; variations; musical notation for 38 songs. Textual discussions show relations with folk-drama and other aspects of folk tradition. Grouped into categories for ready comparative study: Love-games, histories, playing at work, human life, bird and beast, mythology, guessing-games, etc. New introduction covers relations of songs and dances to timeless heritage of folklore, biographical sketch of Newell, other pertinent data. A good source of inspiration for those in charge of groups of children and a valuable reference for anthropologists, sociologists, psychiatrists. Introduction by Carl Withers. New indexes of first lines, games. 5⅜ x 8½. xii + 242pp. T354 Paperbound **$1.75**

Art, History of Art, Antiques, Graphic Arts, Handcrafts

ART STUDENTS' ANATOMY, E. J. Farris. Outstanding art anatomy that uses chiefly living objects for its illustrations. 71 photos of undraped men, women, children are accompanied by carefully labeled matching sketches to illustrate the skeletal system, articulations and movements, bony landmarks, the muscular system, skin, fasciae, fat, etc. 9 x-ray photos show movement of joints. Undraped models are shown in such actions as serving in tennis, drawing a bow in archery, playing football, dancing, preparing to spring and to dive. Also discussed and illustrated are proportions, age and sex differences, the anatomy of the smile, etc. 8 plates by the great early 18th century anatomic illustrator Siegfried Albinus are also included. Glossary. 158 figures, 7 in color. x + 159pp. 5⅝ x 8⅜.   T744 Paperbound **$1.50**

AN ATLAS OF ANATOMY FOR ARTISTS, F Schider. A new 3rd edition of this standard text enlarged by 52 new illustrations of hands, anatomical studies by Cloquet, and expressive life studies of the body by Barcsay. 189 clear, detailed plates offer you precise information of impeccable accuracy. 29 plates show all aspects of the skeleton, with closeups of special areas, while 54 full-page plates, mostly in two colors, give human musculature as seen from four different points of view, with cutaways for important portions of the body. 14 full-page plates provide photographs of hand forms, eyelids, female breasts, and indicate the location of muscles upon models. 59 additional plates show how great artists of the past utilized human anatomy. They reproduce sketches and finished work by such artists as Michelangelo, Leonardo da Vinci, Goya, and 15 others. This is a lifetime reference work which will be one of the most important books in any artist's library. "The standard reference tool," AMERICAN LIBRARY ASSOCIATION. "Excellent," AMERICAN ARTIST. Third enlarged edition. 189 plates, 647 illustrations. xxvi + 192pp. 7⅞ x 10⅝.   T241 Clothbound **$6.00**

AN ATLAS OF ANIMAL ANATOMY FOR ARTISTS, W. Ellenberger, H. Baum, H. Dittrich. The largest, richest animal anatomy for artists available in English. 99 detailed anatomical plates of such animals as the horse, dog, cat, lion, deer, seal, kangaroo, flying squirrel, cow, bull, goat, monkey, hare, and bat. Surface features are clearly indicated, while progressive beneath-the-skin pictures show musculature, tendons, and bone structure. Rest and action are exhibited in terms of musculature and skeletal structure and detailed cross-sections are given for heads and important features. The animals chosen are representative of specific families so that a study of these anatomies will provide knowledge of hundreds of related species. "Highly recommended as one of the very few books on the subject worthy of being used as an authoritative guide," DESIGN. "Gives a fundamental knowledge," AMERICAN ARTIST. Second revised, enlarged edition with new plates from Cuvier, Stubbs, etc. 288 illustrations. 153pp. 11⅜ x 9.   T82 Clothbound **$6.00**

THE HUMAN FIGURE IN MOTION, Eadweard Muybridge. The largest selection in print of Muybridge's famous high-speed action photos of the human figure in motion. 4789 photographs illustrate 162 different actions: men, women, children—mostly undraped—are shown walking, running, carrying various objects, sitting, lying down, climbing, throwing, arising, and performing over 150 other actions. Some actions are shown in as many as 150 photographs each. All in all there are more than 500 action strips in this enormous volume, series shots taken at shutter speeds of as high as 1/6000th of a second! These are not posed shots, but true stopped motion. They show bone and muscle in situations that the human eye is not fast enough to capture. Earlier, smaller editions of these prints have brought $40 and more on the out-of-print market. "A must for artists," ART IN FOCUS. "An unparalleled dictionary of action for all artists," AMERICAN ARTIST. 390 full-page plates, with 4789 photographs. Printed on heavy glossy stock. Reinforced binding with headbands. xxi + 390pp. 7⅞ x 10⅝.
T204 Clothbound **$10.00**

ANIMALS IN MOTION, Eadweard Muybridge. This is the largest collection of animal action photos in print. 34 different animals (horses, mules, oxen, goats, camels, pigs, cats, guanacos, lions, gnus, deer, monkeys, eagles—and 21 others) in 132 characteristic actions. The horse alone is shown in more than 40 different actions. All 3919 photographs are taken in series at speeds up to 1/6000th of a second. The secrets of leg motion, spinal patterns, head movements, strains and contortions shown nowhere else are captured. You will see exactly how a lion sets his foot down; how an elephant's knees are like a human's—and how they differ; the position of a kangaroo's legs in mid-leap; how an ostrich's head bobs; details of the flight of birds—and thousands of facets of motion only the fastest cameras can catch. Photographed from domestic animals and animals in the Philadelphia zoo, it contains neither semiposed artificial shots nor distorted telephoto shots taken under adverse conditions. Artists, biologists, decorators, cartoonists, will find this book indispensable for understanding animals in motion. "A really marvelous series of plates," NATURE (London). "The dry plate's most spectacular early use was by Eadweard Muybridge," LIFE. 3919 photographs; 380 full pages of plates. 440pp. Printed on heavy glossy paper. Deluxe binding with headbands. 7⅞ x 10⅝.   T203 Clothbound **$10.00**

THE AUTOBIOGRAPHY OF AN IDEA, Louis Sullivan. The pioneer architect whom Frank Lloyd Wright called "the master" reveals an acute sensitivity to social forces and values in this passionately honest account. He records the crystallization of his opinions and theories, the growth of his organic theory of architecture that still influences American designers and architects, contemporary ideas, etc. This volume contains the first appearance of 34 full-page plates of his finest architecture. Unabridged reissue of 1924 edition. New introduction by R. M. Line. Index. xiv + 335pp. 5⅜ x 8. T281 Paperbound **$2.00**

THE DRAWINGS OF HEINRICH KLEY. The first uncut republication of both of Kley's devastating sketchbooks, which first appeared in pre-World War I Germany. One of the greatest cartoonists and social satirists of modern times, his exuberant and iconoclastic fantasy and his extraordinary technique place him in the great tradition of Bosch, Breughel, and Goya, while his subject matter has all the immediacy and tension of our century. 200 drawings. viii + 128pp. 7¾ x 10¾. T24 Paperbound **$1.85**

MORE DRAWINGS BY HEINRICH KLEY. All the sketches from Leut' Und Viecher (1912) and Sammel-Album (1923) not included in the previous Dover edition of Drawings. More of the bizarre, mercilessly iconoclastic sketches that shocked and amused on their original publication. Nothing was too sacred, no one too eminent for satirization by this imaginative, individual and accomplished master cartoonist. A total of 158 illustrations. lv + 104pp. 7¾ x 10¾. T41 Paperbound **$1.85**

PINE FURNITURE OF EARLY NEW ENGLAND, R. H. Kettell. A rich understanding of one of America's most original folk arts that collectors of antiques, interior decorators, craftsmen, woodworkers, and everyone interested in American history and art will find fascinating and immensely useful. 413 illustrations of more than 300 chairs, benches, racks, beds, cupboards, mirrors, shelves, tables, and other furniture will show all the simple beauty and character of early New England furniture. 55 detailed drawings carefully analyze outstanding pieces. "With its rich store of illustrations, this book emphasizes the individuality and varied design of early American pine furniture. It should be welcomed," ANTIQUES. 413 illustrations and 55 working drawings. 475. 8 x 10¾. T145 Clothbound **$10.00**

THE HUMAN FIGURE, J. H. Vanderpoel. Every important artistic element of the human figure is pointed out in minutely detailed word descriptions in this classic text and illustrated as well in 430 pencil and charcoal drawings. Thus the text of this book directs your attention to all the characteristic features and subtle differences of the male and female (adults, children, and aged persons), as though a master artist were telling you what to look for at each stage. 2nd edition, revised and enlarged by George Bridgman. Foreword. 430 illustrations. 143pp. 6⅛ x 9¼. T432 Paperbound **$1.50**

LETTERING AND ALPHABETS, J. A. Cavanagh. This unabridged reissue of LETTERING offers a full discussion, analysis, illustration of 89 basic hand lettering styles — styles derived from Caslons, Bodonis, Garamonds, Gothic, Black Letter, Oriental, and many others. Upper and lower cases, numerals and common signs pictured. Hundreds of technical hints on make-up, construction, artistic validity, strokes, pens, brushes, white areas, etc. May be reproduced without permission! 89 complete alphabets; 72 lettered specimens. 121pp. 9⅜ x 8. T53 Paperbound **$1.35**

STICKS AND STONES, Lewis Mumford. A survey of the forces that have conditioned American architecture and altered its forms. The author discusses the medieval tradition in early New England villages; the Renaissance influence which developed with the rise of the merchant class; the classical influence of Jefferson's time; the "Mechanicsvilles" of Poe's generation; the Brown Decades; the philosophy of the Imperial facade; and finally the modern machine age. "A truly remarkable book," SAT. REV. OF LITERATURE. 2nd revised edition. 21 illustrations. xvii + 228pp. 5⅜ x 8. T202 Paperbound **$1.75**

THE STANDARD BOOK OF QUILT MAKING AND COLLECTING, Marguerite Ickis. A complete easy-to-follow guide with all the information you need to make beautiful, useful quilts. How to plan, design, cut, sew, appliqué, avoid sewing problems, use rag bag, make borders, tuft, every other aspect. Over 100 traditional quilts shown, including over 40 full-size patterns. At-home hobby for fun, profit. Index. 483 illus. 1 color plate. 287pp. 6¾ x 9½. T582 Paperbound **$2.00**

THE BOOK OF SIGNS, Rudolf Koch. Formerly $20 to $25 on the out-of-print market, now only $1.00 in this unabridged new edition! 493 symbols from ancient manuscripts, medieval cathedrals, coins, catacombs, pottery, etc. Crosses, monograms of Roman emperors, astrological, chemical, botanical, runes, housemarks, and 7 other categories. Invaluable for handicraft workers, illustrators, scholars, etc., this material may be reproduced without permission. 493 illustrations by Fritz Kredel. 104pp. 6½ x 9¼. T162 Paperbound **$1.00**

PRIMITIVE ART, Franz Boas. This authoritative and exhaustive work by a great American anthropologist covers the entire gamut of primitive art. Pottery, leatherwork, metal work, stone work, wood, basketry, are treated in detail. Theories of primitive art, historical depth in art history, technical virtuosity, unconscious levels of patterning, symbolism, styles, literature, music, dance, etc. A must book for the interested layman, the anthropologist, artist, handicrafter (hundreds of unusual motifs), and the historian. Over 900 illustrations (50 ceramic vessels, 12 totem poles, etc.). 376pp. 5⅜ x 8. T25 Paperbound **$2.25**

Fiction

FLATLAND, E. A. Abbott. A science-fiction classic of life in a 2-dimensional world that is also a first-rate introduction to such aspects of modern science as relativity and hyperspace. Political, moral, satirical, and humorous overtones have made FLATLAND fascinating reading for thousands. 7th edition. New introduction by Banesh Hoffmann. 16 illustrations. 128pp. 5⅜ x 8. **T1 Paperbound $1.00**

THE WONDERFUL WIZARD OF OZ, L. F. Baum. Only edition in print with all the original W. W. Denslow illustrations in full color—as much a part of "The Wizard" as Tenniel's drawings are of "Alice in Wonderland." "The Wizard" is still America's best-loved fairy tale, in which, as the author expresses it, "The wonderment and joy are retained and the heartaches and nightmares left out." Now today's young readers can enjoy every word and wonderful picture of the original book. New introduction by Martin Gardner. A Baum bibliography. 23 full-page color plates. viii + 268pp. 5⅜ x 8. **T691 Paperbound $1.50**

THE MARVELOUS LAND OF OZ, L. F. Baum. This is the equally enchanting sequel to the "Wizard," continuing the adventures of the Scarecrow and the Tin Woodman. The hero this time is a little boy named Tip, and all the delightful Oz magic is still present. This is the Oz book with the Animated Saw-Horse, the Woggle-Bug, and Jack Pumpkinhead. All the original John R. Neill illustrations, 10 in full color. 287 pp. 5⅜ x 8. **T692 Paperbound $1.50**

28 SCIENCE FICTION STORIES OF H. G. WELLS. Two full unabridged novels, MEN LIKE GODS and STAR BEGOTTEN, plus 26 short stories by the master science-fiction writer of all time! Stories of space, time, invention, exploration, future adventure—an indispensable part of the library of everyone interested in science and adventure. PARTIAL CONTENTS: Men Like Gods, The Country of the Blind, In the Abyss, The Crystal Egg, The Man Who Could Work Miracles, A Story of the Days to Come, The Valley of Spiders, and 21 more! 928pp. 5⅜ x 8. **T265 Clothbound $4.50**

THREE MARTIAN NOVELS, Edgar Rice Burroughs. Contains: Thuvia, Maid of Mars; The Chessmen of Mars; and The Master Mind of Mars. High adventure set in an imaginative and intricate conception of the Red Planet. Mars is peopled with an intelligent, heroic human race which lives in densely populated cities and with fierce barbarians who inhabit dead sea bottoms. Other exciting creatures abound amidst an inventive framework of Martian history and geography. Complete unabridged reprintings of the first edition. 16 illustrations by J. Allen St. John. vi + 499pp. 5⅜ x 8½. **T39 Paperbound $1.85**

SEVEN SCIENCE FICTION NOVELS, H. G. Wells. Full unabridged texts of 7 science-fiction novels of the master. Ranging from biology, physics, chemistry, astronomy to sociology and other studies, Mr. Wells extrapolates whole worlds of strange and intriguing character. "One will have to go far to match this for entertainment, excitement, and sheer pleasure . . . ," NEW YORK TIMES. Contents: The Time Machine, The Island of Dr. Moreau, First Men in the Moon, The Invisible Man, The War of the Worlds, The Food of the Gods, In the Days of the Comet. 1015pp. 5⅜ x 8. **T264 Clothbound $4.50**

THE LAND THAT TIME FORGOT and THE MOON MAID, Edgar Rice Burroughs. In the opinion of many, Burroughs' best work. The first concerns a strange island where evolution is individual rather than phylogenetic. Speechless anthropoids develop into intelligent human beings within a single generation. The second projects the reader far into the future and describes the first voyage to the Moon (in the year 2025), the conquest of the Earth by the Moon, and years of violence and adventure as the enslaved Earthmen try to regain possession of their planet. "An imaginative tour de force that keeps the reader keyed up and expectant," NEW YORK TIMES. Complete, unabridged text of the original two novels (three parts in each). 5 illustrations by J. Allen St. John. vi + 552pp. 5⅜ x 8½.
T1020 Clothbound $3.75
T358 Paperbound $2.00

3 ADVENTURE NOVELS by H. Rider Haggard. Complete texts of "She," "King Solomon's Mines," "Allan Quatermain." Qualities of discovery; desire for immortality; search for primitive, for what is unadorned by civilization, have kept these novels of African adventure exciting, alive to readers from R. L. Stevenson to George Orwell. 636pp. 5⅜ x 8. **T584 Paperbound $2.00**

A PRINCESS OF MARS and A FIGHTING MAN OF MARS: TWO MARTIAN NOVELS BY EDGAR RICE BURROUGHS. "Princess of Mars" is the very first of the great Martian novels written by Burroughs, and it is probably the best of them all; it set the pattern for all of his later fantasy novels and contains a thrilling cast of strange peoples and creatures and the formula of Olympian heroism amidst ever-fluctuating fortunes which Burroughs carries off so successfully. "Fighting Man" returns to the same scenes and cities—many years later. A mad scientist, a degenerate dictator, and an indomitable defender of the right clash—with the fate of the Red Planet at stake! Complete, unabridged reprinting of original editions. Illustrations by F. E. Schoonover and Hugh Hutton. v + 356pp. 5⅜ x 8½. **T1140 Paperbound $1.75**

Music

A GENERAL HISTORY OF MUSIC, Charles Burney. A detailed coverage of music from the Greeks up to 1789, with full information on all types of music; sacred and secular, vocal and instrumental, operatic and symphonic. Theory, notation, forms, instruments, innovators, composers, performers, typical and important works, and much more in an easy, entertaining style. Burney covered much of Europe and spoke with hundreds of authorities and composers so that this work is more than a compilation of records . . . it is a living work of careful and first-hand scholarship. Its account of thoroughbass (18th century) Italian music is probably still the best introduction on the subject. A recent NEW YORK TIMES review said, "Surprisingly few of Burney's statements have been invalidated by modern research . . . still of great value." Edited and corrected by Frank Mercer. 35 figures. Indices. 1915pp. 5⅜ x 8. 2 volumes.
T36 The Set, Clothbound **$12.50**

A DICTIONARY OF HYMNOLOGY, John Julian. This exhaustive and scholarly work has become known as an invaluable source of hundreds of thousands of important and often difficult to obtain facts on the history and use of hymns in the western world. Everyone interested in hymns will be fascinated by the accounts of famous hymns and hymn writers and amazed by the amount of practical information he will find. More than 30,000 entries on individual hymns, giving authorship, date and circumstances of composition, publication, textual variations, translations, denominational and ritual usage, etc. Biographies of more than 9,000 hymn writers, and essays on important topics such as Christmas carols and children's hymns, and much other unusual and valuable information. A 200 page double-columned index of first lines — the largest in print. Total of 1786 pages in two reinforced clothbound volumes. 6¼ x 9¼.
The set, T333 Clothbound **$17.50**

MUSIC IN MEDIEVAL BRITAIN, F. Ll. Harrison. The most thorough, up-to-date, and accurate treatment of the subject ever published, beautifully illustrated. Complete account of institutions and choirs; carols, masses, and motets; liturgy and plainsong; and polyphonic music from the Norman Conquest to the Reformation. Discusses the various schools of music and their reciprocal influences; the origin and development of new ritual forms; development and use of instruments; and new evidence on many problems of the period. Reproductions of scores, over 200 excerpts from medieval melodies. Rules of harmony and dissonance; influence of Continental styles; great composers (Dunstable, Cornysh, Fairfax, etc.); and much more. Register and index of more than 400 musicians. Index of titles. General Index. 225-item bibliography. 6 Appendices. xix + 491pp. 5⅝ x 8¾.
T705 Clothbound **$10.00**

THE MUSIC OF SPAIN, Gilbert Chase. Only book in English to give concise, comprehensive account of Iberian music; new Chapter covers music since 1941. Victoria, Albéniz, Cabezón, Pedrell, Turina, hundreds of other composers; popular and folk music; the Gypsies; the guitar; dance, theatre, opera, with only extensive discussion in English of the Zarzuela; virtuosi such as Casals; much more. "Distinguished . . . readable," Saturday Review. 400-item bibliography. Index. 27 photos. 383pp. 5⅜ x 8.
T549 Paperbound **$2.25**

ON STUDYING SINGING, Sergius Kagen. An intelligent method of voice-training, which leads you around pitfalls that waste your time, money, and effort. Exposes rigid, mechanical systems, baseless theories, deleterious exercises. "Logical, clear, convincing . . . dead right," Virgil Thomson, N.Y. Herald Tribune. "I recommend this volume highly," Maggie Teyte, Saturday Review. 119pp. 5⅜ x 8.
T622 Paperbound **$1.35**

Prices subject to change without notice.

Dover publishes books on art, music, philosophy, literature, languages, history, social sciences, psychology, handcrafts, orientalia, puzzles and entertainments, chess, pets and gardens, books explaining science, intermediate and higher mathematics, mathematical physics, engineering, biological sciences, earth sciences, classics of science, etc. Write to:

Dept. catrr.
Dover Publications, Inc.
180 Varick Street, N.Y. 14, N.Y.

DATE DUE

GAYLORD

PRINTED IN U.S.A.